"The Air I Breathe Is Wartburg Air"

"The Air I Breathe Is Wartburg Air"
The Legacy of William H. Weiblen

Edited by Craig L. Nessan

Wipf and Stock Publishers
Eugene • Oregon
2003

"The Air I Breathe is Wartburg Air"
The Legacy of William H. Weiblen
Copyright © 2003, by Craig L. Nessan
ISBN: 978-1-4982-4635-4
Publication Date: June, 2003

Wipf and Stock Publishers
199 West 8th Avenue, Suite 3
Eugene, Oregon 97401

Some articles and papers previously published,
and used here by permission.

Table of Contents

Introduction

I first met Bill Weiblen in the fall of 1974 when I came as a student to Wartburg Theological Seminary. There were many qualities about this man that impressed me immensely. Above all, he demonstrated a deep and genuine interest in the lives and well being of students. Not only did he rapidly learn our names, but he paid attention to each individual person, getting to know each one's personal history in a way that made a lasting connection. Although a seminary president, he exhibited a humility that consistently placed the focus on others rather than himself. He had so appropriated the theology of Paul Tillich that his language resonated with theological depth. He brought theological perspective naturally into our conversations in a meaningful way.

There are many memories of Bill Weiblen that are worth sharing. I recall New Year's Day 1978 when a group of students invited Bill to our version of the Super Bowl, held on campus on a cold and snowy afternoon. He graciously accepted our invitation and chose to play center, hiking the ball and blocking for others. This is a splendid metaphor for Bill's service to the church. Whether as pastor or chaplain, professor or president, Bill seeks his place in the midst of the game, not avoiding its messiness, handing on the ball to others, and assisting them to accomplish the goal. Just as the center of Tillich's theology is grace, Bill Weiblen serves as a living example of what it means to be gracious.

The interviews collected in this volume were conducted in the summer of 1997 and were edited in the fall of 2000. They provide an oral history of Wartburg Seminary and the life of William H. Weiblen. They in no way provide a comprehensive account, but rather offer the memories of a man whose life links the generations at Wartburg Seminary in a unique way. These conversations complement Bill's own more systematic account of the history of the seminary, published as *Life Together at Wartburg Theological Seminary*. I have reason to believe that many others will find these reflections as precious as I do. I hope they will stimulate others to tell their own stories.

This book is divided into four parts. Part One focuses on Bill's recollection of the history of Wartburg Theological Seminary. It was a privilege for me to hear his interpretation of many events, large and small, out of the seminary's past. Part Two includes stories that illuminate Bill's own life, offered in chronological order. I know that Bill, due to his characteristic humility, is hesitant to see these memories in print. But I know that there are many others who share my interest in learning from his biography. Part Three is a collection of theological articles and papers from Bill's academic career. Some of these have previously appeared in various forms, but they are here collected together for the first time. The original sources of the previously published articles are noted and thanks are extended for the permission to reprint them in this form. Part Four offers some representative addresses and sermons. The sermons, in particular, have never before appeared in print. Some introductory commentary appears at the beginning of each of those sections.

The witness of Bill and Ilah Weiblen continues to shape Wartburg Theological Seminary. Especially their commitment to international students and to the cause of peace and justice throughout the world has left a lasting mark. They continue to worship, teach, and model Christian existence. Ilah has been a full and committed partner with Bill every step of the journey in their life together at Wartburg. She has been especially engaged for the freedom struggles in Namibia and South Africa. Her tireless work archiving the materials related to these liberation movements is a contribution that will assist many in the future to document and analyze the miracle that transpired in those countries.

My thanks go out to Ann Filiatrault, Erik Breddin, Val Way, Tiffany Nichole Broman, and Kevin Anderson for their exceptional assistance in the preparation of this manuscript. And thanks to Shannon Jung for final proofreading.

This work is dedicated to Ilah Weiblen and my own wife Cathy, strong and unpretentious women who quietly go about their business and so make it possible for life to continue.

Craig L. Nessan
Easter 2003

Part One:

Conversations on the History of Wartburg Theological Seminary

Introduction to Part One

William Weiblen serves as a bridge between the generations at Wartburg Seminary. Having arrived on the Wartburg Seminary campus as a student in the fall of 1940, Bill experienced first hand the teaching of Reu and the closing of the era led by the second generation of Fritschels, Max and George. Beyond what he learned through his own years of experience, Bill has been an attentive student of Wartburg history. His research into the origins of Wartburg Seminary history has contributed to the preservation of the Loehe tradition at a time when it would have been easy to forget. His recollections of the emissaries of Loehe, who were sent to the United States and eventually to Iowa, are valuable for our own reclaiming of Wartburg's missionary heritage again today.

One should note that this is not an uncritical reading of the past. While Bill is most appreciative of the theological contributions of a J. Michael Reu, his interpretation raises serious questions about matters such as his teaching method and political effectiveness. Weiblen's own reflections on having Reu as a teacher provide a necessary counterpoint to attempts by those from other Lutheran church bodies (especially the Missouri Synod) to appropriate the Reu tradition for themselves.

The thoughts recorded here complement the more historical account chronicled in Weiblen's book, *Life Together at Wartburg Seminary.* In these conversations the reader learns to appreciate many lesser known aspects of the Wartburg tradition. Bill is particularly appreciative of the leadership given to the seminary by Julius Bodensieck at a key juncture in the seminary's history. Other fascinating memories of seminary faculty members add life and color to this account.

The Brothers Fritschel and
The Origins of Wartburg Theological Seminary

WW: There's a little book, which you can look up in the Library. It's written by Herman Fritschel, son of Gottfried. It's called *Biography of Drs. Sigmund and Gottfried Fritschel*. It's about the Fritschel brothers. It's blue in color. The family was from Nuremberg. The Fritschels came out of a family of devout business people. Among other things there was a Christian bookstore. This reflects the strong Christian influence.

CN: Would you say pietistic?

WW: Yes. I'd say it's a story of a pietistic family where the kids responded to a call to mission. Eventually, the Fritschels brought their parents over here and so they all ended up in the U.S. It is a very unique name. You don't find many people with this name in the United States. Anyway, they are significant because they are a part of the historical connection between Loehe's response to the needs of the church in America and Wartburg Seminary.

CN: How much time did these brothers spend directly with Loehe?

WW: I suppose a limited amount of time because at this time Loehe was being over-stretched. It wasn't long before the Fritschels would have been on their own. Iowa became the unique partner with Loehe, because Loehe went to Iowa after the break with the Missouri Synod. There isn't that great expansive mutual participation between Loehe and the Iowa Synod. I think it's partly because Loehe's wife died about this time. If you want to get the whole business of Loehe, going back behind the Fritschels to Loehe, there's a new book by Christian Weber [*Missionstheologie bei Wilhelm Loehe*] that's the most comprehensive thing available. It's got about everything under the sun.

CN: It was published in 1996.

WW: I've been reading a lot of sections of it. I think it is quite reliable. It even mentions a little article I had about Reu in *Currents in Theology and Mission*.

CN: Pretty comprehensive.

WW: One thing that is necessary to get straight is the inconsistency, as you will have noticed, in the dates of the beginning of Wartburg Seminary. One lists it as 1853 and one lists it as 1854. Wartburg College considers itself to have been founded in 1852. Gerhard Ottersberg established that date when he wrote his doctoral work on the Iowa Synod. It's all connected with those early beginnings. In 1852 the need for more schoolteachers became apparent as the colonies began to expand, the colonies like Frankenmuth, Frankenhilfe, and Frankentrost, and so forth. All of those colonies needed school teachers. That's where Grossmann, who already in Germany was an educator and had done advanced work in that area, volunteered himself to

Loehe. With little additional preparation there, Grossmann was sent over to the United States and founded this institution whose main function would be to train school teachers. He had hardly gotten started with that work but the classes had met, so it was legitimate to say that it began in 1852.

CN: In Michigan then?

WW: Yes, in Saginaw, Michigan. He hardly had begun when the whole conflict with Walther blew up. So it became a big decision about who you were going to follow, Walther or Loehe? The bulk of them went with Walther and Walther read Loehe out of the Lutheran Church, so to speak. And it was then that these people like Grossmann, Deindorfer, Amann, and others who apparently were involved in the community there asked: "What are we going to do?" And so they wrote to father Loehe and Loehe advised them to go to Iowa. And so it was in 1853 when they started to Iowa. They got here in 1853 and the first classes were held. A small group of students that were studying in Saginaw made up the party, along with Grossmann, Deindorfer and Amann. They got here and rented this place on Garfield Avenue. Have you ever gone down there to see that?

CN: No, I'd like to do that.

WW: I'll take you there some time, when we can work it in with eating another meal at the Bierstube restaurant. Anyway there's a little plaque along the sidewalk and the building is still there [destroyed by fire in 1998]. So if you follow that rigidly, and say the first educational activity took place in 1853, that should be the beginning. That would be correct. On the other hand, it was primarily those people who were preparing to be teachers and so you couldn't say that it was the seminary. It was during the course of that year, that the decision was made that what they obviously needed more than anything were pastors. And, therefore, that was the work that they decided to do. A call for assistance went out and Grossmann got the help of Sigmund Fritschel. That's why the date for the seminary is listed officially as 1854, because that's actually when the seminary part of it began.

CN: As for the next location of the seminary, when we go up to EWALU Bible Camp to drop off the children at camp, St. Sebald is right there!

WW: You'll find a sign, west of Strawberry Point before you come to turn off for EWALU, the sign pointing to St. Sebald Church. It's only a few miles up there.

CN: And is the church at the same location where the seminary was?

WW: No, the seminary was a little ways from there. It's closer to a farmhouse that you will see, one of the nearest farmhouses to the church.

CN: We should ask the people at the farmhouse.

WW: Well, they may know. I'm not sure who is living there now. You might want to call the pastor and tell him you are coming to see if he is going to be around.

CN: What about the buildings at St. Sebald. Are they gone?

WW: Yes.

CN: So there's not much to see at St. Sebald really?

WW: The thing to see at St. Sebald is the cemetery where the two Indian boys are buried. And there are a few abutments of the old seminary at the original location still there.

CN: If you know where to look.

WW: Yeah. Well, you can go up to that farm nearby. The Schmidts can probably tell you where to go or Albert Hock who lives in Strawberry Point and is writing a history of St. Sebald, one of the pastors there, one of our graduates.

CN: A history of the place and the church?

WW: The whole business. He retired in Strawberry Point and is a very active supporter.

CN: What about the remnants of the seminary in Mendota? Are the buildings used by the seminary still at Mendota or was the seminary in a church?

WW: No. There is a little church there, still like it was. That was called the seminary church. We had an anniversary down there three years ago. It's a church of some little sect now. They opened it up so we could come in there and see it.

CN: Was that the location of the seminary?

WW: That was the church for the seminary. They didn't go to the downtown church. I don't know why the Fritschels thought they ought to have their own Sunday congregation.

CN: The buildings where they had offices and classrooms, that's gone?

WW: That's gone. But the grounds on which it was located is part of the high school grounds now and I think there is a plaque there. It's on the southeast edge of town. That's about all that is there.

CN: And then the graves of the Fritschels are there.

WW: Right. The Fritschels, Sigmund and Gottfried, and Frau von Schwarz

CN: Oh, she's buried there, too?

WW: Yes. She is the woman after whom the Refectory has been named.

CN: Are there any stories about the Fritschels that would have been told, anecdotes, things that perhaps would not have been written down in some of these histories?

WW: A pastor from Neuendettelsau told what it was like when he arrived one afternoon at the seminary at St. Sebald. It was all quiet. He didn't see any students and wondered where everybody was. And finally he went into the building and saw a sister from Neuendettelsau. There was usually one there, one or two, who helped take care of the students. She explained to him that they were all out in the fields. That was the regular routine. They studied in the morning and in the afternoon they had duties, working, making hay, harvesting whatever the case may be.

CN: That must have formed them in a very close community.

WW: A sense of community was enhanced in that way. I'm sure it was a rather rigid community, with not much tolerance for a lot of fun.

CN: No idiosyncrasies or getting out of line. They wouldn't decorate Luther's statue.

WW: I'm sure that they wouldn't do that. But that carried over until even when I was at the seminary in 1940 to 43. Especially in your first year, everybody was expected to do a certain amount of janitorial or yard duty. A certain person was made chairman of this whole operation and they called him the *Spassenkoenig*, the king of whom we made fun. And I remember how angry Ace Schumacher was when he turned out to be the one elected the administrator of all this. He had to line us all up and get this work done. In the wintertime, you had your turn shoveling the walks and he had to have that all arranged. He was not happy that he was elected *Spassenkoenig*. Even to this day you ask him about it and he would be annoyed. But really it was a carry over kind of life together which included a little bit of common labor. It wouldn't be a bad idea now, to get the walks shoveled. It probably wouldn't be too difficult with all the equipment we have.

CN: We just have the clean-up day; it's about the only remnant.

WW: Yeah. That was something that I introduced. My thinking behind it was it would be just great to have everybody working together on different projects. It's gotten to be now a Saturday thing, but everybody—faculty, secretaries, the whole staff—everybody just took a half a day to do something to enhance the beauty of the place. It's a way of recognizing that there are other things that have to be done while you are studying. But the demands now allow for none of this frivolous time off. We've gotten rather rigid about that.

CN: The Protestant work ethic has gotten the best of us.

WW: Right. Because we will not grant easy time off, we have this on Saturday. We get kind of a motley crew, but the whole thing used to be the whole community working, reminiscent of the olden days.

CN: Maybe if it were put in those terms again, it would draw more interest.

WW: Yeah. Because then it was a natural thing. People working were part of the routine. You didn't have to come back for a special day. Now with the way it is, it's another day you have got to add to your busy activities.

CN: There are a couple of things. I was told that the building was torn down at St. Sebald right after they went to Mendota and that the wood was used to build other buildings. Supposedly there is still a garage that has the wood from the original seminary building. They used to find typeset at the site.

WW: Well, there you see, that comes from Gottfried Fritschel, the younger brother. He was more competent in English than Sigmund and also had a particular interest in composition. He

8

spent one summer improving his English by studying at Upper Iowa University, at North Fayette, Iowa. It's a Methodist school. He studied English there. One summer he also went to Madison to learn the art of printing. They had set up a printing press either in the basement or on the ground floor of the building at St. Sebald. And that's when they began printing in 1858. They started printing the *Kirchen-Blatt*.

CN: That was real early after he arrived.

WW: Yeah, he was only here a year. Then he would have students help him with putting out this paper for the whole Synod. It went on that way a few years. But that was also a basis for what became the *Kirchliche Zeitschrift* that was still in operation in 1940. The business office downstairs, the part closest to the post office, was where they duplicated all of Reu's manuscripts. Everybody had a script for their course of the stuff you were supposed to learn. Actually it was preliminary to a book. Sometimes it eventually got in book form. In my day it was always one place where students worked, duplicating material. That was a remnant of the printing press that had been a part of Wartburg. But when they moved to Mendota, the main part of the printing operation, I think, eventually became a separate operation and was the Wartburg Press.

CN: Did they do the *Kirchliche Zeitschrift*?

WW: Yes, and the *Kirchen-Blatt* and then *The Lutheran*, English version.

CN: That was also done by Wartburg Press?

WW: Yes. The Wartburg Press had been in Waverly and at the end it was in Chicago. When the merger in 1930 took place, Wartburg Press was consolidated with the Lutheran Book Concern in Columbus, Ohio. That's what it was known as after that.

CN: The Lutheran Book Concern?

WW: Yeah, sort of like just happened in the merger when Augsburg and Fortress were combined. I used to have a joke with Al Anderson who was the president of Augsburg. He always enjoyed going to the seminaries with books and stuff for the Seniors and attending this banquet. And I was still talking about Wartburg Press. He, of course, would remind us that it was now Augsburg.

I don't know what eventually happened to the printing press of Gottfried Fritschel. I have a feeling that Sigmund Fritschel's daughter's husband may have gotten it, who was named Haefner. Al Haefner taught Greek at Wartburg. He took an interest in one of these little presses. You know how the ink thing comes down over it and it comes up and prints. He had one of those. He printed up very orderly class presentations. I often wondered and I never asked him the question of whether that was the old press that Gottfried Fritschel had got in Madison, Wisconsin.

CN: That would be a real historical artifact now.

WW: Yeah.

CN: Was the *Kirchliche Zeitschrift* printed in Columbus after 1930?

9

WW: Right. And the *Kirchen-Blatt* was continued too for a period of time.

CN: How long did that go on?

WW: Well, Bodensieck went to Columbus, Ohio in 1930 or 31, somewhere in there, right after the merger, to be the editor of the *Kirchen-Blatt*.

CN: This was the German Church periodical.

WW: *The Lutheran* for the German Church. That's the one the Iowa Synod had, and there was also the English version of that. One good source where you can look at this stuff when you get to working on it in the future is in the old volumes of those magazines. They are up in the folio section, where the magazines are.

CN: That would document a lot of the history then.

WW: Yeah. I looked up a lot of this stuff in there. For example, this woman was coming from Mendota, Illinois to the seminary. She had been president when the young people of the Wartburg League presented the Luther statue to the seminary from Mendota. So they wanted to know something about that event. I simply looked it up in the *Kirchen-Blatt* and found an article on it, telling all about the occasion, who spoke and everything like that. There's a lot of stuff in there, dates and stories of what happened. That's the source that I used. You'll find those and other magazines that will be of help to you, too. And then, of course, Wiederaenders probably told you about what they called the *Chronik*, which is kind of a summation of what the Executive Committee of the Synod did, the leaders of the church. That's in the Archives.

CN: That's more of a terse account.

WW: Yeah, but the synod and the seminary, they were one and the same thing. A lot of that is in English, translated by August Engelbrecht who was later president of the Illinois District. He was married also to a Fritschel, whose father was the director after Grossmann, director of the normal school, the college for training teachers.

I also recall a story about Sigmund Fritschel. The congregation in Platteville, Wisconsin, Peace Lutheran Church, traces its heritage back to Sigmund Fritschel. Actually Sigmund was seeking another place where he was scheduled to conduct a service and ended up in that community, actually starting the church there. There are little things about how when he was coming through the snow in order to reach a church, stuff like that. But I don't have a bunch of stories. The main thing I have about the Fritschels is the on-going battle with the Missouri Synod.

They were forced to be very resourceful. Gottfried Fritschel, for example, very early when they were out in St. Sebald, spent part of one summer in Madison, Wisconsin, learning the art of printing. When he came back here he then set up a printing press so they could print their own material, their own church papers, and eventually the *Kirchliche Zeitschrift*. Gottfried Fritschel became someone who was capable of doing the printing press and was kind of a forerunner in this respect. Then for years the seminary carried out its own printing of manuscripts. Later that was by mimeograph. I think Alfred Haefner inherited that press because he had a little hand press in which he printed up things for his classes. You may have seen these presses that they print wedding announcements on, one page at a time. If you had the patience, you could print a book that way.

CN: Maybe that's what I'll have to do with one of my manuscripts.

WW: There's another story about Sigmund Fritschel that is important. It has to do with his father. With his parents' blessing he offered his services to Loehe. Therefore he studied for a while in Neuendettalsau. Sigmund had studied languages at Gymnasium, so he was well prepared. But he had developed a kind of interest not only in Inner Mission to go to the German immigrants but also in Outer Mission while at Neuendettelsau. They wanted to go to the West Coast of the United States to do mission work among the Chinese. That was kind of his plan. But then the request came from Grossmann that they needed a teacher. At that time it was primarily to train schoolteachers who could teach children Latin, Greek and German. Since he was such a good competent person in those languages, Loehe, in response to Grossmann's request, talked to Sigmund. Loehe said that he realized that this dream he had of going with his friend to San Francisco to work among the Chinese was very important to him and was itself in line with Loehe's desires. But now there was this need he believed that Sigmund could fulfill. So would he go? He responded positively.

CN: It was really a visionary notion though.

WW: Yeah. These guys sitting over there in Germany…

CN: Dreaming of doing mission among the Chinese in San Francisco.

WW: Yeah, Wi Jo Kang was interested in this part of Wartburg's history. Well, probably the big thing about the Fritschels was that they both did end up here as founders of Wartburg Theological Seminary. It's interesting how quickly they were embroiled in theological debate. That was the mode in Germany where they came from and it simply transplanted itself over here to this country. Under Walther's wing, the Missouri Synod had most of those pastors Loehe had trained up until the early 1850s. Loehe was also a founder of the Ft. Wayne, Indiana practical seminary. It was interesting that they were soon embroiled in this controversy. It wasn't enough that Loehe was charged once, but here it isn't just Loehe any longer, but the Fritschels were now getting the brunt of the attack. There was one pastor, Schmidt, from Missouri who brought a constant barrage of attacks against the Fritschel brothers.

CN: Was this through pamphleteering?

WW: It was pamphleteering and the church newspapers. A lot of these debates were published. One of them was titled *Iowa and Missouri: A Defense of the Teachings of the Iowa Synod from the Attacks of Herr Professor Schmidt.*

CN: It was published in 1878.

WW: Wartburg Seminary was started here in 1854. They had been closed in Saginaw, Michigan, and count that the first year as the beginning of the seminary. After that they moved out to St. Sebald in 1857. By 1860 they were involved in these disputations. There were meetings between Missouri and Iowa and colloquiums involved. One famous colloquium was in Milwaukee in 1867.

CN: These were public debates?

WW: Yes, they were very public. We were talking about Reu and his position on millennialism. Even Loehe had this strain where he had such a strong hope that the people of Israel would be converted and that Christ would reign a thousand years. So the articles that were published during this period are very interesting to read. Professor Schmidt brought out a whole bunch of articles against our Synod. He had them published separately and so the Fritschels were forced to respond to that.

CN: The title of Schmidt's work was *The Iowa Misunderstanding and Misinterpretation as illustrated by their Actions and Books.*

WW: The purpose of the whole thing was to put the Fritschel brothers under a point of attack.

CN: Well, you see this type of book appear still, especially out of some elements within Missouri.

WW: Yeah, it's polemicized history. On page 2, Schmidt cites that already in 1858 the Iowa Synod accepted chiliasm as a formal doctrine. See how Schmidt interpreted that.

CN: This is really curious.

WW: You know that millennialism came more and more into disrepute, so much so that even Iowa wanted to get rid of it.

CN: I'm surprised that this controversy was so early on and that one of the first controversies was about millennialism of all things.

WW: Loehe made the point that it's there as a testimony of hope in the Scriptures, you see. And it's on that basis that these guys developed their position. The Fritschels respond to this as something that doesn't have to be dismissed out of hand because it expresses the certainty of the hope with which the Christian lives. Christ is going to return and bring about some changes.

CN: Would they both have been authors?

WW: Yeah, they did this sort of thing together.

CN: Kind of equally, neither one is the major contributor.

WW: Speaking of stories, it used to be said that these guys worked so closely together and were such a heart of the seminary at its beginning, they each knew what the other was going to say before the other one said anything. So you could see how they could write stuff together. I suppose they both wrote some of this.

CN: Now what kind of competition existed then on the congregational level between the various Lutheran groups? Were they both starting congregations in the same territory?

WW: They fanned out from around here to different places. Some of those places left the old American Lutheran Church and they are now Missouri Synod. One is in Sherrill, Iowa where there was a small congregation. That was started by these people. Wherever there was a gathering of Germans, people from the seminary would go out in increasing numbers every weekend, often by train. They even went into the Dakotas and the neighboring states around here. But they also had competition, not so much from the Ohio Synod, but I think very early on from Missouri. They got to be defined as an enemy of Missouri.

CN: Would it be like now where two different church bodies would sometimes start two congregations in the same place?

WW: I think some of that happened, the longer the battle persisted. At first there was much work for both of them. It wasn't probably as direct as it later became. By the time, however, when this book was published, they're already an established synod and are probably running into competition for where they would start a church. They wanted to keep the German people away from the heresy of the Iowa Synod.

CN: Was the rhetoric of the Iowa Synod as strong as Missouri rhetoric?

WW: It's an interesting thing as you read this. You come to a beautiful passage, around page 100, in which the brothers Fritschel, I think after the Assembly in Milwaukee, said you can malign us all you want to, but we're still your closest brothers in the faith. We will continue to love you and regard you as our closest brothers no matter what. We know what it is to be subjected to your abuse.

CN: I remember you quoted that in that piece about open questions.

WW: Yes, right. It's as valid and good today as it was then, as a response. When you think what happened to Missouri during the 1970s. All the Loehe people have had trouble in Missouri. John Tietjen did his dissertation on Loehe. They became so narrowly congregationalist that they don't revere the church. The Office of Ministry is made a function of the congregation. Loehe never wanted to make congregations carry such theological weight. Even though the leaders of the opposition are leading these people over against heresy and narrowness, they too may get caught up in a sense of superiority, which leads them to walk out instead of occupying the fort. If they had been occupying the fort, the situation would never have gotten so out of control.

CN: History might have been entirely different. I've noticed that from others who come out of Missouri into the ELCA, that some have a distrust of church for one thing, but also a kind of a feistiness.

WW: Well that's true. We used to say, "You can take the boy out of Missouri but you can't take Missouri out of the boy."

CN: There's something to that.

CN: Now in the teaching of that time, were there distinct areas where Gottfried and Sigmund specialized in their teaching?

WW: It seemed to me that Gottfried, more and more, came in the line of teaching history and Sigmund, more and more, in the line of teaching what today we call systematic theology. Basically, both were teaching all the various subjects in the curriculum, teaching based on the Bible. Gottfried was, I think, the one who usually taught English.

13

CN: They were teaching the students English?

WW: Yes.

CN: But they weren't doing instruction in English.

WW: They weren't teaching in English. One of Loehe's weaknesses was his strong German nationalism, at least with regard to German culture. He was bound and determined that these people wouldn't lose the great language. That meant they were able to retain their identity as Germans.

CN: Which limited mission work to German-speaking people in some ways.

WW: Yes. In spite of that, they went into new territory and did insist on teaching these students English.

CN: Who else would have been teaching at that time?

WW: At the beginning, there would have been Inspector Grossmann, Sigmund Fritschel, and eventually also Gottfried. They would have been the basic faculty.

CN: The entire faculty. It's hard to imagine.

WW: I think Deindorfer, who was a pastor and wrote a history, also was involved.

CN: He would do some adjunct teaching.

WW: Deindorfer did some teaching, too. Primarily, it was Grossmann and Fritschel. Here were these young mavericks, neither much older than 20 something, and they are the faculty of Wartburg Seminary.

CN: And then Reu came.

WW: Yes. There were others helping in the teaching by then. By then, the seminary had grown and some of the children of the Fritschels already were utilized. Max Fritschel eventually was president. He began teaching at the time that the seminary was expanding in Mendota. I'm trying to think if that was about the time they hired their first English-speaking professor for training American, English speaking students.

CN: That would have been near the end of the 19th Century?

WW: That came early in the 20th Century.

CN: I notice here that you've got a Formula of Concord?

WW: This is by George Fritschel who is the son of Gottfried. He's the one who is the father of Doc Fritschel.

WW: His son, Ted Fritschel, was pastor down in Iowa City. I just brought that along if you wanted to take a look at it.

WW: Sigmund was here teaching and then they moved from Garfield Avenue to where now St. John's Lutheran Church is. Deindorfer was the pastor at that time. Times became hard so they sent Sigmund out to serve in a congregation in Detroit in the Buffalo Synod. There were students who hadn't finished their course of study and he continued to work with them while serving this parish. I used to use that as an example of saying that Wartburg from its very beginning was used to doing theological education in more than one place. Wartburg Seminary had experience, in its very early history, of a professor taking some students with him and giving them a theological education. So that's part of our heritage. It was somewhat like that when Peter Kjeseth went West with a group of students and rented some facilities and established the Denver House of Studies. Gradually this model led also to the program in Austin. The one at Denver had reached a zenith in the 1970s. We had the building and facilities, books and resources out there, but we didn't have the money to support it. I don't know why this model couldn't be useful still today. I think Gettysburg Seminary has this kind of program.

CN: Gettysburg has one in Washington, D.C. There's also a cooperative venture in Atlanta.

WW: So, it's still a good idea.

CN: The dates when Sigmund Fritschel was a pastor in Detroit is probably in your book.

WW: It was in the late 1850s. What I think interesting is how in coming to inter-synodical relationships, the Iowa Synod stood apart somewhat. The Gettysburg tradition, on the other hand, with its background considered itself more American and ecumenical. It didn't take a strong confessional position like Mt. Airy Seminary in Philadelphia did.

CN: Gettysburg has Schmucker as their theologian with his American Lutheranism.

WW: That's right, for an example. So Gettysburg would have been the one at that time that would be affirming the Concordat and the various ecumenical proposals. Now today, 100 and some years later, Wartburg Seminary which would have been the opposite of Gettysburg at that time, has already as a faculty affirmed the going ahead with the ecumenical activities and Gettysburg has not yet done that.

CN: Well, I would say if they were true to the Schmucker tradition that they would also be in favor of these ecumenical developments.

WW: Yeah, it's kind of interesting how you can have these great reversals.

15

Wartburg Theological Seminary
at the Start of the Twentieth Century

CN: Bill, what about the second generation of Fritschels. What's your remembrance of Max and George? And we've also got another brother named Herman, and there are probably others.

WW: Herman was the son of Sigmund, who became the hospital administrator. He was the one in Milwaukee.

CN: So he is a brother of Max.

WW: That's right.

CN: So he's second generation.

WW: Yes. He is a direct descendent of Sigmund.

CN: Did he do some teaching here, too?

WW: Yes. He mentioned that in his book. It's amazing how he writes in his book, *Biography of Drs. Sigmund and Gottfried Fritschel* (page 115): "After the death of Dr. Sigmund Fritschel, his widow lived for seven years, when she was called home at the age of 74 years, and was laid to rest at Mendota at the side of her husband and three children who had preceded her." Here he is writing about his mother in the third person. Also he gives the list of the next generation. He talks about the three sons of the original Fritschels in Germany and then tells about the children of Sigmund. Sigmund had 11 children. Those wives were hearty women.

CN: God bless them. Six is plenty for me.

WW: "The four sons became theologians, four of the daughters became pastor's wives. Of Gottfried's ten children, eight were boys. One, however, died after graduation from college, having the ministry in mind. Four entered the service of the church as pastors or professors and two served in other capacities." (page 120). The bulk of them were in the church. "The four sons of Sigmund were Gottfried Sebald, Jr., who after graduating from Wartburg, completed his academic education at the University of Pennsylvania and then went for two years to finish his education at the German universities at Erlangen and Leipzig. At the latter, he graduated with a degree of Doctor of Philosophy, a rare requirement in those years from an American theological student. Upon returning home, he became assistant pastor in New York City for a short time. Suffering from tuberculosis, he returned home at Christmas time and shortly thereafter at Easter, 1880 died at the age of 24 years and 5 months." (pages 120f.). After he was so well prepared. You know that disease was a devastating thing.

CN: So many children, with such potential.

16

WW: The eldest son, Gottfried Sebald, Jr., would have been an important theologian, having studied at Pennsylvania and also with his doctor's degree in Germany.

CN: And it probably would have been his destiny to come back and serve here at Wartburg.

WW: I'm sure that's what his father had in mind. Then you have others like Johannes who taught mostly at Wartburg College in Waverly. Max went to Thiel College in Pennsylvania. After graduating from there, he studied two years at German universities at Rostock, Erlangen, and Leipzig. He returned to Dubuque and became an assistant at the seminary for two years, then professor and finally Director. The total number of years he taught at the seminary was 48. He died at the age of 72. He taught hundreds of theology students in his classes. [cf. page 121].

CN: You didn't have a lot of acquaintance with him, then.

WW: I didn't have direct acquaintance with the sons of Sigmund and Gottfried. But Herman Fritschel, after graduating, came for two years and instructed at the seminary. Then he continued theological studies at the universities of Leipzig and Erlangen. Upon returning to America, he became a pastor of a mission church in Superior, Wisconsin. Then he served as pastor at Brandon, Wisconsin. Next he was called to Milwaukee, as successor to Rev. William Passavant, where he was Rector of the Lutheran Deaconess Motherhouse and Director of the Passavant Institutions. (cf. pages 122f.). He was on the building committee for the seminary. He's the one, it probably didn't happen that way but is alleged to have said, "With a name like Wartburg, you ought to be able to come up with a better design than a square building, with classes on the first floor." But that's just put in our own words. He did insist that it ought to be something unique and forced the architects to think harder about the design. They did think. There's some evidence that they did send a representative over to Erlangen and over to Eisenach who studied the castle. And, of course, the one thing that the architect chose as the organizing principle is the one part of the castle that's a 19th century addition.

CN: It appealed to their aesthetics.

WW: Yeah, the tower. So it was like you were there when Luther was alive. Except you were able to see a Wartburg that Luther never did.

CN: Was the old mansion where the seminary was located still standing at that time?

WW: Yes. It was standing, but not very long, however. Maybe within the first year, I think it was 1916 that it was taken down.

CN: Was it intentionally demolished?

WW: It was intentionally demolished. Mrs. Salzmann, Reu's daughter, always told me that Max Fritschel was worried that the church officials would turn it into old folks' home. And he didn't want old folks' home on the same campus as the seminary.

CN: That's a curious twist.

WW: It was quite a usable building yet. There are a few pictures that show the new construction done and the old building still standing there. A few years ago when they built

17

those duplexes down there, they got into the corner of the area where the old mansion stood and there were some artifacts, just bulldozed and covered up. All kinds of finds there. They found old bottles, obviously some stuff from the bathroom.

CN: That was down on the ground floor, according to Patty Gottschalk-Shaffer's account, which she got from Mrs. Salzmann.

CN: Was the house that the Holms lived in (385 Wartburg Place)—earlier Zeilinger had lived there and then Salzmanns lived there—moved to that location or was that the original location where it is now?

WW: I think that's the original location.

CN: Because on the map it looks as though it were further to the north.

WW: Well, I don't think so. The first houses built were the two brick ones. And then to accommodate more, they built the two wooden ones. They were built two years later.

CN: And the so-called English professor was named Zeilinger.

WW: Yes, that's the one some people had problems with. He didn't seem to be the right caliber for Reu, so he got kind of a rough deal. If you want to see how that works out, my roommate in seminary was a descendant of Zeilinger. He is still living. There wasn't that great a love for him, by Reu or the Fritschels.

CN: Are you aware of any other significant events between the time of the Fritschels and the time when you came as a student?

WW: Did we talk about how student dissatisfaction with George Fritschel reached the point where there were student protests, asking the Board of Directors and so forth to get somebody else?

CN: Would that have been in the '20s?

WW: That would have been in the '30s.

CN: Shortly before you came, then.

WW: Right. Very shortly before I came. And my pastor at home, he was one of the ringleaders, Merritt Bohmhoff who is now retired and in Waverly, whose last position was as the Development Director at Wartburg College. He was one of those involved. There was some fret because the faculty involved pushed the question of whether they should be kicked out and not recommended for ordination. That's the way they handled it in those days. You know, that was quite a thing for students to try and go over the head of the faculty.

CN: That marks a big transition in the structure and the authority of the seminary.

WW: And the fact that those students had that kind of determination. I think it was a healthy sign for the future developing life of the student body at Wartburg Seminary.

18

CN: They certainly felt strongly about it.

WW: Yeah. And it is amazing that they could actually go to the Board of Directors, or whoever, and talk about it.

CN: I read your history of Wartburg Seminary. It seemed like the student organizations and the institution itself developed in the late '50s and '60s. Ewald seemed to have had a fairly significant role in formalizing certain procedures.

WW: Before that, however, in the '30s, was when they called the first full-time president, Emil Rausch.

CN: Prior to that the president would have been part-time director and part-time faculty?

WW: Right. Max Fritschel was Director of the Seminary. The first Director was George Grossmann, who also taught a class. The Director always taught. So up to that time, or even now, Wartburg Seminary's president has always taught something. I think that's a good tradition because the president has his foot in the classroom. Like at the present time, Roger Fjeld's competence in the field of American church history just fits in beautifully for him to teach that course and give him the interaction with the student body. I always thought that was a necessary thing. But Rausch was the first one to devote his major energies to being president and so I would say that the structural development of the seminary got a start under him. But it didn't have a long opportunity to develop because he died already in '38 or '39.

WW: Well that brings us then to Reu, the main one of all. Sigmund Fritschel became ill after having moved back to Dubuque in 1889. Reu came to Wartburg Seminary after serving as a pastor.

CN: He had been in the parish?

WW: In the parish at Rock Falls, Illinois.

CN: For about ten years?

WW: It would have been about 10 years that he was involved, first being *Rektor* or assistant pastor, and then pastor of Rock Falls. It was one of the little churches William Streng later served as a pastor.

CN: Both of them served in Rock Falls.

WW: Yeah. Streng was in the big church in Rock Falls. He had students at his church. There were two congregations, I think.

WW: Mrs. Salzmann reminisced and talked about her father as a pastor. He was highly regarded because he was used to help students in the languages, Greek and Hebrew.

CN: That's rather exceptional in and of itself.

WW: So that's where he came from before the seminary. You might just follow that as your own line some time if you get to dig deeply into Sigmund's letters, how he assessed Reu. I can't

19

imagine him, with the power he had, having anyone coming to teach who didn't have his stamp of approval. He must have approved Reu. Nevertheless there seems to be kind of a lingering irritation between the Reus and Fritschels.

CN: The change of generations, maybe?

WW: Yes. Because the second generation of Fritschels were not at the same level of competence as the two older brothers.

CN: It kept it from being a family dynasty in some ways.

WW: You know, I liked Reu as a teacher. He had kind of a hypnotizing voice, a real deep voice. He knew how to modulate it very well. He must have had a photographic memory because everything was so precise and carefully conceived. There was not any deviation from it. He had these long, convoluted German sentences, and he could spew them forth in beautiful German. I could not help but be impressed by the sound of it. Also when speaking English, he sounded formidable because of his accent and his pronunciations.

CN: He must have had a very systematic mind.

WW: A very systematic mind. I think that was his field. He actually taught everything there was on the curriculum at one time or another. He did a lot of biblical studies. He was very proficient in the language. He was used by Neuendettelsau to teach Hebrew because he could do it well.

Well, the course consisted of this. You got this script, and that is really all you needed. He did not encourage you to go out and read. He could tell you what was wrong with Schleiermacher, for example, and that he was not to be trusted, and so on and so forth. Barth was now coming on to the scene and we thought we should read something about it in the *Kirchliche Zeitschrift*. He simply told us it is in danger of becoming Biblical *Schwaermerei*.

CN: He would want you to just take it on his authority then.

WW: Yeah. He expected that. He knew what he was talking about. He used the script that he had written of his lectures. He departed somewhat from it but not too much.

CN: So you could sit in class with the text in front of you.

WW: We would just add the elaboration as he made it in various places. He had a great proliferation of Bible passages. Sometimes he explained some of those nuances and applied the different possibilities. So you could add that. What you were required to do on the test was give back as much as you could on those various parts that he asked you about.

CN: These were written exams.

WW: Yes.

CN: Was that typical in all the classes, to have written exams?

WW: Yes. In class we didn't yet have these blue books which I learned about later when I went to graduate school. If you went in to Reu for an exam you could write for two hours solid, as fast as you could, and wish you had more time.

CN: To try to demonstrate all you had memorized.

WW: And that is kind of what he expected too. He did not have much tolerance for the guy who could reduce it to one or two pages. He expected more than that. He expected you to be able to expound some of these crucial biblical passages.

CN: How much room was there for disagreement or offering an alternate interpretation?

WW: I think that he pretty much had his point of view on everything and would expect that returned, although he could surprise you. We talked about baptism, and in regard to baptism, he said, "Now don't forget as pastors, that this Baptist woman living down the street from your church is just as genuinely a member of the body of Christ as all of your sisters and brothers in the Lutheran Church." He was certainly not as narrow as Missouri. Missouri was fighting him all the time. Some guy down the river in Muscatine was attacking Reu. He wrote a little pamphlet that was against Reu's position on chiliasm, the thousand-year reign, and so forth. That is one I never could figure out, why Reu moved in that direction. It just did not seem to fit in with the kind of person he was.

Well, this was the first year I was here and everybody was kind of concerned about whether they wanted to be in the Army or not. It was a hard struggle to say no. My first year in the summer time it was all we talked about. We couldn't even think of the future. All of the colleagues would be subject to the draft. That was the hardest thing.

CN: That would have been difficult. That would have been more difficult than the Viet Nam decision, because that was a different type of war.

WW: Right. The issues were clear-cut. It was needed.

CN: For Germans, especially to feel that divided, as German-Americans to feel a certain division in their soul.

WW: Well, I don't know what more to say.

CN: There must be some more detail about Reu, things that you have learned about him, maybe during the years before you were a student here.

WW: I had always heard about this Reu. I remember how surprised I was when I saw him. He is not a large person at all. He was a figure bigger than life. He was very small. He had a big moustache. His dominant thing was the curly black hair. We always speculated on whether or not he dyed his hair. I think really he did. He was 72 or 73 years old when he died and I can't believe that he had only three gray hairs.

One of the things that I think one must reckon with when it comes to Reu is that he was a babe in the woods when it came to ecclesiastical politics. Somehow he had a way of giving the impression that he belonged much farther to the right than he actually did.

For example, towards the end of his life he wrote on Luther and the Scriptures. In that work he had specific quotes from Luther in German, many of them which you can find, which have Luther as an advocate of plenary inspiration. But he ignores a host of others, which to be fair to Luther, you have to add also. Luther's insistence is on the living word in these written scriptures. His book on the church and the means of grace gives a much truer picture of Reu's understanding. But you have to remember it was the age of pure doctrine and everybody was out to get it straight that you are more genuinely Lutheran than another.

CN: Where was that coming from?

WW: Well, I think that originally started after the Reformation, with the whole development leading to the Formula of Concord and has never stopped since.

CN: Just a continuation of what I would call hyper-Lutheranism.

WW: Yes, exactly. I think that created some problems for him, like when the American Lutheran Church was formed in 1930. He gave this very emotional speech, that he could not be a member of the Lutheran Church anymore. He felt he was being bypassed. This did not amount to anything and he continued to teach here. I think there was some kind of substance to it, a kind of a jealousy over against the Fritschels. The Fritschels are the original forebears and they had a larger family here. Reu was in some ways raised by his mother alone. He always felt a little fragile and vulnerable against the Fritschels.

CN: Almost a sense of inferiority somehow to that tradition?

WW: Theologically he was far superior. He demonstrated beyond a doubt that he was. But Reu's position on such things as the debate going on about Wartburg Normal College was very unsettling. The schools had been together and eventually separated out. The two parts, the seminary and the college, continued to function together until the 1860s, when they were separated and the college part went to Galena. Financial disaster struck there. The director of the college apparently was not competent and it seemed to be in trouble. So they eventually closed the place at a great loss of money, I think.

CN: In Galena?

WW: In Galena.

CN: And then it was restarted?

WW: When they saw that it didn't work in Galena, they brought the two schools back together at Mendota, Illinois. And when they moved the seminary here to Dubuque in 1889, then the college part of it was separated. They moved toward establishing the college in Clinton. I think I've got a section on that in my history.

CN: Clinton, also, for some time.

WW: You see, the Iowa Synod wanted the seminary to come back to Dubuque, as things were growing again. Then they also wanted to establish a substantial, dignified, legitimate, viable college preparation. I think the fathers saw that it would be necessary to have a good academic institution. That's what they set out to make in Clinton, that it would be like the Gymnasium in

Germany. It would take students already in high school and continue their education. And, of course, this was being done by Missouri Synod anyway. They simply took the European model and implemented it here.

CN: Like what's at Concordia, Missouri.

WW: Yes. Well, that's what the Iowa Synod fathers looked for and they considered Clinton to be that kind of academic institution. Waverly, at the same time, would be a place for those who just wanted a practical education. The church needed that, too, for seminary preparation, a school where they would get the essentials like Greek and a few things like that, but mainly learning how to be a pastor. So there was always a little jealousy between Wartburg at Waverly and Wartburg at Clinton. It all came to a head by the time of the depression in the 1930s, when they simply had to consolidate all these schools. Clinton was, of course, closed. Here's one point I think I may have mentioned to you when we talked about Reu. The descendants of Sigmund Fritschel, even Gottfried for that matter, tended to go on for additional education and these respectable courses of study.

CN: Would they go to Germany to study?

WW: They would even do that, but also at institutions here in the U.S. And so they were interested in Wartburg at Clinton becoming a college of high caliber, which it did. But when Reu was asked about the issue when things came to a crunch and institutions had to be closed, he thought differently about the whole matter. He kind of waffled and said, "I'll have to say that the students who come from Waverly are equally well or better prepared when it comes to classical languages than they are from Clinton." And it simply was not true. First of all, Waverly didn't have the caliber of students that they had at Clinton. The caliber of students that went to Clinton was the children of the Fritschels and just brighter kids. You would want to understand how there was not always the great enthusiasm for Reu on the part of the Fritschels.

CN: There's another contributing factor, then?

WW: That is part of it. Gerhard Ottersberg told me very personally, just like we are sitting here, "We could not understand how Reu would not be for having an institution that really prepared these people."

CN: Do you think that had to do with his own being a self-made man?

WW: I think that maybe it did. He was going to say that they could do it in different kinds of ways. I think that's probably one of the prices of being a self-taught theologian. You eventually tend to believe your own rhetoric.

CN: And you may not value the credentials of others.

WW: Yes. And you don't bump up against the credit of others. That helped me also to understand how people like Haefner, cousin of Ottersberg, who was Dean of Wartburg College for a long time, was simply a person of the highest integrity when it came to students waiving any requirements or things like that. He hewed a steady line of excellence about what grades meant and so forth.

CN: So the standards from Clinton were absorbed into Waverly?

23

WW: Yes, into Waverly. Like Haefner said the day we drove him to Waverly in 1932. Every town has its little slogan. They still do that somewhat. When you came to Waverly there was a sign out there that said, "Waverly, a city that's going somewhere." And Haefner said to his wife, "Well, I hope it's still true when we get there."

CN: He had been at Clinton?

WW: Yes. He had been at Clinton but then he was at Wartburg Seminary here. At that time he was the librarian and taught some courses in Greek. But his main job was fixing up the library and organizing it.

CN: What became of the property in Clinton?

WW: They sold it to the Veterans Administration. There were some beautiful properties there. One of the great causes of sadness for people in the church and its institutions was the closing of all these schools in the merger of 1930. The depression was setting in at the same time that this merger was being undertaken, so there was just no way they could support all these schools. In addition to Wartburg College at Clinton and Wartburg at Waverly, there was Hebron College in Hebron, Nebraska. There was Eureka College in Eureka, South Dakota. Wiederaenders' father was out there and that's where he met his mother. And there was Luther College and Seminary in St. Paul, Minnesota. They were all merged together into this one school at Waverly. So you can imagine there were a lot of unhappy campers.

CN: All of the historical ties that were interrupted.

WW: Yeah. And all of the little jealousies that got wedged in between. "He's a Clinton guy." Or, "he's a Waverly guy."

CN: Even today, we make such distinctions.

WW: Yeah. Some of the professors did a better job of rising above the whole thing than a lot of the loyal fans out in the church did. Mathematics professors, for example, that I had in Waverly, came from St. Paul. There was a young guy who graduated from St. Olaf, who took some courses at the school in St. Paul while he was beginning his teaching. He was my math teacher and was at Waverly until he died a few years ago. He became a loyal Wartburg supporter and saw the whole effort consolidated together. When I was at Wartburg College in 1936-40, there were still big movements for putting Wartburg somewhere else, anywhere else, than this little nest of Waverly. St. Paul people made a lot of noise and, of course, they had a nice facility. They had beautiful land on a lake, which is in a different part of St. Paul from where Luther Seminary is located. It was a more beautiful physical location, though probably not large enough. There was that one and then there was another campus at Hebron, Nebraska and one in Eureka and one in Clinton. The one in Clinton was sold to the Veterans Administration. It was, for a while, the Veterans Hospital.

After the merger, Hein was President for some time and I think he first expressed the idea that as long as you have all of these different empty schools around, you are going to have protests for opening them up or moving the institution there. When he died, Henry Schuh became President from St. Paul Lutheran Church in Toledo, Ohio. He was more of a business administrator than an ecclesiastical person, a tough old business person. He said, "We've got to get rid of these campuses." And so the church got rid of them at any price. They sold St. Paul as just pieces of ground. I guess there is one building that was converted into an apartment house that is still up there. And the properties at Hebron and Eureka were not extensive enough. The old buildings may still be there, but used for something else, I don't know. But that's what happened after the merger. Except it was still being considered until after that war in the late 1940s, whether or not Wartburg should be moved. It made some sense to move it to Des Moines. As it turned out, however, it doesn't depend all that much where a school is located. Instead, you are talking about what kind of program you have.

CN: Sure. And Waterloo has grown so far to the north that you have a metropolitan connection there. Was the Clinton program called Wartburg College too?

WW: Yes.

CN: And Waverly also?

WW: Wartburg at Waverly was called a Normal College for a long time.

CN: That's shows the emphasis on preparing teachers.

WW: Yes. And it was only a two-year college. It was not a four-year college. And the one in St. Paul was also a two-year college. You see, they were following the old pattern like was followed by Missouri and Ft. Wayne, which used to be at Springfield, Illinois, where you studied a couple years at the college and then went to the seminary. And so you didn't have a full BA degree. It's like what we used to do, when pastors were urgently needed around the time of World War II and in the '50s. You would let a guy into the seminary who did not have a complete college education, but he was expected to pass and take all the courses that everybody else had to take.

CN: But he did not necessarily have the degree.

WW: Yes. If he didn't have a BA, he couldn't get a M.Div. He could get the Diploma of the Seminary.

CN: But Clinton was graduating after four years of study?

WW: Right.

CN: And Waverly was graduating two years, and Reu made this comment that he didn't see any difference.

WW: He actually believed it. I believe I was stating it cautiously. I think he actually said that he would have to say that the people who came from Waverly were better prepared than the ones coming from Clinton. And that simply couldn't be true and it made a farce of everything the people at Clinton were doing. The people like the Fritschels came from classical education. Gottfried Fritschel had studied at Erlangen and other places. Both Fritschels had Gymnasium, which Reu had up to a certain point, but I do not think Reu was able to finish. He was thus a self-made man. They were deciding about Clinton and Waverly. Clinton was set up to be a typical respectable academic institution

CN: That wouldn't win a lot of points for the people in that corner.

WW: Reu would get himself in those kinds of things. I think that's part of that mystery which is Reu.

CN: That his political acumen wasn't all that well developed.

WW: He should stick to writing another book.

Reu gave the opinion that the students coming from Waverly were better prepared to study theology than those coming from Clinton. It was exactly the opposite. Such a statement flies in the face of those who were descendants of the Fritschels and even the Fritschel brothers themselves, who were trying to get Wartburg accepted as a very solid academic institution, one that could measure up to any in the states.

CN: This would not add to the credibility.

WW: No. You are talking about a two-year preparation at Waverly instead of four years, and more languages. Reu thought if you taught them Greek and Hebrew that would be enough. You certainly did not need Latin and you certainly did not need all this science they were taking. So I think in ways like that, he made life kind of miserable.

Another example was how he treated people who came from St. Paul Luther Seminary. They had one theologian on their faculty who was fully trained in Germany. Like you and me, he had his doctor's degree from Leipzig or Erlangen. Reu said there was not anybody on the faculty at St. Paul who we could use here. So imagine when it came to those people in that part of the Ohio Synod, who thought they had a first rate theologian who could have been utilized here and was needed here. So there are those little things.

CN: It seems like he had a real affinity for people who would be self-made like he was himself.

WW: He demonstrated that he was indeed competent and there was not any question. Lowell Green and others want to emphasize why we should publish him as an American theologian. By the very prodigious amount of material he dealt with and covered, he does have some claim to importance. But we would be doing a disservice to be selective. I know Bodensieck struggled with him at length.

CN: When I go back and look at the dogmatics, and some of the other writings of Reu, it is just amazing how dramatically different that style of theology is from where we are today. Yet I think that Pieper is in that same mode and his books are still being used in the Missouri Synod.

WW: Yes. It certainly has validity and can be used historically. I would think that if Reu himself were alive today, he would have a different approach. I think it is a disservice to simply repristinate.

J. Michael Reu:
The Iowa Synod's Theologian

WW: I thought we could talk a little more today about Reu, just a couple sources. I don't know whether you have seen this. This is supposed to be the final, memorial edition of the *Kirchliche Zeitschrift*. There are a couple of good things in it. Conrad Bergendoff, the Augustana Synod historian, has an article.

CN: He's just having an anniversary.

WW: Yeah, he's 100 and something. He's been a worker for Lutheran unity in this country for a long time. He's quite a good critic of theological streams and in this article he has some things about how the Lutherans tended to remain tied to European theology. I suppose Reu is an example of that. What I wanted to talk about is that each one of these Lutheran traditions somehow was bound to Europe, especially from the middle 19th Century on, the time of the great expansion. So they were, indeed, bound to the mother Church. They looked upon their children being gathered here in America. But I don't know that they were ever really connected with the major theological strains that were permeating the life of the church in Europe. I mean they were certainly opposed to all the things they called non-confessional. Reu in a special way stands deeply connected with the theologians of Europe. I guess you'd have to say simply Germany. This connection is basically to Johan Christian Konrad von Hofmann [1810-1877] and that tradition. He made a great deal of that.

CN: Would he have been the generation of Reu's teachers?

WW: Reu's teachers were primarily these professors that he had at Neuendettelsau. He never had many of the actual professors. He began to have contact with them, I think, after he began to be accepted because of his writings. You know he introduced this prestigious collection on the Catechism. And that was acknowledged.

CN: But more as a colleague than as a student.

WW: Yes. That he was. That's why I wrote that little article ["J. Michael Reu—A Self-Made Theologian, *Currents in Theology and Mission* 16 (1989): 341-345], but it doesn't go into depth, indicating that Reu was a self-made theologian. He knew all these people and he started getting all their books. I am sure that von Hofmann was an influence for him when he was down in Erlangen.

CN: This was a traditional, confessional approach to theology?

WW: It was the one that emphasized the history of salvation.

CN: So it was a biblically rooted.

WW: Yes, strongly. When I first went to Germany and was settling on a dissertation topic, I talked with Kuenneth. I wanted to compare Reu with some of the contemporary people in the European situation, dominant people like Werner Elert and others on the doctrine of Scriptures. Kuenneth informed me that Reu would not be considered to be a creative theologian, because he copied basically the attitude of people of his time. So he didn't think it was a good project to work on. I still think it would have been.

CN: But he discouraged it.

WW: So I worked on Kaehler instead.

CN: Today you could do it as a history topic more than a theology topic.

WW: Reu didn't talk much about Theodor Zahn [1838-1933]. He was a professor of New Testament at Erlangen. He was still teaching into the Twentieth Century. He's the one who was perhaps, the most significant for Reu in his biblical approach. Zahn would be one you would think of as a progressive biblical scholar, making use of the best in New Testament history and research, but still somewhat along the Confessional, conservative line. I suppose he had been in opposition to David Frederich Strauss who came earlier than he did. In understanding Reu, it's important to get that connection with Zahn. And I would say that any of the commentaries you want to look at that Zahn has written, or his articles on biblical criticism, he would have been one who follows "lower criticism" as they divided it at that time, which was mainly textual criticism. They did many good things in coming out with what we finally have as a good New Testament text with all that research in the 19th Century particularly. Zahn was the master for Reu. Reu praised him in class quite often.

CN:: He would have been the main professor then at Erlangen who influenced Reu?

WW: He would have been the main professor in New Testament. I suppose his influence came, not so much when Reu was a young student at Neuendettelsau. He only stayed there until he was 20. But Zahn influenced him more as he developed who he was in his research and studies here at the seminary.

CN: Through his readings then.

WW: Yes.

CN: I've seen books by Zahn here and there.

WW: They are worth looking at. The theologian who was normative for him in his systematic theology, I would say, would be Christoph Luthardt [1823-1902], the guy who wrote the compendium on dogmatics. A lot of people used that for a text. That was significant for Reu, too. We talked about von Hofmann the last time we met. The only thing I didn't mention is that von Hofmann also would have been greatly influenced by Schleiermacher. You have the emphasis that doing Systematic Theology was about developing the consciousness of the believer from within the Christian community. Von Hofmann stressed that the Christian reality, the Christian life, was communion between God and humanity. You know Reu's theme was very similar. So you see that emphasis was deeply embedded in him.

CN: It's kind of ironic that Reu got that theme from Schleiermacher, since Reu uses Scripture so differently than Schleiermacher.

WW: Yes, and Reu would distance himself from Schleiermacher, criticizing his emphasis on the inward disposition of the believer. Reu followed the usual negative criticism that this referred to the emotional center of people rather than, as it really does for Schleiermacher, the whole center of their being.

CN: I hadn't put those things together before, but it's not that big of a leap from what Schleiermacher intended by his feeling of absolute dependence to this communion with God in Reu.

WW: Yes, I think they are showing that there was a kind of a common reality. I suppose, as these nations and people were seeking their identity, they find it in relation to God. Schleiermacher so profoundly stressed how the Christian reality impacted the community. Certainly above everything else this was his systematic principle. A lot of our people forget that Schleiermacher was the one for whom systematic theology was organized from the standpoint of feeling dependence upon God.

CN: If you don't read *The Christian Faith* and only read the lectures on religion you fail to get the whole viewpoint.

WW: Those lectures on religion are good for an introduction but we need to go on to his systematic theology. There ought to be a seminar sometime on Schleiermacher.

CN: I did an independent study with Professor Cochrane on Schleiermacher when I was here as a student.

WW: Well, I imagine Cochrane criticized him from the standpoint of Karl Barth.

CN: He was very appreciative of Schleiermacher.

WW: He liked Schleiermacher?

CN: I don't know if he liked him, but he was appreciative of him. Maybe he provided a critical foil in contrast to Barth. I wanted to ask you again about the circumstances under which Reu left Germany.

WW: I obtained some information from two fellows who were here for a semester from Neuendettelsau. One was a young fellow who was married and had a baby with them. The other fellow was a New Testament professor on sabbatical in the States, who spent a good deal of time here at Wartburg. When they came, a little afterwards, they gave me this information. They showed me the records and gave me a copy of Reu being rebuked for an indiscretion. He was mostly rebuked for not coming forth and telling that he had sinned, for having this relationship with a young woman. I don't know whether that took place right about the time he left. I think it did. He was baptized in 1869. He came to this country in 1889. So he would have been only 20 years old when he was first arrived at Mendota, Illinois where the seminary was located at that time. Reu was then given a congregation of his own. I think that followed upon this occasion. They showed the records to me and were kind of joking about it.

CN: It would have to have been about the time he came to the United States.

WW: It would have been so nice if his grandson, Richard Salzmann, would have been able to know that about his grandfather. It made him much more human.

CN: It puts the human touch to it all.

WW: But that was one thing. These guys were all so serious and you could find very little sense of humor among them.

CN: In that generation.

WW: Yeah. Bodensieck was the only one with a sense of humor. The others were very serious.

CN: It wasn't professorial somehow?

WW: I don't know. They must have engaged in a little banter here and there. Surely they had a sense of humor but didn't know how to express it.

CN: It'd be interesting to know how their faculty meetings were, if they would have that kind of humor among themselves, even if not in the classroom. Are there some other things you were thinking about Reu?

WW: Reu is criticized for his attitude to Hitler and the Third Reich. The basis of that criticism rests primarily on the statement he gave at a meeting of the American Lutheran Statistical Association in 1934, their 17th annual convention. Reu began with these words: "You asked me to say a few words about the Lutheran Church in the Third Reich. Let me at the outset repeat what I said about two years ago about a year before his rise to power when someone inquired concerning my opinion of Hitler. [That would have been 1932.] I answered, 'If I were a German citizen, I would vote for Hitler.' This is still my position today so far as the political situation in Germany is concerned. Beyond question the leadership of Hitler and the Third Reich has been a source of blessing to Germany. Under him the centuries old dream of a united Germany has been realized in a measure few hoped possible. The nationwide process of housecleaning in politics, education, current literature, amusements, and social life is carried out with astonishing thoroughness. The fervent wish of all those who stood for moral decency, a square deal in business, and a distribution of opportunity and influence in keeping with the percentage of population, namely the relocation of the non-German elements, especially the Jews, was realized. The Third Reich brought about the complete rebirth of an entire nation, leading it back to its better self." He goes on: "But you have asked me to speak, not about the Third Reich, but about the place of the Lutheran Church in the Third Reich." He goes on to show that basically the Lutheran Church, as he understood it, no longer existed. There was no longer any Lutheran Confessional Church, especially with the German Christians under Bishop Mueller.

CN: So he was critical of the German Christians as well.

WW: Yes, he is very critical of that. Totally critical of that and he agreed with the confessional people like Sasse who made the criticism. So in that respect, I think one would need to grant

30

him that he saw that the position of the Church at that time was weak and powerless and helpless because it had lost its courage to stand up for the faith.

CN: Does he refer to the Confessing Church?

WW: He doesn't say anything about that. By that time the Confessing Church was just getting going. So it's hard telling where he would have been.

CN: Where did he get his information about the Nazis and the political situation.

WW: Well, I think from being there and I suppose from faculties with whom he corresponded.

CN: Did he travel back and forth regularly?

WW: He did a number of times for the Lutheran World Assembly and other things. I think it must have been from what he learned from the papers here, as well as from the people to whom he wrote over there

CN: It'd be really important to know with whom he corresponded.

WW: Yeah. If only one could get that correspondence. I suspect that that was all eliminated. I had him for two years here. I don't remember him saying much or anything about the whole situation in Germany. But it's true, I don't think we can find any later disavowal of this thing, although he must have done so according to his widow. He recognized that Hitler had deceived him and destroyed the people and everything. There still is a question. It would be good to seek out whatever correspondence is available.

CN: In what you just read there, it'd be easier to excuse him from what he says about supporting Hitler if you didn't have that reference in there about the Jews. That's the most troubling part to me because I can understand how someone, especially from a distance, could see Hitler kind of rallying people for economic reasons or even political and military reasons.

WW: Yeah. Dr. Cochrane said that Hitler came to power by affirming all the right things – patriotism, motherhood, virtue, hard work. But that, too, is the troubling thing. It shows, I think, the deep-seated kind of hostility there was with the German people, because the Jews had succeeded quite well economically in Europe.

CN: An element of resentment then.

WW: Yeah. Where he says, "the distribution of opportunity in keeping with the percentage of population, namely the relocation of the non-German element."

CN: Of course, when he uses the word "relocate" there's no way he could know what that would come to mean later.

WW: No, he would have no idea of that. I brought along something for you to look at, just to give you a feeling of the breadth of his scholarship. Here's a bibliography that John Burritt did in 1969 when we celebrated Reu's 100th birthday.

CN: Where do you think he got this kind of energy? This is almost like Luther in terms of output.

WW: Yes. Well, I think he was deeply imbued with this sense of industry and desire to succeed above all others. He was a man of small stature. His father died when he was young. He had a mother that was determined he was going to be cultured and educated. So he started violin lessons at a very early age.

CN: How did he maintain this type of drive to publish.

WW: I think he was driven to demonstrate he could provide the answer for everything by connecting it with the Scriptures.

CN: He became the Iowa Synod's theologian.

WW: He soon became that. He started publishing very early in his career, after he came to Dubuque. That's where he was different than Fritschel. Fritschel didn't publish that much. Reu got started, I suppose, because the book concern was looking for people to publish books and he could come up with manuscripts. So when any issue would arise, soon Reu came with a final, definitive answer. I think by the time that he was 30 years old he was beginning to be accepted as an authority for ecclesiastical, theological answers. I would say that he keenly sensed, the shrewd little Bavarian that he was, unlike the kid who may become a great pugilist or soccer player, that when it came to the classroom, he could outdo them all.

CN: That was his niche.

WW: This is where he could defeat everybody. I suppose that played a role for him. He soon developed a kind of capability that drove him. It must have petered out at the end, I came here in 1940 and that year he had the only sabbatical that he ever had. Just as an aside, if anybody from Wartburg ever feels they are disadvantaged about sabbaticals, have them look to Reu who gave 43 years of his life and had one sabbatical in the whole time.

CN: I'd just as soon that not be too widely known.

WW: He wanted to do a commentary with some prominent New Testament theologians. That included Franz Pieper who was married to a Jewish woman. Also a New Testament scholar from Germany who had to leave, like Paul Leo did. He left earlier and was at Princeton. Reu had set upon the idea of coming up with a contemporary commentary on Galatians and eventually the entire New Testament with people like Pieper. Reu had a whole year free compared to what he had always put out beforehand. It is strange that there was not more produced. You wonder what he did with the whole year.

CN: Whether his powers were waning.

WW: Yeah, or whether he just had to be in the thick of things all the time and couldn't get away from it. Perhaps he felt out of sync. He had been Acting President in the months before Bodensieck took office. He was the one with whom I corresponded about coming to the seminary.

CN: He was energized by all the activity.

32

WW: Yeah, he needed students so he could lambast here and there. But it's strange that there wasn't more published with things developing in Germany the way they were.

CN: Are there stories about Reu that especially typify who he was as a person and as a teacher?

WW: I suppose we could tell a myriad of stories of him and his finely chosen lectures. There are several stories about how Reu would help a student whose father or mother had died and had to go home suddenly. Reu took them to the train. So behind all the rest was a warm, tender heart, although he was strictly always business. I didn't have to write a thesis when I graduated. Most people didn't. You could get the diploma from the seminary. But if you wanted the Bachelor of Divinity, you had to have no grade lower than a B. Then you had to give a thesis. I wrote one, a study on Paul's use of participle. It was a lot of work just trying to classify all of the various uses of participle that Paul made in his writings. So I was talking about that and said, "How did you like it?" He said, "Es hat mir Freude gemacht [I liked it]." I guess I was looking for a little more discussion. I said something and he answered, giving me the same words again.

CN: End of the discussion.

WW: End of the conversation right there.

CN: So he wasn't overflowing with praise?

WW: No. But there were the occasions where he would invite students down at Christmas time to sing carols and so forth at his home. The student body was small.

WW: Well, I guess most of the stories that I have heard are about how tough he was, but still a good teacher. Everybody wants to demonstrate that they had Reu and that he was really a tough teacher.

CN: How they survived it.

WW: Yes, "I survived and what a fine boy I am."

CN: He started teaching here in what year?

WW: In 1900.

CN: So just think of all the pastors who were shaped by his teaching.

WW: There is a story of him that he was a dominant force at St. John's Lutheran Church. There had been a very close relationship between St. John's and the seminary. It was founded about the same time as Wartburg so it's always been close there. He considered himself, I suppose, a patriarch and authority at St. John's Church. So when they would be singing hymns and he didn't like the tempo at which they were singing, he would with his deep bass voice try to re-direct the whole congregation. And often he would succeed. Everybody would be expected to fall in line with him.

CN: What about Reu and the Missouri Synod?

WW: Reu was severely criticized by certain, more conservative elements of Missouri. But I think Reu personally tended to feel that he needed to justify his existence with Missouri and felt more at home with some of the people in the Lutheran Church Missouri Synod than with others. And I would like to think that that was not the reactionary, rabid kind of fundamentalism that Missouri represents in some ways, but the more evangelical, in the best of Loehe tradition.

There is one specific illustration in that Reu felt the need to provide graduate study for aggressive and serious, creative thinking students. So in the 1930's, he started a graduate school at the seminary, a Master's program. A number of people came to various short courses that were connected with that. This included one of the Kretzmann brothers, O.P. Kretzmann, who became the president of Valparaiso. He studied with Reu under this graduate program where you could come and spend time and then read a bunch of books, digest them and come and meet with Reu. So our S.T.M. program, that was formally started in the 1960's, revived what had originally begun in 1933. It was about the same time as the Lay Academy began, another one of Reu's ideas. So he saw the value of theological education taking place in many ways.

CN: With these different expressions at different levels.

WW: Yeah. It seemed to me that he was seeing the task in continuing to train theologians. I think some people in Missouri tended to look to Reu as a real leader, a colleague. Others down in Clinton regularly attacked Reu. But Reu got too impatient with Missouri. Richard Salzmann told me many times when he would pick him up at the train and ask him how things went at a meeting with Missouri, Reu would be extremely frustrated.

CN: Pastor Hock mentioned a love/hate relationship between the Iowa Synod and Missouri Synod.

WW: I think it was mostly a hate relationship. But I think there was also a strong bond there, because of their common ground in Loehe. Even though Loehe got dumped on by the Missouri Synod, there was still enough of Loehe in the best of the Missouri Synod that Fritschel was speaking the truth when he said, "You are our closest brothers in faith. Malign us as you will, we still look to you and will pray for you." But what they might expect in reply was to be accused at every turn of being heretics. Somehow, this is just my own personal imagination, Missouri developed a kind of aristocratic arrogance, and I don't know where this comes from. It always considered itself superior in every way, superior in doctrine, superior in institutions. But that kind of collapsed with the recent debacle at Seminex. All this has showed is that now Missouri has in the third or fourth team, with the first string sitting on the bench.

CN: There's this emphasis on pure doctrine.

WW: Yeah. I don't know how that became so prominent, although I think that Loehe could also be an arrogant guy. He was pretty convinced that he knew what God wanted and had a close line to God. It would be important to see how others who have studied Loehe feel about that. Yet he was amazing to pull off what he did, to get this congregation to be the people of God in mission.

CN: Hock mentioned how appreciative the articles are in the *Lutheran Cyclopedia*, Missouri Synod's encyclopedia, especially the articles about Loehe and Reu and the Fritschels as some evidence of this love/hate relationship. Of course, that would have been after the time of the controversies. It was in the '50s that those first would have been published.

WW: And we can be thankful that Bodensieck was the editor who selected some of the authors for the articles in *The Encyclopedia of the Lutheran Church*. There were a lot of good people in Missouri and he had the clout to ask them and they were happy to respond. He also had good contacts in Europe. That's why I think it turned out to be a good encyclopedia. I believe it is especially good for developing churches. I gave my last copy to a student from Africa. I just figured it was good thing for them to have.

CN: Was Reu involved in the open questions controversy?

WW: No. That came to the fore at the time of the Fritschels, but Reu continued in that approach. He emphasized that and he was criticized for it. As we talked last time, one of the things I never quite figured out is why Reu understood the millennium the way he did. Martin Heineken had all of his theology under Reu.

CN: He did?

WW: Yeah. His first training was with Reu. He's one of our graduates. He talked about the fact that Reu never encouraged us to go beyond what Reu himself could provide. Reu could give you a lot of accents to any of the European theologians, backwards and forwards, through the centuries. But what you got was always a Reu interpreted point of view. He did not encourage independent scholarship. For that Martin Heineken was annoyed. He had been deprived. He said Reu did make clear that the foundation out of which we stand is the doctrine of justification. He said that was healthy and good that he was well grounded in that. But he knew as well that he had also been deprived. I thought that too. How much better it would have been if he would have sent us scurrying into the library to read Schleiermacher himself instead of saying that he is nothing more than modern biblical enthusiasm. Or that we should read Barth, comparing him with Luther. We only got Barth in footnotes from him.

CN: Was he ever challenged by students in the positions he took?

WW: You never heard of challenging him.

CN: That would never happen.

WW: No. You see that's why Bernard Holm and I talked a lot about Reu at one time. He said that's the problem with a self-made theologian, that he doesn't grow up with having graduate seminars in which you are blasted to smithereens. You take a position and find it attacked from all sides and you have to defend yourself and see how well you can do with it, how thoroughly you studied the matter. So that's one of the things you miss when you yourself choose only what you're going to study and present. It gives you a distorted perspective. I think there is something to that. That's why the Germans have always moved from school to school in their education.

CN: Cross-fertilization.

WW: Maybe it happens too much in their case. They always leave behind one strand of theology before they've even digested it to study the next new thing that is emerging on the scene.

CN: When you read Reu's *Dogmatics*, it has the sense of a propositional system. And if you are going to build this up and defend it, it doesn't invite taking up alternative positions, other than to refute them or absorb them.

WW: Mainly to refute them. We talked about his system of lecturing. He set up all these particular theological answers to the specific topic that you were dealing with. We always thought we were getting down to the real one, but discovered that we had to go through at least four or five alternatives before we got down to what really was the truth.

CN: Well, there's a longing for that kind of theology but it doesn't hold up anymore.

WW: The students wouldn't tolerate it. At least I would hope not.

CN: One would hope. There are church bodies where that's the way it's still done.

WW: I wonder what it's like to be a pastor in the Lutheran Church Wisconsin Synod where the dogmatics is based on the propositions that are, at least, 100 years old. That's what you have to learn and that's it. If you are looking for security, that's the place to go.

CN: We talked a little bit last time about Reu feeling somehow displaced at the formation of the old American Lutheran Church. What about his relationship with the Ohio Synod in general?

WW: I think he considered that they were second-rate compared to him. I think that he felt that his theological competence exceeded the Ohio Synod. I think he probably would have acknowledged that the Ohio Synod were good politicians, good church statesmen. He was a babe in the woods politically. Every time he ended up in a battle, he ended up losing.

CN: Because of the politics?

WW: Yeah, he didn't know how to proceed in the world of politics. I think there was a feeling that the Ohio Synod was closer to the more rigid thinking of the Missouri Synod.

CN: That if you put them on a continuum, they'd be closer to Missouri than to the Iowa Synod.

CN: They had been at it longer.

WW: Yeah and they had C.C. Hein, from which the lecture series comes. He certainly was accomplished. They produced those kinds of people.

CN: Who were some of the others?

WW: Well, there was August Ernst [1841-1924] and, of course, their own theologian was Gerhard Lenski. A lot of the conservative groups are using his commentaries again. In that respect, he was somewhat like Reu. He didn't write as much, strictly the commentaries, but he certainly wrote a lot there. Then in modern times there's Henry Schuh who was in the office of stewardship, I think, when the Church was formed. C.C. Hein died. The vice president was Emanuel Poppen. When the next election came up, Henry Schuh was elected president of the old American Lutheran Church. Henry Schuh was president when the American Lutheran Church came together with the Evangelical Lutheran Church and formed the new American Lutheran Church. Schiotz was the first newly elected president. Schuh was a good politician. I think maybe the Ohio people, in some respects, had a little better grasp of evangelism than we did in the Iowa Synod. Ohio produced people like Fred Meuser. His little book on the formation of the American Lutheran Church was his doctoral dissertation from Yale.

CN: Did Reu have significant relations with any others, like the Norwegians or Swedes?

WW: I don't know a great deal about what extent he did have conversation there. I think that he carried on a dialogue with Conrad Bergendoff. They should have known each other.

CN: That wasn't the focus by any means.

WW: Al Rogness, a pastor in Ames, Iowa, knew a great deal about Kierkegaard. That's where Bodensieck came to know him. Bodensieck got him to lecture here. He gave some lectures on Kierkegaard. Al Rogness could appropriate Kierkegaard in such a way that he himself could communicate out of his insights.

CN: In a way that connected with people.

WW: Yeah.

CN: How about the relationship between Wartburg and Luther Seminary?

WW: You know that when I was a student here, I was not even aware that there was this big seminary in St. Paul. That's how oblivious I was.

CN: The language and the ethnic differences still played so largely.

WW: Then I eventually married a Norwegian-Swede and she happened to come from the ultra-conservative little group known as the Shell Rock Synod, from which Jack Preus also came.

CN: That's an irony.

WW: But Ilah, of course, really had no conscious awareness because she grew up in other towns and most of her life in the church was spent at St. Paul's in Waverly. So she wasn't actually reared in it. When I first went up to meet her grandparents, these people from the Shell Rock Synod Church as they always called it, had to pass muster on you. Of course, I couldn't go to communion there.

CN: You met her in Waverly?

WW: Yeah. We went up North to meet her grandparents. Her grandfather was a venerable old Swede. I know he didn't swallow the smallness of the Shell Rock Synod. Like they used to say, the only church that he would be happy with was one in which he and God were there alone.

Augie Engelbrecht was going to be a model replacement for Reu. But then maybe his interests went in another direction. Then he married into the Mattes family and that firmly established him in his own right.

CN: Well, it would be hard for anyone to carry on in the stature of a Reu.

WW: Well, it would have been interesting to be able to put together all the little squabbles that really played into major decisions.

J. Michael Reu
and Church Politics

WW: This is Fred Meuser's book. This is his doctoral work.

CN: *The Formation of the American Lutheran Church.*

WW: In here he's talking about the inspiration controversy and Reu on pages 226-230. He gives a nice statement on page 186: "It is important to notice exactly the nature of Reu's protest. Neither the existence of difficulties within Scripture, nor the claims of critical research were behind his opposition. It was based solely upon the conviction that the Scriptures themselves claimed to be absolutely inerrant only in matters pertaining to faith and Christian life. He was convinced that the very passages used by the ultraconservatives to 'prove' complete inerrancy supported his own view rather than theirs. Throughout the period of disagreement he and his followers insisted upon proof from the Scriptures before they would accept the stricter viewpoint and rejected the claim that absolute inerrancy was a necessary corollary of the whole Christian faith."

CN: That's a nice quote.

WW: You'll see how Reu takes a position. He is for the right thing. He doesn't want to get that inerrant statement in there and he takes a strong position. Then you'll read some of the intrigue about how there was a statement about the Scripture that floated around and nobody really knew where it came from. It was somewhat different than Reu's position. Some people thought, nevertheless, that Reu was the brains behind it. That stirred up people and it kept this thing fomenting. Some wondered whether the merger would take place. Hein, at one point, thought the merger was all set. Then he gets Reu writing him a friendly, but firm letter that he couldn't go along with the idea of inspiration as it was presented.

But I think you will discover what I mean when I said that Reu was no politician. He was in the midst of those controversies and took positions but sometimes he left an openness and an equivocation that people could walk around. Now if you would talk to Wiederaenders, he would tell you that Reu took this strong position at the formation of The American Lutheran Church convention in Toledo, Ohio. Reu does talk about how he felt it was the end of his career. Since they were voting for a merger and it was going to go through, he had taken the position that he probably would be out.

CN: Out as a professor?

WW: Yeah. He would probably be out and have to leave. I mean it was kind of strange. It indicates what they were talking about in his character when as a young student at Neuendettelsau. He became infatuated with a young lady, but he didn't have the guts to come forward and admit what the thing was. Maybe it's the same character flaw that comes to

39

expression here, that only shows itself in the middle of political intrigue. Politically, he was a babe in the woods. So it's kind of interesting to see. Those who make Reu say more than he does, like Johnson and Lowell Green, who never studied under Reu but heard stories and read his stuff, they don't recognize that he complicated a lot of things by seeming to agree to almost everything but then would come back with a position against it. I think he basically had the right position. He only really got in trouble when he tried to be more conservative than he really was. That's when he got in trouble. If he had been faithful to his true nature, he would have been consistent.

CN: He would have been a better politician, too.

WW: He would have been a better theologian and politician, too. And maybe, I don't know whether anything along that line played in here as well. Some people have always talked about the fact that he didn't take strong enough positions against the Nazi regime. Well, the words of Reu that we have about that all came before it came clearer on *Kristalnacht* what it was all about.

CN: Right. It was very early in the '30s.

WW: Meuser has got a lot of stuff in there about Reu. But on the same subject of Reu, I have the material I was referring to and I want to show it to you today. I have the record of that civil case here. Here is a copy taken from the records at Neuendettelsau. I was telling you about Reu being censured for his relationship with this woman. Here's that whole account.

CN: It's handwritten. So this is a copy of the original.

WW: This is a copy of the records from Neuendettelsau. In the document it points out that Reu was put under censure because he had maintained a relationship in secret. He really was to be suspended, but they granted him the opportunity to take his final exams, which he did then in the fall of 1888 and came to this country in 1889. So the whole thing basically says that according to the rules of the Mission, he broke the house ordinance by establishing a relationship of love, the punishment for which is suspension from the seminary. Not only did he keep this a secret, but in view of the vocation he was following for his life, he should have come forth and confessed. But it was only when it became clear that he might be suspended that he took any action on it. So he was faulted for that also. So it's kind of interesting. Mrs. Leo said he's a sinner, too.

CN: At least early in his life.

WW: Yes. I have not let this story be well known. This is the only copy here. I told those guys who gave me this that Mrs. Salzmann was still living then, and I didn't know whether it should become known. Really, it's a moot question because he was not finally dismissed. He was on the verge of dismissal. I think they all recognized that he was such a good student.

CN: They let him complete his exams.

WW: They let him complete his exams and he came over here and served with these people. And, of course, I suppose you could say that his indefatigable drive might have come from the fact that he was going to make amends for his foolhardiness. But he ended up marrying someone who he met in New York on his way through, no connection to this other relationship.

CN: He got a wholly a new start then.

WW: A friend of Reu's was in Australia and in 1934, this fellow wrote down many things from his correspondence with Reu. I also have copies of Reu's baptism and his confirmation. What's more important is this correspondence which is a copy by Reu's friend, which documents what he wrote back and forth for all those years. This guy says that his remembrances of Reu go back to October 1886 as he entered the Mission Society. He talked about his appearance and so forth. In here he talks about things in the United States, such as the problems he endured.

CN: Had the friend visited in the States?

WW: No. This is from correspondence. They wrote back and forth.

CN: What was the occasion for his writing this?

WW: Reu was given an award in 1934.

CN: For the catechism research?

WW: And for his overall contribution to the Mission Society.

CN: This is from Neuendettelsau?

WW: Yes.

CN: An honorary proclamation. And so these were the things that were said about him at that occasion?

WW: No, this is the remembrance of this guy in Australia who wrote those things for this occasion and presented them, I think, at Neuendettelsau. I'm not clear about whether he himself was present or whether he simply sent them.

CN: So that's all in German then, too.

WW: Yes, but you can easily read it.

CN: He would have been pretty frank writing to someone in Australia.

WW: He was very frank and there comes out his feelings of lack of confidence in George Fritschel who taught history. Bodensieck then devoted most of his time doing things for Reu. Now after the merger, Bodensieck was appointed editor of the *Kirchen-Blatt*, still printed in the English language like *The Lutheran*. Reu saw that as a way of making life miserable for him. You see a kind of paranoia.

CN: So there was a sense of competition or stealing from his influence?

WW: Well, no, just that they made life harder for Reu by not letting Bodensieck remain here. He saw the Synod leaders trying to make life difficult for him.

CN: I see. Bodensieck actually left to do this new work.

WW: Yes, he moved to Columbus.

CN: Was he already on faculty and assisting Reu as a faculty person or a junior staff member?

WW: Well, the lines were kind of fuzzy, not like they are now. People came and worked at the seminary. Outside of the regular professors, who were in their positions, they used others without sometimes mentioning them. Bodensieck was more or less in that kind of situation. He did a lot of things for the old Iowa Synod because of his ability in both English and German. And so Reu considered him, I suppose, his own assistant. He didn't realize that Bodensieck wasn't always happy with being under his thumb. When he got to Columbus he could blossom for himself. Probably in many ways he was relieved to be out from under Reu, who was such a dominant force. Those are all the things that are never directly said. You only get it here and there. You get some of what Reu really felt in those letters.

CN: So Bodensieck would have come into the picture of helping out in the 1920s?

WW: Yes, I would say.

CN: Prior to the formation of the old ALC.

WW: Yes, right at the time. I am sure he played a big role with Reu, helping him with his English speeches, things like that.

CN: Would he have been teaching also at that time?

WW: Yes, he did some teaching. He taught at Wartburg College in Waverly, too. That's why I say that they moved people around in institutions. The basic faculty members were permanent in their positions, but there would be a lot of what we would call today temporary faculty.

Another thing in there I thought we could talk about was Reu's attitude toward the Scriptures. He felt that he could not go along with the merger, because of the position on inerrancy. He even thought for a while that when the merger of the American Lutheran Church in 1930 took place, it would be the end of his career. He made testimony that he felt he was being forced out. Fred Meuser refers to that, too. In this letter exchange, one can read about that. But Reu was overreacting, because people weren't in any mood to kick him out or think he didn't belong. He was opposed to putting that statement on inerrancy in the Confession of the ALC and I take that as the one crowning piece of evidence that Reu remained open in his scriptural attitude.

CN: He opposed the word inerrancy?

WW: He was opposed to including absolute inerrancy in all matters of faith and life. There were issues where you could have various opinions.

CN: I need to get this straight. He opposed the word inerrant?

WW: That's where there is a kind of subtleness on the part of Reu. He would affirm that the Scripture is inerrant, but he opposed it being a matter of the confession of the church that it is inerrant in all matters of faith and life.

CN: So he was for more latitude.

WW: He was for a more differentiated view. He wanted to be very confessional and took confessions of faith very seriously. Reu thought there was no longer a Lutheran Church in Germany, since the Lutheran Church came into existence after the Reformation with the formation of its confessions. And these were no longer being followed. Yet he was opposed to a Missourian attitude that took a quantitative approach to inspiration.

CN: It's a fine line. So he was much more open to historical/critical methods of interpreting Scripture.

WW: Yes. I think you'll want to look into Meuser to see how far that went. Reu gave a great deal of attention to these questions. He felt that a great many of the inconsistencies and errors that are apparently in the Bible were often resolved by the serious scientific study of the Scriptures. But he would come out in a different place then the Jesus seminar people do now.

CN: More of a confidence in the ability of scholarship to discover the truth.

WW: They looked forward with confidence to historical/critical studies. But you couldn't put Reu or any of those theologians in the category with David Frederich Strauss and his efforts. Reu, you would have to say, was representative of the Iowa Synod's theology and the theology of Wartburg Seminary. There was an historic emphasis. If you are dividing 19th Century theology into various categories, you could come up with one position, which is strongly confessional. Then there's the viewpoint that has been termed liberal theology. And then you could come up with a mediating position. That's the position, I think, in which Reu stood when he was true to who he really was and when he was at his best. When he tried to prove that he was more legitimately confessional and conservative than anybody else was, then he was not true to himself.

CN: So if he slipped out of the mediating position, it would be on the side of the strongly confessional stance.

WW: That's right because that's where the pressure was. He was hounded consistently by Missouri. He believed that he had to prove that he was more confessional than Missouri.

CN: He would never have been confused as a representative of liberal theology.

WW: No. There, too, he brushed it off too easily. He only said of Barth, that he is in danger of becoming a *Schwaermer* [enthusiast] with regard to the Bible.

CN: You could hardly say that about Barth if you studied him very long.

CN: Do you recall him commenting on any other theologians of that era, Brunner or Gogarten? That would be fairly early for him to have commented on Tillich.

WW: Yes, although Tillich was in the U.S. for some of the same time. Reu could have met some of these people, because he had a connection with Pieper at Princeton.

CN: Which would have been closer to the place at which these people would have entered the U.S. on the East Coast.

WW: Right. Pieper did do a lot to help these people. He was the one who was responsible for helping the Leos. He helped Paul Leo obtain a position at the Presbyterian Seminary in Pittsburgh before he next got a place in Texas, and eventually came here. Reu was in communication with Pieper. Reu was intending to edit this new commentary on the New Testament that would be more up-to-date than the work of Theodor Zahn and would take advantage of the best historical scholarship, written from the perspective of the American people. He looked to Pieper as being a partner with him. Of course Reu, unfortunately, died in 1943 and the thing was never finished.

CN: The project never came to pass.

WW: But you can read what he was doing with the Book of Galatians. Reu was finished with the first book of that series. That's the book that this Paul I. Johnston wanted to publish. Mrs. Salzmann didn't want him to publish it, because that was at the time when Richard Salzmann was still alive. He was kind of a liaison of Reu affairs between the seminary and his mother. They just felt that it might seem somewhat – embarrassing isn't the proper word – a little bit antiquated, that this older work would be considered as a modern, contemporary commentary.

CN: This would have been years later though.

WW: E. Clifford Nelson – a big worker for Lutheran unity and a prominent professor in church history at Luther College, basically of UELC background – always chided me about Reu being more connected with this fundamentalist in Minneapolis than he was with his own people. Meuser has that in there too. And he sees Reu embracing this American fundamentalist. But I think, as Tillich pointed out to us, when you are talking about the fundamentalism you experience here in America, you have to distinguish that from conservatism in Europe.

CN: Especially in Germany.

WW: Very much so. And I think he is right about that.

CN: You would say that Reu would be more taken with German conservatism rather than influenced by American fundamentalism.

WW: I think he would, but he gets himself in trouble by latching onto these characters.

CN: And perhaps he himself doesn't realize the distinction thoroughly enough.

WW: Yeah, it was in early '40 or late '39 that he was starting to plan this stuff with Pieper.

CN: And when did Johnston want to publish it?

WW: That was in the last few years, I suppose about five years ago. He had it all prepared. So the thing is available in the archives, but I think it did more justice to Reu not to publish it. I suppose a lot of people today would have found it quite useful, at least that's the thinking of guys like Johnston who are trying to publish Reu's works.

CN: He's the same one who did Reu's sermons.

WW: Correct. And now he's publishing an anthology of Reu's theology. He got into it through Lowell Green.

CN: I know the name, but I don't know who that is.

WW: Lowell Green is one of our graduates who went to Erlangen and did his degree in the history of dogma and on Melancthon. Mike Rogness is the son of Dr. Alvin Rogness, the former president of Luther Seminary. Five years later than Green he too was a student at Erlangen and did his study on Melancthon, proving how wrong Green was in a lot of his exaggerated assumptions about Melancthon. Lowell Green, who is kind of a radical conservative, urged Johnston to work on Reu.

CN: Is Johnston a pastor?

WW: Yes. I think he hoped to get accepted on the faculty at Concordia Seminary in St. Louis when they had that exodus, but he was never picked.

CN: He has his doctorate then?

WW: Yes. But it's from Illinois in history. It's not in theology. He did a comparison between Reu's ideas on education with an educator by the name of Hebart.

CN: That was his doctoral work?

WW: Yes. That's how he got started. Wiederaenders helped him with it. Wiederaenders strongly feels that not enough was ever done to indicate Reu was the greatest theologian that Wartburg Seminary has produced. Probably it is true.

CN: These are books that are not going to have a very wide circulation.

WW: No. One shouldn't get sidetracked from real contemporary theological investigation. You don't need to give an apologia for Reu.

CN: No, I don't think I'm tempted that way. But the idea of doing a theological history of Wartburg Seminary, one that would have some impetus into the present might be valuable.

WW: Yes, it would be very good to show that there is, beginning from Loehe, a continual stream which is mission. Wartburg was born from the commitment to mission. And it's had a strong mission thrust. Even now, as you know, with the changing world view and taking into account the relationship to other cultures, which may be completely contrary to what Reu was living, but not contrary to the inner spirit of what really moved Reu and what was driving him. That would be a contribution to serious theology.

CN: To see the continuity with the present. And also to explore the connection between mission and worship. To me is a very important connection.

WW: Exactly and this would be an interesting chapter. Examine how it happened that we became so low church when we came from Loehe. For a long time we wore only the black robes.

CN: I wonder how much that had to do with trying to appease Missouri.

WW: Yeah, except that when you look at Missouri, it has a strong strain of high church. They were people who came from the Loehe side of the tradition. Some, like John Tietjen and John Damm, carried it to an extreme. They wear clerical collars all the time. Anyway, there is a very small work that Salzmann did once about what is at the heart of Wartburg's theology. It was published in one of the issues of the Ambassador. Wiederaenders has them in the Archives. They were prepared for Founders' Day or something. Salzmann gave a lecture in which he emphasized the various points about Wartburg Seminary's theology.

CN: That would be very interesting.

WW: I think theology comes from certain spiritual motifs, like when Luther said about Karlstadt, that we're of another spirit. There's something to that. I think that there is a spiritual *Geist* out of which we live and move and have our being. To articulate that would be a useful thing. And it would be a very interesting thing, too.

CN: Well, it's exciting to me because I think that *Geist* is still alive. And there is the continuity, as you named it, with the focus on mission. That seems to me to be a thread throughout, even into the present.

WW: Yes. I don't know whether we should move from there to get to Salzmann.

CN: I wanted to ask about Salzmann a little bit. I know he was the son-in-law of Reu.

WW: Right. His wife was Hedwig, the second daughter of Reu.

CN: And she's the one that Patsy Shaffer-Gottschalk interviewed.

WW: Yes, she had a very good memory, very precise and clear. So that's a very reliable account. Her husband, Sam, was not a deep scholar but he was a hard worker. He was appointed professor of homiletics, liturgics, Christian education, and pastoral care. That was all in the practical field and was concentrated in one person. I suppose he became professor because, first of all, he was the son-in-law of Reu, and, secondly, he was pastor of St. John's Lutheran Church here. When he first graduated he was pastor at Grinnell, Iowa. I think it was there that they were married. By the time I was here, he had been on the faculty for seven years or more. He was never known as an in-depth scholar or anything like that.

CN: He drew a lot on his parish experience.

WW: Yeah, he drew a lot on his parish experience. His main problem was that he felt obligated to parrot Reu, you know. Anything he taught in homiletics was what Reu had said.

CN: He would have used Reu's books then?

WW: Reu's book on catechetics, Reu's book on homiletics. For liturgics, there wasn't any book by Reu, so he was a little more free there. I think we all felt that Sam was a good friend of students and he would go miles to help you and struggle with your problems. He was trying to gain understanding and insight into the latest psychology. He said, for example, he remembers how dumb he was as a pastor here in Dubuque. A bright young man came to him all disturbed and depressed. So Sam suggested that he take some time off and go home. So that's exactly what the guy did. He walked into the river down there and ended his life. So Sam said that's when I bought Freud and started reading and trying to understand. And I realized that I had done exactly the wrong thing. So Sam was the kind of a guy that sought to bring in that dimension into his teaching. He was there for students and so forth.

Many of the old timers will remember with joy some of his antics. Like in my class on homiletics, up in Room 208, that was where he usually had his lectures. I remember Salzmann saying to one student, a classmate of mine who later became an assistant to the Bishop, he said, "If you preach like that, you'll drag your congregation down into hell with you." He was known for those kinds of remarks. That, too, is kind of a German characteristic.

CN: Particularly in preaching then, but also in other subjects?

WW: Other subjects as well. For example, when dealing with liturgy, he would be in the Chapel and we'd have to practice reading from the Bible. Someone would stand up there and say: "The Gospel is recorded." Or somebody would say: "The Gospel is found." And he would jump out of his seat with his old bald head bobbing and say: "Isn't that nice, brethren, he found the Gospel. He found it. Shouldn't we be happy?" And he went on like that for five minutes. In your life you would never again make that mistake. Then he would say, "Why don't you just say what it is, that the Gospel is written in...."

CN: He made a big deal out of that?

WW: Yeah. He was a steady influence here. Reu was here but near the end of his term. And then the War came along, with accelerated classes. Then Bodensieck, the president, left to go to Europe. After the War Salzmann was kind of the continuity through that period.

CN: Yes, and he would have extended the influence of Reu much longer.

WW: Yes, oh yes, he kept that going. The person who was hired to replace Reu was such a devotee of Reu that he refused even to correct the grammar.

CN: Who was that?

WW: That was Emil Matzner. He was afraid he might distort the meaning if he started fiddling around with trying to improve Reu's English. He only made little editorial changes that had no great change in meaning.

CN: So Matzner continued to use Reu's *Dogmatics*?

WW: He used Reu's *Dogmatics* and basically read it in class. The good students would find something there. Rather than just being irritated by it, they would go beyond it. But there were a lot of people for whom dogmatics was just a lost cause.

CN: Would there be electives in theology?

WW: Not much. The course was pretty well prescribed. But beginning after the War, that started opening up. Well, anyway, Salzmann was the next generation and stands with the Reu tradition. The Reu contribution was not necessarily loved in the Fritschel tradition. We've already talked about the tension there between the Reu side of things and Fritschel side of things.

The Post-Reu Era of the 1940s

CN: When did you first come to Wartburg Seminary?

WW: In the fall of 1940. We were on the verge of war and the students were exempt because of their student status. It was kind of a unique era for Wartburg because a new president had just been elected, Julius Bodensieck.

CN: So that was his first semester also.

WW: That was his first semester as president. He had been here at the seminary before as a young professor of New Testament and at Wartburg College too. He is an interesting guy himself. He came to the United States as a young person, just about finished with the Gymnasium, from the little town of Hamlin.

CN: Where is that?

WW: In northern Germany, where the guy led the rats out.

CN: The Pied Piper of Hamlin?

WW: Yes that is where he was born. His father had died and his mother came over here and settled in Charles City. He worked in a factory for a few months. The pastor suggested that with the kind of training he had, he ought to go to seminary. So he came here and completed his work. He was very bright. He decided to be a teacher. He taught part-time here and part-time over at Waverly. He did some graduate work at the University of Minnesota. Then he was here for a while. Then the old American Lutheran Church was formed by the merger of 1930. Then he went to Columbus and was editor of the *Kirchen-Blatt*. They still published that.

CN: That was the American Lutheran Church publication.

WW: Yes. That was the German publication. The Lutheran Standard was the other one.

CN: Were they both being published at the same time?

WW: Yes, they were for a few years. The Iowa Synod had had the *Kirchen-Blatt* and it also had an English version. Anyway, that is why he went to Columbus. His wife died and he had two children. Then just before he came here he was married again to a schoolteacher from Bryan, Ohio. Her dad was a pastor there for 48 years, Pastor Henkelmann.

CN: One of your predecessors as pastor there.

49

WW: Let me show you this *Festschrift* for Bodensieck. It was put out in 1975, especially in relation to what he had done after the war.

CN: When he was over in Europe.

WW: Yes. It has some good material in it on other matters. For example, if you wanted to know something about the Germans in Russia, how they got there, and how they were treated, you can find a report on that in here. It gives a very succinct statement of how they came by the invitation of Catherine the Great. It talks not only about Bodensieck, that is useful in itself, but something about the situation right after the war, that is historical and theological in general. There are also some words here from theologians of note.

CN: Bodensieck was as well known in Germany, or maybe better known in Germany than here.

WW: Probably better known in Germany than here. He was never looked upon or regarded here as any thing other than just another Lutheran. It's true his career did not facilitate a continuing theological growth and development. He became kind of enmeshed in the whole history of the church at that time. You can't say that he developed into a contributing theologian. But he was responsible for setting a new direction and a new tone, I think, in theological education at Wartburg. And there is one little personal reference there. When I was a student here, of course, the lodge question was a burning issue. You can imagine. Now we take their money, as much as we can get.

CN: We try not to look at the source.

WW: At that time it was a big issue you know, whether you could allow lodge members in the congregation. Even if you didn't allow lodge members, could you have fellowship with churches that you knew did accept lodge members? Of course, that was right in line with the whole pure doctrine emphasis that the Missouri Synod emphasized so strongly. These churches back and forth whether it was ULCA or ALC or Missouri, whenever they could accuse the other of some laxity in regard to the lodge, they did it with delight.

CN: Because it was an issue where they could claim a little one upsmanship.

WW: Yes. Everybody had to point to this or that. Well, Bodensieck did something very wise for us. He taught a course, kind of as a predecessor to what you and Norma Cook Everist are involved with in Church Administration. He was the president that started it back then and it continued with Ewald to the present time.

One afternoon in class, Bodensieck came and read us an account by Ogden Nash about what it means for men to dress up and be lodge members. Nash set this forth very beautifully, that there was this desire in all of us to be kids again and act out some of the fantasies that we had never had a chance to express. It was the opportunity for a little regression and to celebrate that innocent time when we could be the grand potentate. So he read the whole thing without making a comment. It was obvious what he meant was that we should not be exercised over the issue. He taught us about the lodge with pastoral care. With other pastors we spent a lot of time talking about this, whether you could let lodge members come to communion, whether you could let them do this or that. So he simply read us this thing. He could not say it publicly because he would be in trouble. He was not worried about the lodge. That is what he was really saying.

CN: He was saying do not get preoccupied with this because there are bigger issues?

WW: I happened then to get a call to the Michigan district to the church in Bryan, Ohio. This is where his wife was from, Justine Bodensieck, who would have been Justine Henkelmann. That was her home. So they used to stop and see us because from the time that I got the call, she was very interested. Her father had been a pastor in Bryan, the only place he ever served for 48 years. He wasn't very aggressive or mission minded. He was concerned that you didn't violate the consciences when getting people into church. They could hear the church bell and they knew what the church was, that was enough.

CN: They could find their own way.

WW: That it was not fulfilling a mission if you violated them by coercing them to come to church. So that is what this guy thought, so she was interested that I had received a call there. They used to stop there on the way. She had a sister also, over in Poland, Ohio. We happened to be there one time when the Bodensiecks came. We got into a discussion and Bodensieck couldn't help but represent his opinion on the lodge issue. But this guy Huter, married to Mrs. Bodensieck's sister, was an archconservative. He had earlier been a missionary to New Guinea. So the two of them got into a violent argument about all of this stuff, the lodge and so forth. I guess I had come over to see Huter about the lodge issue regarding some members. Bodensieck and Huter argued and I just sat there and listened. Nothing was resolved. The next day then, Bodensieck stopped and said I had to realize that his brother-in-law was very conservative on that. He would probably also be opposed to my taking part in a ministerial organization. Bodensieck had advised us at school to do that, of course. He said probably in Bryan here, you could get to know the clergy by meeting them in the post office and things like that. He was trying to make sure I wouldn't get into any conflict with Huter.

You could see that he wanted an open attitude in his students. I think he got it from most of us. We did have a lot of students that came through and thought the lodge was the big issue. And that they were serving God and humanity when they rescued somebody from the lodge.

CN: He was also counseling moderation in terms of how to deal with those who wouldn't agree.

WW: So it was kind of interesting. Bodensieck was always most helpful. He retired here and was doing research. He always gave me the greatest respect. I tried to raise the recognition level of the emeritus people, by at least giving them a hand or remembering them at Christmas time. He appreciated things like that. He is a person, whose whole life was given to the church and to the vision of the church and the Iowa Synod. He gave a great deal of his time and energy to helping Reu. He was the assistant who could do all kinds of stuff for Reu. Translate for him and many other things. We talked about that last time. But it never enhanced his own position very much. Bodensieck was full of life, vim, vigor and vitality. He had been a student of Reu, of course. The first year I was here Reu was on sabbatical so I did not see much of Reu that year.

CN: Didn't Bodensieck edit the Encyclopedia of the Lutheran Church?

WW: He did this due to his capacity in knowing both German and English and having been an editor of the *Kirchen-Blatt*. He had kind of a general knowledge beyond his ability as a New Testament scholar. I do not think that he really ever kept up with New Testament in the way you would expect. He was trained by Reu, and had many jobs along the way, and teaching at seminary and college level. He also taught Hebrew. That is where I had him, for Hebrew.

CN: What kind of a classroom teacher was he?

WW: Well, he was kind and helpful but still had some of the old German practice in that he used a lot of ridicule.

CN: Putting down people he did not agree with?

WW: Well, it was not so much those he did not agree with, but rather trying to have a sense of humor and sometimes using that humor a little bitingly. For example, in class we had one student who would come to class with a bar of candy. You know what noise the paper would make when you are trying to be quiet about it. We could see that Bodensieck was getting irritated. All of a sudden he just stopped and said, "When are you going to drop the other shoe?"

He was not a sustained lecturer. He inserted more discussion. With Reu you went to class and sat there and it was mainly a very chiseled, refined and beautiful lecture in which there were no questions. Reu anticipated most all questions, as Germans do. He would go ahead and read though his lecture. Bodensieck tried to tie things in.

He was just newly married and he brought a sense of freshness to the church. He was in favor of the new American Lutheran Church and was maybe glad to be out from under the kind of stuffiness of the Reu generation in which he grew up. So he was excited about being president and wanted to give us a positive direction. He tried to initiate some social life with his wife, who was a very good hostess. He would invite people down to the house.

CN: Which house was that?

WW: Bodensieck's was the former President's house, the last gray one at 485 Wartburg Place. Reu lived next door in the house that was built for him. It was built by collections made by students in 1938 and 1939. The seminary deeded a piece of property to Reu and the house was built. That is where he was. That all happened that year I first started in 1940. The house had been built in 1939.

CN: Well, Reu did not live there that long.

WW: No. He moved in 1939 and died in 1943. It was not long. Even as it was built, I don't know if you have ever seen the study. There is an inside stairway down to the basement that was made for Reu. He had an unbelievable number of books. He was editor of the *Kirchliche Zeitschrift* and was sent books by publishers in Germany.

CN: To write reviews and things?

52

WW: Yes.

CN: Who else was here at that time?

WW: Bodensieck taught Hebrew. Another teacher who was most significant was Augie Engelbrecht. He had just graduated from seminary in the spring of 1940. I came in the fall of 1940. He was asked to teach because Reu was on sabbatical. He was the grandson of Sigmund Fritschel. His mother was a Fritschel. Engelbrecht, his father, was the district president.

CN: So he was well-connected by family.

WW: Right, and a great guy. He lived in the dorm with us. He made his lectures very understandable and gave time for discussion. He taught us the difficult subject at that time called "The Life of Christ" using a book by Alfred Ederscheim.

CN: I have seen it, *The Life and Times of Jesus the Messiah.*

WW: The book speculates on all these facts about Jesus and purport to give a life of Christ.

CN: They are still using that text in some conservative circles.

WW: I bet they are. There were all kinds of theories about Jesus performing miracles as a little kid.

CN: Right, as in the New Testament Apocrypha.

WW: That was one of the main courses that I had from him. Augie was liked by students in the succeeding generations. After I had him and when Reu came back, then he took a parish. He went to Pennsylvania and served there for a while. Then he went to Yale, I think, for a year or so. Then he was brought back here to teach and continued to teach here until he died in the fall of 1959.

CN: So that was just before you came back again.

WW: Yeah. It was an unnecessary death, a real loss for the church. By that time he had specialized in the Old Testament and taught it exceedingly well. I did not have an eye on the Old Testament to the extent that he did. He was just an excellent teacher. That was when polio was still a threat. It had been virtually conquered by the polio vaccine but because of his age, he was about 45 then, he was told he did not need a polio shot. So he had never been vaccinated. He contracted polio and died.

CN: That is tragic.

WW: It is a sad loss for the church. He had just gotten back the year before. He had a two-year sabbatical in Germany so he could complete his degree under an Old Testament professor there.

Then in New Testament and Church History we had Albert Jagnow.

CN: I have seen the name.

WW: He was the first one of the Ohio Synod who was made professor in the old Iowa Synod.

CN: So he was a path breaker in that respect.

WW: Yes. I think there was a deliberate effort. He was also one of the first who trained in a so-called secular university, or non-Lutheran university. He went to Yale. He was a graduate of Yale in Church History.

CN: So that was another breakthrough.

WW: Yes, although there had been people with an American Ph.D. who taught here going back to the turn of the century. At this time there was not that much love between the Ohio Synod and the Iowa Synod.

CN: This was about ten years into the American Lutheran Church already.

WW: Right. Jagnow was a fastidious, hard-working guy. His most severe expression was, "My, my." He knew his church history backwards and forwards and in addition to that he was a very good organist. He usually played the organ here on festive occasions. He was the organist. He was the organist also down at St. Matthew, which is formerly an Ohio Synod congregation.

All of this history keeps coming before you, you know. Pastor Heinrich Luz started St. Matthew Church after he was dismissed by St. Johns. He simply moved up the street a few blocks. He was the pastor who took the initiative to get the City of Dubuque to buy this estate and invite Wartburg to come back here. That is the kind of interest he had in the church and the consciousness of the city that he had. But he had a fall out with St. John's, which considered itself the mother church, in Dubuque. St. John's would have been started at the same time as the seminary.

CN: That is how you got these two churches so close together.

WW: Yes, he started an Ohio Synod church.

CN: They must have taken him in then.

WW: That same old process goes on today. If you get mad at the church, you go out and start a new one somewhere.

CN: Well, I've heard Pastor Miller down there say practically every Lutheran church in town was started by St. John's.

WW: That is true. That is often the way. Luz had a good graduate level education but was not dynamic. He was an intellectual.

CN: You know you are in trouble then.

54

WW: There was also Sam Salzmann. Of course, he is a legend in himself. He is the son-in-law of Reu. He was from South Dakota.

CN: Where in South Dakota was he from?

WW: He was from the central part of South Dakota. He always said that the only sure crop from South Dakota was the people it produced for the church. He was a very good friend to students. He came to Dubuque as pastor of St. Johns. He was called from St. John's to be the professor of the church and Preaching and Christian Education. He taught the practical part of the curriculum.

CN: So he made good use of his years as a pastor then.

WW: Yeah. He was known for his expressive way of speaking. Like others, he would also use this method of ridicule. It seems to be a German characteristic. He said about one of my classmates, "If you preach like that you will drag your congregation to hell with you."

CN: It gets your attention.

WW: Yeah. A regular part of procedure was learning to do the liturgy. We were in the chapel and he would give us instruction and make it clear that when you wore a black robe, you did not wear brown shoes. Then there is an experience that all who studied with him would remember. If you stood up there and were going to read the gospel and said, "The Gospel is found," he would jump out of his seat in the back of the chapel and say, "Isn't that nice brethren, he found the Gospel. Just think of that, isn't that wonderful." You would never open your mouth again. The same way with "record." "Oh, did you go down to the court house to record it?"

CN: What did he like then?

WW: He said, "Why don't you just say, 'It is written.'?"

CN: I was taught that here too, but probably not with that much sarcasm.

WW: Let's see, that would be Poovey and Pirner.

CN: Right. They themselves probably would have been taught by Salzmann.

WW: Yeah, especially Pirner. Yes, Pirner would say that. Salzmann taught catechetics from Reu's book. Salzmann spent so much time on the development of the Roman mass over the centuries that whenever he got to the modern age, all of a sudden he realized it was the end of the term.

CN: It was kind of the Luther Reed approach.

WW: Yes. Well, that was Salzmann. He was the one who put emphasis on the sermon, that it had to have a coherence to it, an inner core, a red thread that would go all the way through. He would say, you bring these points together. He had these big old hands, big fingers. We used to call them "milking mice." The students had all kinds of expressions.

CN: Did he advocate three point sermons?

WW: Yes, indeed. Although he did not insist that it had to be three, but they usually turned out that way. His system of doing things was old fashioned. In teaching how to preach, the first thing you had to do was take down the sermon that he presented in class. Then by that process you were supposed to be learning how to write a sermon. Then, of course, we all had to write that same sermon and give it back to him.

CN: He delivered a sermon.

WW: He presented it in class. He went into detail, showing its relation to the text and stuff like that. It was kind of a running commentary or a homiletical exposition.

CN: Like a case study of a sermon that he prepared.

WW: Then you were to give back the same thing. Every class member had that sermon. A lot of them would use these sermons when they went out to preach, because that is what we were told to do. Part of his idea was that he would not let you preach until your second year. You had one course in homiletics. Finally one congregation said, "Don't send us people that preach the same sermon."

CN: They had heard it more than once!

WW: They had heard it again and again.

CN: What about law-gospel in preaching? Was that an emphasis?

WW: Yes that was a great emphasis of Salzmann. In addition to Salzmann, then another professor, who was new the year that I came in 1940, was John C. Mattes. He came from the ULCA in Pennsylvania. He was what we called high church. I think if he had had his way, he would have used historic vestments. We had the custom of only wearing black robes. In many ways you would say he was a forerunner of Gordon Lathrop. He placed great emphasis on presiding.

CN: It sounds like the vestments were regionalized in terms of what was customary in different parts of the country.

WW: Well, I think it was in the ULCA that they were accustomed to the alb and chasuble. I do not recall anyone at that time, in the early 40's or late 30's, who worked with historic vestments. Mattes was very concerned about the mission of the church. He helped start the mission congregation that is Holy Trinity Lutheran Church today.

CN: He was involved in that start?

WW: Yes. Augie Engelbrecht was very much in on that too. I came here in 1940. They were doing a survey about starting a congregation "up on the hill" as it was called, by Washington Junior High. From there on, it was countryside. There had been several ideas about starting a congregation closer to the seminary. One was actually begun on the corner of Grandview and Dodge Streets. I helped with the survey. The mission pastor there was by the name of Zibbell and never had much success, with the synod and the shortage of funds and everything. They decided to close it down but Mattes insisted that he would do it for nothing. So we started worshiping in a store there right next to where Holy Trinity is now.

CN: Up at the five corners there.

WW: Yes, that little brick building right next to it. It was a store at that time or had been. Mattes was very active in that. Mattes had three daughters and two sons. The girls urged their father to invite all the seminarians, hoping that they would land one. One of his daughters did marry Augie Engelbrecht.

CN: I was going to ask you before about what you said about Salzmann. Did he meet one of Reu's daughters then after he was a pastor at St. John's?

WW: They met here at the seminary. They used to meet behind Reu's house.

CN: This is when he was a student then.

WW: Yeah. After high school she was eligible to teach and got a teacher's certificate. So his wife taught here for a year. That is how that came about. Mattes taught Confessions. I thought it was a tedious way of teaching. He just sort of went through it. We talked and raised issues. Reu dictated the notes to us. Mattes too was very Lutheran. He was confessional, from the ULCA and General Council.

The librarian at the time was also the archivist, Bill Goetz. He was an excellent student, a little older. I think he had taught school for some time. He decided to run the library. He also ran the bookstore. At that time already we were making provisions so students could buy books at a discount.

CN: That was the first bookstore?

WW: Except after that, it was not doing too well. The students themselves, during the time of Buchheim and others before him, incorporated it as a nonprofit corporation in order to do business and rebates. You did not get your discount when you bought your books. Your discount for the whole year was figured out at the end when they figured out where they stood financially. All of that ended with a screeching halt during my years when one of the people that had been elected by the board of governors of this co-op charged $2,000.00 to the Wartburg bookstore as a down payment on an airplane.

CN: Oh, goodness.

WW: Goetz taught German for years. He would preach in German. As a student, I wrote an essay for him talking about whether we should or should not require German for pastors. I wrote a blistering article on how stupid it was to spend all this energy and time bothering with German, when we were about ready to go to war with Germany and so forth. What reason could there possibly be for it? I never heard any more about it. When I came back here and was installed on the faculty, the very day I was installed, Goetz came to my office and brought me this essay.

CN: He still had it?

WW: He had it.

CN: This is after you had studied in Germany then.

WW: I had studied German and struggled through it and even written in it. He had the last word.

CN: I guess so.

WW: That was the kind of man he was.

CN: The instruction at that time was in English or German?

WW: Even prior to that, most of it was in English starting in the 30s. Reu always had lectured in German. As I said, when I came here he was on sabbatical. The next year, I was in the first class when he lectured in English. I think he regretted that he did not start lecturing in English sooner. He realized that he would eventually be forced to write in English and do the translations for himself that previously he had everybody else do for him.

CN: So the works of his that are in English are all translations others did.

WW: Many of them are. There are some that he had written himself which then were proofed. I think basically the catechetics and the last dogmatics were written by Reu himself. He had good students like Augie Engelbrecht to help him with the English part, making it more readable. Reu was the last one to change. Bodensieck, I think, insisted on it ultimately, that he give up the German. This was ridiculous because most of the people could not get that much out of a lecture in German.

CN: I think being at war with Germany added to the temper of the times.

Wartburg Seminary After World War II

WW: Bodensieck began his tenure as president the same year I began seminary. And then he functioned as president until 1945 when the War ended and they wanted him to go as liaison between the German Church and the military. He accepted that position, which was partially subsidized by the government. It was a very necessary one and Bodensieck was exceptionally competent to do it, because he handled foreign languages very well and knew the German Church. So he did a very large and important ministry during those years. When I went to Germany to study in '58 and they found out where I was from, the first thing they would say was "Bodensieck." There wasn't a pastor who didn't know Bodensieck because he had been so involved in helping to provide extra relief during the hard times after the War. So they looked to Bodensieck as one of the heroes who helped Germany recover. His wife did a lot of the work also. So he served in that whole ministry, from '45 to '50 or however long, he served there.

CN: And then he came back to the faculty.

WW: He came back to the seminary but I don't think he functioned as president. I think that in the meantime Salzmann and others had been acting presidents. When he came back, he didn't take up the duties of president, as I recall. It was during that time that Bernard Holm was called. While Holm was not as strong as an administrator, he did a lot of things that set the course for the seminary, moving into the modern age.

CN: The faculty began to expand during those years.

WW: Yes. The student body grew like wildfire. It went from being a seminary of less than 100 to over 200, including interns, during those years.

CN: Right after the Second World War.

WW: In the '50s to '60s. Big time. Those were heady times because they were all enthusiastic young students. Most of them came direct from college, here to study theology, mixed in with a few people who had served in the military, whose coming to the seminary had been delayed. So they were exceptionally good students, bright people. You could find that all over. Up at Luther Seminary at the same time were Kent Knutson, Carl Braaten, Gerhard Forde, and Clarence Lee. All of those who became professors got their degrees from Harvard and other major universities. And from this time, a large number of people from Wartburg went on to graduate school and studied at Harvard, or Princeton Seminary, or at other secular institutions.

So it was, I think, Holm's course to direct the seminary to get ready for an accreditation visit. That had already been done for the first time in 1944 with the ATS. But then Holm had some difficulty making decisions. Streng and Engelbrecht used to talk about some of the funny things he used to propose in dealing with faculty members, because he was a typical absent-minded professor. And then came the merger in 1960. By that time Holm was resigning as president and going back to full-time teaching, which he did. After he resigned in about '57, Alfred Ewald came as president.

You had asked if the students back in previous years ever heard anything of Brunner or other theologians. So I just brought a copy of the student publication from that time. At least starting in the '50's they were beginning to hear other voices. Here is an article in the student *Ambassador*, a critique of Brunner. Then there was a later publication by Manfred Meitzen who was a graduate of Wartburg, went to Harvard and got his Ph.D. with Tillich. He had written about Tillich. So, they were starting to experience those kinds of things.

CN: This is well after the Second World War. This particular edition is 1955.

WW: Right. They were beginning in the early '50s to get more into that kind of material.

CN: This would have been post-Reu then.

WW: Right.

CN: It probably needed his passing before this transition could take place.

WW: Yeah.

CN: How long was the *Ambassador* published?

WW: Well, this went on from the '40s up until, I suppose, the '60s.

CN: I've never heard of the *Ambassador* before. This is Volume 4 in 1955 so it started around 1951, unless they had volumes that covered more than one year. And this was a student publication?

WW: Yeah. That's an article by a student there.

CN: William Streng was the consultant.

WW: Yeah. He was the faculty contact.

CN: Wayne Stumme was theology editor.

WW: And that's why in the centennial edition, there's an article by Reu's son-in-law, a professor at Wartburg, named Samuel Salzmann, on the theology of Wartburg Seminary.

CN: Oh, there is an article on that. It appeared in 1954.

WW: It was the centennial of the founding of Wartburg Seminary.

CN: In a picture of the faculty in '57, there are Holm, Leo, Jensen, Mengers, Streng, Nyholm and Bodensieck.

WW: You see, that's the time when the whole integration of the Danish tradition came in.

CN: That was Jensen and Nyholm?

WW: Jensen, Nyholm, and Mengers. There is also a little unpublished history about Ewald and how he became president. Part of the merger in 1930, of course, was getting the Buffalo Synod into the whole thing. And that was accomplished. But then there was always the effort to be sensitive to the fact that they were part of the merger, since they were a small synod. And so people like Ewald were then elected to being District Presidents.

CN: He had been District President.

WW: Right. He was District President in Minnesota of the old ALC. Then when the merger came in 1960, in order to assure Ewald's support for that merger, there were assurances made that he would be given consideration for a position of leadership in the next church. Some of the old Ohio Synod people and some of the old Buffalo people up in St. Paul weren't very hot about this merger, because back in the '30s it meant the closing of their school up there. So when it comes now for the time of the merger of the '60s, some of these lingering problems persisted. They knew they needed to have the support of the District President, Ewald. So the way that was obtained was by the negotiations of Henry F. Schuh with Ewald and other leaders, that he would be given a position of leadership in the new church. It was obvious he was not going to get it by election to any of the Bishops' offices, because he did not have a large enough political base for that.

CN: To move up in the hierarchy?

WW: Right. So Schuh turned to the idea of him becoming the president of Wartburg Seminary.

CN: How would they be able to pull that off?

WW: They pulled it off by the fact that he is elected by the Board, with the President of the Church presiding. And if the President of the Church is making a strong plea, that has persuasive power. And I think Ewald was flattered by it and he accepted it gladly. He did many good things. He did not come in, however, with the joyous welcome of the faculty. They had kind of hoped that Doc Fritschel from out in Colorado, George Fritschel's son, would be the one elected as president, because he had proven himself as a good leader, aggressive and ambitious.

CN: So Ewald was an outsider to Wartburg.

WW: He was an outsider whom they didn't know or didn't want to. They knew he was from Buffalo. They knew he was more aligned with the former Ohio Synod people and with a group of kind of reactionary pastors up in Minnesota who had gone to Luther Seminary, which they considered superior in every way to this seminary here.

CN: Good for them.

WW: Yes. And so they didn't really welcome Ewald at all. But Ewald did his darndest to accommodate himself to them. If he had any fault, I suppose it would have been that. He tried too much to find a way to be liked by them.

CN: What struck me in your history was the institutional development of the infrastructure during his presidency. Fritschel Hall was expanded and Blair House was built.

WW: Yes, those things. He had a sense for art that he also determinedly brought into his whole effort. This was a time for development of educational institutions, sort of like the Seminary Appeal for colleges and seminaries, after the War. So there was money to do this kind of stuff. Ewald was in the midst of that and that was his forte, I think, that he knew something about building and architecture. So he was very interested in that.

But his greatest contribution, I think, was his contribution to the ecumenical movement. Without being a supporter of any kind of ecumenical activities and probably never having been involved very much, Ewald simply came onto the scene here and had interest in developing ecumenical relationships. He was president and took the position of leadership for the developments which occurred in the formation of, first of all, the Association of Theology Faculties in Iowa and later the consortium that became the Schools of Theology in Dubuque. The eventual loss of Aquinas was very regrettable.

Ewald was president when I was elected. Gerhard Krodel was here and we were quite close, good friends. He was in favor of this merger and so we sensed that Ewald was a very lonely guy, because there weren't many people that were around supporting and welcoming him. So we supported him in the direction he would go, including the ecumenical relations, and tried to anticipate his suggestions in every way we could.

CN: To keep things moving in that direction.

WW: Yeah. And he welcomed our interest in our discussions with him. He was happy to have someone take the time to encourage him.

CN: Vatican II was coming in right at that time, too. This *kairos* moment.

WW: Yeah. And I remember now, many years later, Gerhard Krodel was complaining about some president somewhere. I told him, "Well, which is better or worse? Remember when you were at Wartburg, we would go in and talk to Ewald and he would listen." And he said, "Well, in some respects that was probably better." So Ewald fulfilled, I think, a role here.

CN: Did he teach at all?

WW: He taught one course. That was Church Administration. And at that time, it was pretty much prescribed what that course was going to be. Because the visiting "firemen" from Minneapolis, leaders from every Division, came down to meet with the seniors and spend one period with them.

CN: So it was a course done in consultation with others.

WW: All of them had to be heard and Ewald coordinated that. He was present in all of those classes and had them do some things himself, talking about administration, the responsibility of the church at large. That's what he taught.

CN: Who were your colleagues when you came as professor?

WW: Salzmann was still teaching and Holm, Streng, and Poovey. Bodensieck was still here and taught one course.

CN: Was Benz here yet?

WW: Benz had just been called, but was not back here yet.

CN: I read that Dr. William Streng was a guiding influence in getting internship going. What do you recall about the early years of internship?

WW: Well, I recall it this way. In my day, it was a possibility.

CN: It was an option?

WW: There were several internship possibilities. Sometimes need dictated the internship.

CN: Where they needed someone to go?

WW: Where there was a place that needed a pastor. The seminary had always done this since its beginning. We sent people out sometimes when they weren't quite finished to be able to serve awhile and then when the crisis was passed, after a year, come back.

CN: Would these have been students that only went out on Sunday, then?

WW: No, they came out of the seminary and went full-time in the parish and later came back to the seminary.

CN: Did they call it internship then?

WW: No. I can't remember what they called it in the very beginning. It was called internship when we came back to Dubuque. I investigated an internship as a student and one was suggested to me, a street ministry in Pittsburgh. There were a couple of internships that, by that time, had gotten to be a regular thing. Pastor John Becker of Fond du Lac, Wisconsin, whose brother later was president of Wartburg College, regularly had interns. He needed help, but he also was a good pastor. The guy who went there got a lot of insight. So there were things like that. But it was after the late '40s and '50s when Streng came here that it was getting emphasized more and more. More and more people were going on internship. Wartburg was one of the first ones to require it.

CN: That would have been in the early '50s, according to what I read.

WW: Yeah.

CN: So it was more of a makeshift thing in a sense.

WW: The concept of it was. When it started with Streng, it was primarily to integrate learning with experience.

CN: The earlier ones would have been more out of the need of the parish.

WW: They were based just on the need of the parish. They were to fill some vacancies here and there. But as you said, Streng would have played the major part in it.

CN: I haven't had this discussion with my colleagues who do internship work, but my hunch is that Wartburg is the first seminary of the present ELCA seminaries to require this.

WW: That's true and, I don't know, probably of all the Protestant seminaries in the country.

CN: Wartburg would have predated any of them?

WW: Most of them. There may have been one or two there. Everybody was pushing it, but to make it a requirement, that was something new. I suppose Streng is primarily responsible for that.

CN: So that would have been a very significant innovation in theological education, coming out of Wartburg.

WW: It was indeed. The same thing began to happen with what has developed into the whole business of Clinical Pastoral Education [CPE]. Along with this emphasis on internship, in a few years, there began a developing interest in CPE and an increasing number of our people going and becoming qualified in that. Then Bill Hulme came here and virtually set up the system that prevailed for a long time, where you had required courses in pastoral care which included regular participation in an institution of one kind or another. Or you would go into a church setting in which particular professional attention was given to other areas of healing and medicine.

CN: That would have been local sites?

WW: Well, it also meant driving sometimes, for instance, a group went over to Independence. Dave Solberg was one of those. People drove to Mendota once a week, in Wisconsin to Mendota Mental Health.

CN: Near Madison.

WW: Yeah. So Wartburg was very vital in that and was one of the first, if not the first again, to require this CPE.

CN: And Hulme would have been giving it oversight.

WW: He was the key person in developing that whole thing. He came to Wartburg College fresh out of Boston University where he had gotten his Ph.D. in pastoral psychology. They needed a college chaplain and somebody to teach other courses. So Hulme with a Ph.D. was the logical choice. And you can imagine, students now having the chance to talk to somebody who is looked upon as having certain kind of expertise in psychology and counseling, he was simply overwhelmed. He also had the material with which to write books. His first book was dealing with a lot of the issues that were plaguing young people. He wrote a little book, *Face your Life with Confidence*.

CN: He was just the right person at the right time.

WW: The right person at the right time with the desire to do it and he did it. And it wasn't long before all the seminaries had to have a professor of pastoral care.

CN: He didn't stay at Wartburg College that long.

WW: Well, then he came to Wartburg Seminary, but he didn't stay here that long. Then he went to Luther Seminary, because they didn't have anything comparable. I think maybe he felt the challenge of the city and that was of interest to him. But he felt badly that Luther had nothing and so saw it as an obligation to give them something in this area.

CN: What memories do you have of that faculty when you came?

WW: Well, they were very helpful in coming in. I have good memories of that and felt I was accepted. Then, of course, there was Gerhard Krodel in New Testament and also Horace Hummel was the Old Testament professor. So it was a lively bunch. New blood had just come in and there were sort of factions. I, of course, had known Salzmann from way back as a student and the other older professors.

CN: Was Salzmann the strongest connection to the previous era?

WW: Yes. He goes back to Reu and to the Fritschels. So I have good memories except that I couldn't help notice the difference between what it is to begin in a seminary and what it is to begin in a congregation. You know, when we first came to the parish as a young couple, we were warmly welcomed, met at the train, set up with the whole house spotless for you.

CN: Tell me about it.

WW: Yes, then coming to Wartburg after having been in Germany for nearly two years and with our furniture stored, we moved into 465, the second brick house, and it was dirty and hadn't been cleaned or anything. And here our furniture came on a hot day like this, hot and humid, and the truck arrived to unload our furniture at about 7 o'clock in the evening. I felt so sorry for these guys. Everybody was sweating, and we just had them drop stuff wherever they could. It was just utter chaos. And the next morning, we had an all day faculty meeting.

CN: Welcome!

WW: And so I went to the meeting and poor Ilah was stuck with the kids and having to get ready for school. You couldn't help but think of the difference. It isn't that people don't think of it, but they are just not oriented in that direction. Whereas, in the parish the nurture is there and the welcome. I remember the beginnings with Hummel and Krodel and Poovey, all these people. There was a lot of activity. The younger faculty members like Krodel and Hummel and myself would have social events, dinner, evenings together. Burritt would also have social events.

CN: The younger faculty.

WW: Yeah. We always did things together, to which the old ones weren't necessarily invited. That was because they wouldn't have enjoyed it.

CN: Was Hummel the one who ended up in Missouri?

WW: Yes. He came from Missouri and he, of course, rebelled against the rigidity of Missouri. So he became, at least so everybody at Concordia thought, a flaming liberal. He espoused the latest teachings of all the great Old Testament teachers, like von Rad from Germany, and so forth. And was very high church and enjoyed putting that on at services. There was a service with Hummel presiding, an evening Communion service, and he had Burritt as incense bearer with a long procession. Burritt was swinging the smoke. Dr. Salzmann was sitting right behind me, with Mrs. Salzmann and their daughter who is deaf, and I heard him say to her, "Ich kann es nicht mehr aushalten [I can't take it anymore]." And they got up and left. Horace delighted in presiding at High Mass. And, or course, that was in line with the Loehe tradition, but you still have that other piety that prevailed.

CN: The black robe tradition.

WW: Yeah, you need to find out where that came from.

CN: Was it daily Chapel at that time?

WW: Yes.

CN: With faculty presiding once a week?

WW: I think that's probably right. They were preaching every week, but we didn't have Holy Communion that often.

CN: More emphasis on participation in the parishes?

WW: Yeah. I remember when it started being more and more common to have communion services. But there used to be the philosophy that we should be active in the churches downtown, which was a good thing.

CN: What about other memorable times either with the faculty or in the life of the seminary during those first years?

WW: Well, it was an overall exciting time because there was a new theology coming in with Krodel and Hummel starting a graduate school. Beginning in the '60s, they revived or started again, however you choose to designate it, the Master's program. And there was the starting of the ecumenical cooperation together. But the big thing was the summer school. There always had been the Luther Academy, which was started by Reu. That was for continuing education and evolved into the program that is now the Luther Academy of the Rockies.

But mainly there was an emphasis on continuing education. We had a program in the summer. The Dubuque Seminary and Wartburg cooperated together in doing some of those things jointly. You know that cooperation with the Roman Catholics was especially exciting. And that's when I first encountered Arthur Cochrane. Cochrane and Cletus Wessels and I taught a course on the Church. And we had a mixture of about 25 or so from each tradition, 20 to 25 each of the Reformed and Lutheran and Roman Catholic. It was a big group. We would have a lecture as part of it and break down into discussions because it was a couple of hours each day.

CN: This was in the summer?

WW: Yeah. And so it was really an exciting thing. But with that we always had some visiting fireman, some prominent theologian to give a serious lecture. So, for example, we had Paul Holmer from Yale and John Macquarrie from Scotland.

CN: That would have been exciting.

WW: That was exciting. People were turned on and enjoyed the summer school. That was fun. Go out and have a beer with these guys in the evening and vital discussions, and arguments in class. Fun time.

CN: Can you think of any other memorable experiences?

WW: This is one of the old books I retrieved when they were throwing stuff away and we went to salvage books at the dump.

CN: That's a story I want to hear.

WW: Pastor Burritt, the librarian, was going to clean up the shelves as they brought books together and remodeled Fritschel Hall. The Library had a lot of books that hadn't been reshelved, old German books especially. Many came from St. Paul, Minnesota and they just dumped a bunch of them down in the area which is now the staff lounge. That was one big old room. All those books were there and they decided they were going to get rid of them and hauled them out to the dump.

CN: This was a *fait accompli* then, they were already there.

WW: At the dump. We heard about it and so Gerhard Krodel and I went out there. I was just a young, assistant professor, just starting here. It was during my first year or so here. That was a terrible thing, so we went out there and saw all kinds of books that obviously ought to be kept. So we rescued as many as we could, but some were filthy because the bulldozers were covering them over. Most of them probably belonged there. Later we had to make more storage for them up in what is now faculty offices, storing them up on the third floor.

CN: This one says it was withdrawn from Luther Seminary.

WW: Yeah, that's Luther in St. Paul, that merged here.

CN: How was the instruction at the seminary different from the time you were a student in comparison to when you came back as a professor?

WW: As students we read Reu for dogmatics and ethics. I can't even remember being referred to Schmid's book on Lutheran doctrinal theology, which seems strange. You were simply given Reu's dogmatics and expected to learn that. We were given a lot of references to von Hofmann and Zahn. And we were expected to look up passages in the Bible. A good deal of the dogmatics was spent in talking about the teachings of the Bible on these particular subjects. So it was difficult to separate theology from exegetical work.

CN: A big overlap between theology and Biblical studies.

WW: Right, very much.

CN: What difference did it make when the Danes came in from Trinity Seminary in Blair?

WW: Oh, I think that was a continuance of a number of shockers that started after World War II. There was the upsurge of different students coming in with war experience and students from other places. But then especially when the Danes came, they were well beyond these fellows as far as knowing contemporary theology, even in the field of New Testament. C.B. Larsen was not a raving liberal or anything like that, but he knew well the modern biblical field and taught New Testament in that way. So that was a step beyond Reu and Theodor Zahn.

CN: So for curriculum it was very influential?

WW: I think it played a role in stimulating new thought. The Danes used to say when they came here, they were shocked to see how sophisticated Wartburg students were in regard to things like being able to go out and drink beer and stuff like that. And how narrow they were in their dogmatics. That's an excessive statement, isn't it, but basically true because they had people like T.I. Jensen who also taught contemporary theology who would have used some of Brunner and other kinds of theologians.

CN: He translated the dogmatics of Prenter.

WW: Yes, Regin Prenter. But that never took off. You would think that would be the kind of solid dogmatics that one would be able to use. But it is so ponderous and being a translation makes it even more so. But at least they had exposure to some new streams. I think that did make a difference. The whole world was changing in such a rapid way. The events following World War II just catapulted all institutions like ours into a new age.

CN: Even if there had not been that Danish connection?

WW: Yes, because you had people who were coming to teach here who brought with them a bibliography which was different than the old one. There was eagerness to get on with something new. I can remember in college when we were getting those stimulating teachers in college more than we ever had here. For example, I had Haefner in Greek, Ottersberg in history, and people like that. So already from there you were thinking in relation to the future. In my own case, however, I liked Greek very much and was interested in that and thought the best thing I would like to do would be to go on and study Greek and teach it sometime. But then also at the same time, I was anxiously waiting to get married. First of all, you weren't supposed to be married and secondly, there wasn't any realistic possibility of getting married and going to the seminary, too, out of sheer costs and so forth. But anyway, by the time we graduated from the seminary, we were just enthused about starting life and being married and all this. But then, I think, that kind of spirit of looking to something new and maybe going to graduate school attracted a lot of people. A few of us had a chance to do something about it.

In my own case, it was simply that I had wanted to be in military chaplaincy when I was at seminary and couldn't get in. I did, then, later and through that had some GI Bill coming. So after I came back and the family had been in Waverly, staying there while I was overseas in Korea, they called me to the church in Waverly as associate pastor. So just returning from the experience of being separated for a year, it seemed like a pretty good deal to me to stay there. So that's what we did. But having done that, then comes along the possibility of utilizing the GI

Bill. So the Senior Pastor Schmidt also was Chairman of the Board of Theological Education. He knew that there would be need for an increasing number of people who had gone to graduate school. So he helped in arranging a year off for me to go to Harvard and that's what kind of got me into the whole thing.

CN: Into the theology realm.

WW: Into new theology. I guess I've told you, I went there with the intention of proving what a heretic Tillich was.

CN: Wrong!

WW: When I first heard him, you know, I felt that's what I've been waiting to hear all my life. That's what I think!

CN: It was like finding yourself.

WW: Yeah. So having had that year there and the long experience in parishes of several different kinds—the double parish in Ohio which merged, St. Paul's in Waverly, the Air Force—they were looking for someone to replace Matzner, who had parish experience and some scientific study in theology. So just having completed that Master's, I suppose that's why I was selected.

CN: The two came together.

WW: Schmidt didn't like to drive the car, so he had been down here in Dubuque for the Board of Theological Education that did the electing. And I drove down to Waterloo to meet the train to bring him to Waverly. He said, "Well, I hope you are ready for a shock." I said, "Why?" And he said, "Well, you were elected."

CN: Had you sent in an application?

WW: I had gotten stuff ready. I delayed and delayed at sending it in. But I did send it in. Then the very last days before the election, I had written a letter that it is never too late to correct a mistake as long as there is a possibility and that I realized it would be a serious mistake for me to leave this parish now and leave the ministry now. I almost had it in mind to give that to Dr. Schmidt, but then events started happening quickly after that. First thing we were in Germany and studying there. But I think I was helped a lot with my inquiry and interest through that one year. That was a refreshing time. It was a great time to be at Harvard, first of all, because they had just beefed up the Divinity school and had people like Tillich. Stendahl had just come there and Richard Niebuhr. It was just an exciting place to be. So, in many ways, my theological education started there for all practical purposes. But I had no thought of studying systematic theology.

CN: At that time.

WW: Yeah. I thought of teaching in college, teaching Greek, something like that.

CN: Doing that in Waverly?

WW: Going on to school in Greek. I found in Tillich a good expression of what I was looking for and took all of that I could. I found that I could get by and cut the academic mustard. I was very apprehensive about that after being out of school and never having really been severely tested.

CN: Yeah, you'd been behind, then, in terms of knowing the current theological scene.

WW: Yeah, some of these names were unknown. I did some fast learning.

CN: I'd like for us to go into detail about your own biography. Maybe even starting from your early years.

WW: That's a good thing for next time.

CN: I'm sure appreciative of this, Bill.

WW: Well, thank you. It's great to remember some of those things and think about what they mean in relation to each other.

Wilhelm Loehe, parish pastor from Neuendettelsau, Germany, who provided the vision and prepared the first pastors and professors for what was to become Wartburg Seminary. His spiritual direction and emphasis on mission lives on today.

Johannes Deindoerfer, pastor, early founder, historian, and president of the Iowa Synod

Georg Grossmann,
first seminary president

The Frischel brothers, Sigmund (left), who came to Dubuque in 1854, and Gottfried (right), who came to Dubuque in 1857, as professors. They were known as "Professor Senior" and "Professor Junior" respectively. Together they would be the faculty of Wartburg for most of the first three decades and helped shape the direction of the Iowa Synod.

The Iowa Synod in 1860. The Fritschel brothers are in the front row, on either side of the crease (Sigmund, left; Gottfried, right). Grossmann is the tall person in the back on the far right.

(Left) St. Sebald, Iowa, the second site for the seminary.

(Right) Some of the students from the St. Sebald years. This group was circa 1868.

Emerson Mansion, the site of the seminary upon its return to Dubuque in 1889. A gift from the city, the property is still the site of the seminary today. Little remains from this early period except for houses built for the faculty and now used by students.

The second generation of Frischels – Max (left), son of Sigmund, and George (right), son of Gottfried. Both served as Wartburg professors, with Max also serving as president.

The seminary got its stone buildings starting in 1916. The stone was quarried right on campus. The cornerstone (lower photo) was laid on November 10, 1914, on Luther's birthday.

Students (left) and a student room (below) from the early part of the 20th century. Note that German identification was still prevalent.

75

A young J. Michael
Reu, ca. 1900.

A familiar portrait of Reu.
A self-made scholar and
prolific writer, his
influence would extend
well beyond the boundaries
of the Iowa Synod and,
later the American
Lutheran Church.

Reu, ever working in his office.

Julius Bodensiek, who served on the Wartburg faculty from 1921 to 1930, was called as its president in 1940. His tenure as president was limited, however, as he was called in 1945, with his wife, Justine (above), to serve as a liaison between Allied governments and German churches, and later to service with the new Lutheran World Federation. Bodensieck's role as statesman took his influence far beyond the walls of Wartburg, and he is fondly remembered in Europe for his work.

Professor Paul Leo (center) at his installation service. Bernard Holm, then President is behind Leo (far left), accompanied by Schluetter (back), with Schmidt presiding (right).

Part Two:

Conversations on the
Life and Times of
William H. Weiblen

Introduction to Part Two

William Weiblen was born on March 2, 1919. In these autobiographical reflections the reader gains a glimpse into the family, childhood, education, and career of a modest man. Bill would in many ways prefer not to see these memories come to print. "There is only one thing worse than being undervalued by your peers," he often has quipped quoting his own Professor Alfred Haefner. "That is to be overvalued." Yet for his many friends and former students, these recollections are a treasure.

One obtains a glimpse into Bill's early life. One learns of the influence of his uncle, Franz Matter, one of the original missionaries to the Native Americans in Wyoming. Stories are shared about his college days at Wartburg College in Waverly, Iowa and the courtship with Ilah. We hear about his pastoral ministry in Bryan, Ohio where a large room in the church was subsequently named "Weiblen Hall" in their honor. There are memories of his time as a chaplain in the Air Force, serving in Korea. We learn something about the profound influence the person and thought of Paul Tillich has exerted on his life, beginning with his year at Harvard. There are reflections on the years at Erlangen, particularly about the various theologians Bill encountered there. Finally, we read some personal memories of his teaching and administration while serving as a professor and president at Wartburg Seminary. Notice how the ecumenical and international dimensions of the church have come to the fore through his ministry.

The life of William Weiblen has been interwoven with the history of the Iowa Synod and its Wartburg Seminary from beginning to end. Although baptized by his uncle, Pastor Franz Matter, in a congregation of the Ohio Synod, the congregation of his Miller, South Dakota childhood was rooted in Iowa Synod soil. He attended both Wartburg College and Wartburg Seminary, the chief educational institutions originating in the Iowa Synod. The two congregations that Bill served as a pastor both have Iowa Synod roots. He has labored for decades as professor, president, and emeritus at Wartburg in Dubuque. In the years following their retirement, Bill and Ilah have remained foundational influences on the history and life together of the seminary. It is only fitting that the gathering place at the seminary connected to the Refectory is now called "Weiblen Commons." How many hours have Bill and Ilah ministered at table to the community of Wartburg Seminary over the years? Looking back on a lifetime of service, one stands in wonder at the mystery of God's providential guidance of our days and in praise of the goodness of God's grace!

William H. Weiblen: School Years

CN: I'm wondering, Bill, if you would be willing to talk about your own life story with me. Maybe we could go chronologically back to the beginning.

WW: I was born 2 March 1919 in Miller, South Dakota.

CN: Miller is where?

WW: It is in the central part. It is northwest of Mitchell, straight west of Huron. It is about 70 miles east of Pierre. It is right where ranching begins and farming ends. My parents had lived in Miller from the time they were married. They were not young when they got married. My mother was 33 and my dad was 37 and they were both part of the homesteading colony that a pastor in the Iowa synod had laid out at Orient, South Dakota which is about 30 miles north of there.

CN: So there was this connection with the Iowa synod there in South Dakota.

WW: Yes. This pastor was a relative of mine and one of the last people to work with the Indians. So my parents were both from that settlement which had come from Polk City, Iowa out to Miller, South Dakota. I was the third child. My oldest brother, John, was a Downs Syndrome baby. He died when he was four years old. My brother, Don, who is two years older then I am, became a chemist. He kind of set the tone for all of us later. He was an outstanding student. I never could measure up. I always felt that teachers would say, "That was good, but not quite like your brother Don." And then I had two others younger than me. My sister is two years younger than me and there's a younger brother who just now retired. Those younger than me are my brother, Richard, and my sister, Dorothy. She is in Brazil, married to Richard Wangen. She has been a missionary all her life in Brazil, serving as a teacher. My brother Paul is a geologist. He is the one who just retired.

CN: He is the one in Minneapolis.

WW: He just retired from the science department at the University of Minnesota. I suppose I could tell a little about what I see came together in my mother and father. My mother was a most serious, pious person but also a very inquisitive, with an insatiable appetite to learn. She didn't have much opportunity. The only schooling she had was the parochial schooling that went with the religious instruction that you would see in this community. But my mother was very serious and it was hard to get her to relax and have fun. She came from northern Germany up by Stettin. That's where her parents came from. My dad's family was from southern Germany, Württemberg near Reutling, not too far from Stuttgart. That was more of a fun-loving group. On my dad's side, it was interesting that my grandmother came out in that group as a widow with five kids. The oldest was twelve and the youngest was one-year old. She came along because her husband had died the year before they came out.

CN: She was the one that emigrated then.

WW: Yes, she came out to South Dakota. She had emigrated from near Reutling and came to Polk City and that is where she married my grandfather Weiblen. Her husband had died before they ever left. I think it is quite a testimony, again an indication in my mind, of how the really strong people of the frontier were the women. They had to carry the burden of this enterprise. I think they were endowed with a kind of inner strength and even physical stamina, prepared to endure what the frontier had to offer. My grandmother Weiblen was a good example of that kind of determination.

I think from my mother, I got the idea of wanting to know and learn. And from my dad's side I got the determination of faithfulness to the job. Rely on your word and also on your genuine sense of humility, as I look back. Anyway, that is the strain I came from.

CN: Could you tell me a few things about your mother, her name and her siblings.

WW: My mother's name was Anna Augusta Fransesca Bellin. Her family home was near Stettin in Germany. Her uncle was one of Loehe's trainees. He came over here and served with one of the last missionaries to the Indians. His name was Franz Matter.

CN: She had some siblings too?

WW: Yes, she had a brother, Martin Bellin who inherited the farm and so forth. The oldest girl was Marie, then my mother Anna. Louise was after my mother and then after Louise was Helena. So there were these four girls and one boy. Whereas in my Dad's family were four boys and one girl. The interesting thing is that my Dad and his oldest brother married Bellin girls. My Uncle Charlie, my Dad's oldest brother, married Marie and my Dad married Anna. So I have double cousins there.

CN: From gender they could have all paired off.

WW: Yes, right. Marie worked on the Indian Reservation with the Episcopalians at the Rosebud Indian Reservation. Louise was a nurse who died of tuberculosis which she contracted somewhere. Then there was Helena who was married quite young.

CN: There were so many deaths to tuberculosis.

WW: Yes. My parents now were living in town from the time that they were married, so all of us never actually lived out on the farm. They went there to work.

CN: This would have been your grandparent's farm then?

WW: It would have been my parent's farm by this time.

CN: But they were living in town and farming.

WW: Yes, they lived in town. My dad did other things. He was involved with my uncle running a garage. They had the first Chevrolet-Buick garage in Miller, South Dakota. My uncle was a land sales person. My dad helped with that and managed some farms and things like that.

CN: Did your parents meet in South Dakota?

WW: Yes, I suppose that is where they met. My mother would have been—this was in 1883 that they came out from Polk City, Iowa—she would have been two years old. My dad was not yet ten years old at the time. So they knew each other. They got to know each other from then on, after they lived there.

To bring that up-to-date. The colony was established by this guy, Franz Matter. He was the one who came from Germany. He stopped in Neundettalsau and was sent to the seminary when it was out at St. Sebald, around 1860 something. He finished his preparation and was designated then to be part of that group that went out to bring the gospel to the Crow Indians in Cheyenne in the 1860s.

CN: Is this the group that was out in Wyoming and Montana?

WW: Right. My mother got her piety I think from the way the church was inculcated up there. There was obviously an ongoing battle between pure doctrine and some of the liberals, because already my uncle, Franz Matter, had this in his craw. It wasn't too long and he felt that the Fritschel brothers were too liberal. After the Indian enterprise failed, he was involved in several congregations. His doctrinal position led him more and more to move away from Iowa. He wasn't quite ready for Missouri, so he became part of the Ohio Synod. That's what he was when he went out to South Dakota, the part of the Ohio Synod that maintained a Lutheran college and Luther Seminary in a trailer park in St. Paul.

He tells the interesting story of how he landed in the United States here in Dubuque and took a wagon out to St. Sebald. He came upon the place and it looked absolutely dead. There were no signs of life in the building and he wondered what had happened. It so happened it was the afternoon, when the students were all out doing their work in the fields. And then he came inside and was welcomed by a Sister. She was one of the sisters, one of the several during the course of years that came from the Diaconal Work in Neuendettalsau with the Wartburg people, and she gave him some refreshments and introduced him to Sigmund Fritschel. He told how deeply impressed he was by the warmth and kindness of Sigmund Fritschel. He finished his course there, went to work with the Cheyenne in 1863 and made a second trip back in 1865. They came back once after Braeuninger was killed.

CN: So they went back another time after that.

WW: He was part of the colony there. He served as a missionary with the Indians. This was with the Cheyenne in Montana. I have a little diary that he kept from the very last trip. After they went out there, that didn't succeed either. So they came back and there were three Indian young people who came along with an associate of my uncle's.

CN: It was after his second trip when the Indian boys came back.

WW: Yes, they were baptized and two of them were buried out at St. Sebald.

CN: I saw their graves.

WW: Even after that, Franz Matter and a graduate named Krebs who had made two of the journeys before, were asked to go out there one more time. To see what kind of connection they could make, if not with the Crow Indians or the Cheyenne, then with the Ogalalas. And so this diary I have is an account of his trip, the last effort made to try and reach the Indians. It's mainly an account about how on a certain day it is very cold and there is a lot of snow and stuff like that.

CN: But it is a tangible connection to that period.

WW: Yes. Then he came back and, of course, was eventually sent to a congregation. He served for a while in parts of Ohio, Minnesota, and several other places. He served in Des Moines a long time. That is where he met my aunt and they were married. Des Moines, you know, is in the same county as Polk City, Polk County. From Polk City, he went up to South Dakota. I think he felt maybe he could make this one last effort on his own with the Indians. It is rather sad to listen to his stories, as he writes a reflection about his work with the missions. He said, "I was undoubtedly not created to be a missionary. I simply did not have the stuff to do it." You know he had been there and been part of it. I suppose he felt that he had failed or something.

CN: It is amazing for me to even imagine how you would begin.

WW: Yes and how they learned the language. Those guys, you know, learned things like printing themselves on the side that helped their ministry and also the seminary here. Gottfried Fritschel had developed the printing press and he had the students help him put out the publications. That is where my uncle learned to use one, on these hand presses. He put out regularly a publication called the *Das Schifflein, The Little Ship*. The University of Minnesota has copies. The archives here has a copy, too.

CN: Who was the audience of that?

WW: That would have been the members of his parish, the little parish in Orient, South Dakota. They were treated not just to hand-written stuff. It was better than many of us had later. It was genuinely printed. It was amazing.

CN: So he was following in the footsteps of the Fritschels then.

WW: Yes. I'll have to get the diary to get the exact date of the last journal. I think it was '63. After that then, his energy was sort of being consumed in the doctrinal controversies of the church.

CN: Like predestination and chiliasm.

WW: Right. By his conscious decision, he joined the Ohio Synod.

So technically I was not born in Iowa but Ohio. When Gerhard Ottersberg, historian and also a grandson of Sigmund Fritschel, gave a lecture on the history of Wartburg, he mentioned that I was from the Ohio Synod. He said that I was from the Ohio Synod because I was baptized in a church that had been started by my great uncle, Franz Matter. That is technically correct. But the roots were all Iowa except this uncle who had become part of the Ohio Synod and had baptized me.

He was one of the last missionaries to the Indians in Wyoming. After his death many of the books from his library were donated to the rare book room. However, he felt the Fritschels were too liberal and eventually left the Iowa Synod and became part of the Ohio Synod. And so he started this homestead and church and school in South Dakota. That's where I was baptized. So it was on that basis that Ottersberg said what he did about my roots not being in the Iowa Synod. It was as though you weren't genuinely part of the whole Iowa tradition if you had your baptism in Ohio, even though I was raised in an Iowa Synod congregation. Ohio was somewhat larger and I think more powerful in inter-synodical dealings.

CN: So it is only formally accurate.

WW: Later a church was started in Miller by the Iowa Synod. My mother was a charter member of that parish, so I came back into the Iowa Synod in the 1920s. I was out of it only for a short while.

CN: Just in your early years, then.

WW: Yes, my very early years. Franz Matter was an interesting pastor. Very strict. I didn't get to know him. He died before I was born. As a kid, I never liked to go to the Matter home. It was always too proper.

CN: Stifling.

WW: Yes, very stifling. I'd rather go to our farm where I could be free to run as I chose and ride the horse and do things out there. My mother revered proud posture. Franz Matter couldn't do anything wrong. He was the ultimate.

CN: So her piety originated from him.

WW: Yes, I think it did. I think my dad didn't like that too much either. Nor did any of the Weiblens because they were not from that kind of church. Not too many years after they came to South Dakota, the mother died and so these five kids had to function by themselves. They grew up to want to have a little more fun. Dad knew how to play the violin a little bit for dances. So they had these dances in the houses, which Pastor Matter was opposed to, of course.

CN: The dances were something he wouldn't care for.

WW: No, he wouldn't.

CN: It is an interesting tension, though.

WW: I've felt it in my life, you know. I realized that the strength of the home was primarily from my mother. She had me registered in college even before I knew it and without any funds. She had written to Wartburg College and told them that I was going to

87

come. And she asked if there would be some help, if possible. So that was an example of the fact that she was going to make damn sure her kids had what she didn't. She had an insatiable quest for knowledge.

CN: Did she read?

WW: Yes, she read as much as she could, but she was busy maintaining the house. Everything was such heavy handwork.

CN: Labor intensive.

WW: There were no washing machines until much later. I remember by the time we kids were able to earn a little money, with paper routes and so forth, my older brother and I and our next younger brother, we joined together and gave them the money for the down payment. The down payment helped the family buy a Maytag washing machine.

CN: That was a great event.

WW Yes it was. My mother was so proud of that thing. It still exists up in my brother's basement in St. Paul, Minnesota. It's one of those cast aluminum tubs that will last from here to eternity, you know.

CN: After the other ones are long gone.

WW: So that didn't give her much opportunity to learn. But she also wanted to know how to play the organ and the piano, so she learned that, too. We had a little reed organ. Though she couldn't play very well, but she didn't care. She would play in church and that would make me so embarrassed. She missed all kinds of notes. She was determined, so I realized the strength of her. That is a tension I felt. I felt the same thing when Tillich started talking about the differences between his parents. His fun-loving mother from the Rhine, you know. His Dad a strict, proper Prussian.

CN: Just had the genders reversed from your case.

WW: Yes.

CN: Did you say your father's name?

WW: My father's name was George Daniel Weiblen. He was a twin. He had a twin brother, Philip. There was a William in that family also and the oldest was Charles. The youngest then was a daughter, Dorothy.

CN: Tell me about your school years.

WW: I enjoyed school. We only lived one block from the school so we could run from home to there. We didn't have the great burden of walking, you know the stories people tell.

CN: Walking through the snow and the slush for six miles.

WW: We went to Miller Public School, which was only one block away. So we didn't have any great stories of going through six feet of snow to get to school. I always regretted that because the other guys always brought their lunch. That looked like kind of a fun thing to do.

CN: You would go home for lunch?

WW: Yes, we'd go home for lunch. They didn't have kindergarten there. I started when I was six years old. My mother had the idea that I should skip one grade, so I skipped the third grade. My most notable year, or the brightest for me as I would call it, was when I was in the sixth grade and I got all A's. I remember fifth grade as a good year. I had a good teacher, Miss McKay. She would interpret nature and the weather for us and it was very interesting. She had us learn Helen Hunt's *October's Bright Blue Weather* on a beautiful day in South Dakota. You had many that were so blue.

CN: Do you remember that teacher's name?

WW: Yes, that was Miss McKay and the sixth grade teacher was Miss Hurley. In seventh grade, where I suppose I was starting to come to life, there was so much activity because of the teacher. She was kind of a live wire. Pepper Martin, we called her. Her name was Martin and she wanted to do many things. She did such unusual things as having us dissect a rabbit, even though you didn't have the proper laboratory facilities there in the regular classroom.

CN: She found a way to do it.

WW: We did it, even with that horrendous smell of when you open guts and everything. I had the feeling that she about passed out but she was intent on doing that. At that particular juncture I didn't have as much interest in grades as such. I didn't have any problems. I got satisfactory with B's and stuff. If I had followed the course that I was on in the sixth grade, I suppose I would have ended up like my brother, Don. He had the highest record you could get from the school and all kinds of scholarships to colleges. I remember when he graduated that Don was a little slow in getting up to come for one award and the superintendent said, "I suppose if you get as many scholarships as this, it seems they don't amount to much after awhile."

I chose a different course by seeking to be part of the group. In eighth grade I had a very good teacher, a man teacher, Mr. Nikisch, whose father had been part of the Prussian army and he regaled us with all kinds of stories. He told how with his white gloves he would wipe across the horse and there wouldn't dare be any dirt on it. They had to keep their horse so perfect. He was a good teacher and a lot of fun after class. We were coming alive then. As one example, I still remember what the boys in the class did in music, a subject that was taught by one teacher for the whole school. She would come in for a half-hour every week or so for music. She was apparently kind of sexy to some of the senior guys in high school. So we men in the eighth grade took turns going up and asking her a question. Because as she bent over the desk, they could see her breasts. So it was all arranged that we would go up and ask these questions.

CN: It was a plot. That's the first time in history that eighth grade boys liked music class.

WW: Overall though, what I remember of South Dakota was the land. I felt an integral connection of being part of the prairie. It was something that was so vast and rolling that I felt somewhat mystically the connection with the rolling prairies of South Dakota. I enjoyed one summer in high school that I spent on the farm, living on the ranch, herding cattle, keeping the cattle out of the corn and stuff like that. One of the interesting things that happened was that one time, the neighbor's bull got out from the other side of the fence. It must have gotten away from one of its cows in heat or something. It just came through the fence on this side like there was nothing there and rammed his head together with our bull on a steel fence post and bent it over. I could still show you that today. When I got married, I took Ilah out there and showed her.

CN: The post was still like that?

WW: It was still bent. When they started going at each other, the cattle, the cows, heifers, calves and everything lined up in a great big circle around them, just like kids watching a fight at school.

CN: Something very primal about that.

WW: Yes, there is, to watch this violence or something. So I got scared and headed for home to get the bachelor who farmed our land. He wasn't there so I rode back again and by that time it was all over and the cows and the cattle were in the corn. That was kind of an interesting summer. We cooked our own meals. The house had bedbugs in it. I remember the bedbugs being so bad that I would get up and go out and sit in the car trying to sleep.

CN: How old would you have been?

WW: I must have been about thirteen. When I came home, my mother made me go out to the toilet, we didn't have an indoor one, and change clothes because she didn't want any of those bugs in the house.

The first time I went to a hotel was on the way to Wartburg College. I turned on the light and went up to the room there to go to sleep. I noticed there was a little animal crawling back there, so I pulled the bed out to the middle of the floor as far as I could and put the clothes away. I had had enough of bed bugs.

I can appreciate a little bit what it was like with lice and stuff for these people in concentration camps.

CN: It is nearly incomprehensible, I think.

WW: I told you how my Dad had motivated me to go to school and not become a cowboy. In South Dakota after the eighth grade you didn't have to go to high school.

CN: So there was a decision to be made right there.

WW: Yes and it was the year before that I had been out on the range. Having spent one whole summer out on the ranch riding a horse and herding cattle I decided that is what I wanted to do. I flatly announced to my parents that I was not going to high school and was going to go out on the range. And my Dad said, "What are you going to be, the dummy of the family?" It was very pointed, practical advice. It worked very well.

CN: That was a pretty clear motivation.

 WW: My brother, on the other hand, was already earning money at that time. He always earned money by delivering papers and then working at the hotel. Don said, "I'll give you the $3 that you need for laboratory fees if you go to high school." I was playing this part. I was sure inwardly I would probably go but I guess I enjoyed at the moment acting like I wasn't.

CN: All this to get you to continue with high school.

WW: So he was bribing me and my Dad was shaming me.

CN: This is the way God works.

WW: I've used that sometimes. It's just as holy and sacred as if there had been kind of triumphalistic intervention.

CN: Like the lightening bolt.

WW: But then in high school I got particularly interested in mathematics and the sciences. We really had good teachers then because it was in the depression. The guy that we had for chemistry and physics had been a college teacher. He lost his job because there were cutbacks. So here he is teaching high school. We didn't have just any ordinary flunky and he let us do experiments. So when I came to Wartburg College for the first year of chemistry I already had everything that we were studying.

CN: Did you go with the same group of kids all the way from elementary through high school? How large a group was this?

WW: From third grade on. There were about 50 kids.

CN: That is fairly large.

WW: So you did get to know each other particularly well. We had classes and you very definitely felt yourself a part of those classes.

CN: So there would be more than one classroom at each grade level.

WW: No, there was one basic classroom in which you were together and that would hold all the students. There weren't as many in the grade school as there were in the high school because when you came to high school, then the whole gang of kids from the country came in who had been going to one of rural school houses.

CN: Okay, so the 50 were in the high school group.

WW: I suppose we had about 30 in the grade school.

CN: Which would be manageable in one classroom.

WW: When I was speaking of classes, I meant the social classification in which you were assigned, according to financial standards. This was true even in the church somewhat. The socially superior churches were the Methodist and Presbyterian.

CN: Is that right?

WW: The Lutherans only came in afterwards. The Lutheran church was started when I was still a kid. In my early years I went to the Methodist Sunday School. Of course, my mother always made it very clear that we didn't get involved in any of the inner motivations and spiritualizing that went on in the Methodist church. For example, do you remember that the Methodists had a kind of preaching mission every year? They would have services every night and get people stirred up to join the church.

CN: Probably with altar calls.

WW: And the kids got special little pins if they brought somebody to the services. One of my friends asked my brother Don and me if we would come because we would get credit for that. So we went. And my mother gave instructions as we left, "Now the service will come to a point where they will be praying about people and they will ask them to come forward and stuff like that. When that starts you come home." We were there during the service, but we happened to be sitting up towards the front and it was crowded and we couldn't find a way out. So here we were and the mother of this friend was praying for him and crying and everything. We were just standing there, kind of dumbfounded and we didn't go up to the altar. But we did have all these people praying about us. So I always said that I had a partial blessing.

CN: Your heart was strangely warmed.

WW: Yes.

CN: I had an experience at a Pentecostal meeting that is a notable memory for me as well.

WW: In high school, I did go out for track. I didn't got out for other things. I ran the mile and the two-mile. In the last lap of the two-mile run you felt as though you were going to collapse before you could get across. A guy at the hospital asked me what it felt like the first time we were doing this exercise during my recovery and I said, "I feel like I am in the last lap of the two-mile run."

CN: That pushes you to your physical limit.

WW: I played the tuba in the band, as did my older brother.

CN: That would have been in high school.

WW: Yes.

William H. Weiblen:
Study at Wartburg College
and Wartburg Seminary

WW: The summer before I came to Wartburg, I luckily got a job on some kind of a WPA project. I painted the Main Street of Miller, South Dakota. The city had some funds that provided work. They did mainly WPA projects and they were hiring. Usually, it had to be the head of a family, but for this painting job they were hiring high school graduates, too, so I got on there. That was really hard work. We had to carry these steel forms. Instead of picking them up and moving them by power, you had two guys carrying them.

CN: You earned your salary that way.

WW: Yes, but they were heavy. I would come home at noon, fortunately I could go home and mother had a nice dinner prepared. But I would just go and lay on the bed and get whatever rest I could so that I was strong enough to finish that afternoon, because I was small, smaller than I am now. But I stuck with it. When it was all said and done, I had about a hundred dollars saved from the summer. That is what I had when I headed for Wartburg College. The whole thing cost about $200 per year. I found part-time work.

CN: After you got there?

WW: Yes. With the summer work and that, I made it up there. At that time then, the church school was cheaper than the state school. And of course they needed the people. They would fight for enrollment. Wartburg had a particularly hard time because it had just been consolidated with all of these other colleges. There was a lot of resentment towards students who should have been coming there but didn't.

CN: Because the campus had been moved?

WW: Yes. But that was a good experience. I was just going to go to Wartburg for one year and then hopefully transfer to where my brother was staying. In the summer I was working in St. Paul and living with Donald. I was a busboy in a restaurant. I got a call from a professor of mathematics who said that there was a job available with board and $5 a week.

CN: This was after your first year, when you were not intending to go back that you got this call.

WW: Yes. And so I thought about that. I guess it might have been the pull of seeing people that I knew and so forth and the certainty of having something. So I went back and had to be there about a month before school started. So I quit my job that I was doing with my brother and came back. During those few weeks, some of the students working on the campus crew asked me, "Have you ever thought about studying to be a pastor?" I hadn't thought about it at all! Up to that point, I hadn't been really interested in a lot of the usual church activities, Luther League and so on and so forth. I was following my father's footsteps. It was just kind of a strange decision. I don't recall any religious experience of it. I decided I would try it. I was planning to keep on with my interest in math by taking the next major course, which at that time was calculus. But at a small school like that and so few male students other than those studying for the seminary, as most of them were, they had no problem putting calculus at the same time as first year Greek. So I had to decide right there.

CN: This would have been the first semester of your second year.

WW: Yes, so I decided to do that. Never having taken a language, I launched into first year Greek and discovered that the interest I had in math transferred also to studying Greek. I discovered I liked the subjects better than I did when I was in high school. So that is simply the way it happened.

CN: What was it about these people who talked to you about being a pastor that moved you?

WW: I guess when I stop to think about it, it is the sense of community and camaraderie. It meant first of all that I would be one of them. Secondly, it looked like something that would be engaging and challenging, with a certain romance about it, the idea of being a pastor. I guess partly it was also remembering a couple of our pastors whom I liked who were nice to me.

CN: You could imagine yourself doing what others had been doing.

WW: Yes. Like this one pastor, I don't remember what grade I would have been in, but I was shoveling snow going around from house to house to make money. I came by the church then and snow was all around it. I just went ahead and shoveled it. He was there for some reason and saw me. I was already late for dinner so I had decided I had better head for home, but he came out and picked me up and took me to the hotel and bought me dinner and gave me some money for the shoveling. I always remembered him and people like that. So it was kind of the call of the community and association with the other fellows, kind of mundane things like that and the plea to preach the Gospel.

CN: Did you see yourself becoming a pastor, as that was the career path you were on?

WW: At that moment I was more interested in Greek. As I got closer to the time of actually coming to the seminary I began to have second thoughts because the seminary seemed like sort of going into the monastery. I was a little apprehensive, so then I began to think of graduate school and teaching Greek as a vocation.

CN: That was prior to coming to Wartburg Seminary?

WW: Yes, but it wasn't going to happen. Then suddenly I was already engaged to Ilah. That was a prime consideration. We were not engaged officially but we were promised each other. So I was anxious to get out too and the surest way to get out was to go ahead and go to seminary.

CN: You once mentioned something about a first love at college.

WW: I was going to tell you about my first love when I came to Wartburg College as a freshman. I don't know if I had really had a date up until that time. We were compatriots together in school for so long that you didn't tend to think of boys and girls. You thought more of just being part of a group.

CN: That is healthy.

WW: It was kind of fun. But then the drive came to want to associate with a girl. I can remember at home that when I tried to indicate something about that, I was ridiculed. That was the common way, you know. That wasn't something that anybody would waste time doing, bothering with girls. So I didn't get much encouragement there. So I broke away in college. The college had partially existed in St. Paul, Minnesota. It was a junior college with the seminary close by. That was Luther College and Seminary of the old Ohio Synod. That is where my brother had started. He could have gone to a lot of different schools, but my mother wanted him to go there and he did. He later transferred to Minnesota after spending his first year there because then they closed the school. I came a year after that, two years after my brother. There were several girls who had been there. One of them was one of the two Glueck sisters, Vivian and Irene. Vivian was in my class and she was working in the library and I was working in the library. So here we were thrust together and it just kind of came naturally that I invited her to go to a show or something. Then came the big social event of the fall at the college, homecoming. So I had a date with her for homecoming, my first actual date.

CN: During your freshman year?

WW: Yes. So from then on, it sort of became a natural thing. We started talking about going steady and so we did. And so we would meet for breakfast and do a few things. We would play tennis and horseshoes. She was very athletic. So that was Vivian who I was with the whole freshman year.

When the year ended I was hoping I could go to some other school. My brother, Don, had gone to Minnesota so I thought of that. The only place I could get a job in the summer was in Minnesota. He worked at a restaurant as a busboy and he got me a job there. So he and I lived together in a room in St. Paul and I worked there. I hadn't made the move to officially line up to go to any other school like Minnesota and probably wouldn't have been able to go financially. But then I got a telephone call from the Dean of Students of Wartburg College telling me about what was considered the best paying job in Waverly, because it was at a restaurant and you got your meals plus $5 a week. So I could have the job if I came right back. So I did and decided to stay there.

CN: That kept you at Wartburg College then.

WW: I was already working at the uptown cafe the day that Vivian and her mother and her sisters came back. During the summer I hadn't heard from her very much, so I was a little teed off. And there they came. I supposed what I should have done was jump over the

95

counter and greet her with a kiss or something, but I was kind of mad at her and a bumbling idiot and so I just ignored them. I thought somebody else would take them as customers but they didn't. It was inevitable that I had to go and wait on them. So I did.

CN: It was awkward then.

WW: Yes and here I was not saying anything. Vivian was looking down and her mother said, "You are awfully quiet." I didn't say anything. I took their order and served them and didn't think anything about it until a couple of weeks later when I had the opportunity to be with her alone. I told her that I thought it was best that we didn't go together steady anymore. But I've often wondered how things might have been, you know, the decisions you make.

CN: Yes, there are always these turning points in life. Did you ever know what happened to her?

WW: Yes, I see her at college reunions. She became a teacher and she married a guy from her hometown. She retired from the University of Wisconsin in the library's German department because she knew German. So I always see her at reunions.

And then of course, I met Ilah. I met Ilah before my senior year. So Ilah and Vivian got to know each other in school at Wartburg too. Yes, we see her. She has a fine family of boys. I used to help her with her chemistry and stuff like that. I thought the chemistry professor at Wartburg College was not so great, but when I came back there as pastor he was perhaps the most active of all the professors with the whole business of the Sunday School. He was a Norwegian amidst all these Germans. So I learned that I was wrong in my assessment of him.

I've thought back about Vivian that I must have been deciding that she was eventually going to dump me anyway and so I thought I would beat her to the punch. I don't know if that was the underlying fear with which I was operating. It was also just a few weeks before that I, in discussion with guys working on the campus crew, reached the decision that I would switch to pre-seminary. Vivian thought that was the most ridiculous thing because I was shy and she couldn't conceive of me being a pastor.

CN: So she wasn't real supportive of that change.

WW: She wasn't much enthused about that. I had a chance to talk to her a number of times at meetings. But I think that played into the decision about her too. I probably thought, with my mother's conscience working through me, that I had wasted too much time in that relationship during my first year at college. Now if I was going to be a pastor this was a whole new big change. I would have to be thoroughly diligent in every respect.

CN: Do you recall feeling that too?

WW: I discovered that just as you needed discipline to do your mathematics work every night or you didn't learn anything, so also with Greek. The same skills that made me succeed with math and sciences were applicable when I started studying Greek.

CN: Analytical skills.

WW: Yes and so I liked Greek very much. I majored in it. Alfred Haefner was a good teacher. I also liked history and Gerhard Ottersberg was a good teacher of history. There was also an excellent math teacher by the name of Chellavold.

CN: You had some fine teachers there.

WW: Yes, I really had the cream of the crop. They contributed much. For several years they only got a small portion of their salary because the church was not taking in enough money during the depression. As the church later became more fiscally prosperous, they made no effort to pay the back wages of these people.

CN: They served them well.

WW: But it was people like that who made these colleges. Whether you think of Luther College or St. Olaf, you can look at the histories of these places and see these dedicated pioneers who gave themselves, never giving any thought about personal advancement. They just saw their calling as being there. They really made the institutions what they are. I think it is kind of a Lutheran characteristic. I said during the seminary appeal several times that in reality the Reformation really began in the study, Martin Luther's study of the Psalms particularly. So that's why we have always been a church that supports education and rightfully supports our schools. Sometimes too many of them had to be cut back and that causes a lot of pain.

The only problem was that sometimes the church then didn't see its responsibilities to secular state institutions. I think the Norwegians and Swedes did a much better job at that than we did as Germans. And I suppose that is partially because Germans tend to be a little embarrassed about being Germans in the American scene.

CN: What was the nature of pre-seminary study at Wartburg College?

WW: They had a very specific course laid out. You had to have at least two years of Greek and another foreign language, preferably German. You had to have so much science and you had to have philosophy. There was a whole curriculum prescribed but you had a great deal of latitude in the elective courses. But what was especially recommended was a major in languages, or if not a major than at least a minor in languages and a major in something like history or English. Occasionally, one could do a major in science. But there was a curriculum. That's why when you came here you were already prepared to go. You didn't have to take any time with Greek.

CN: Right.

WW: Everybody had Greek but they didn't teach Hebrew in college. They could have done that differently. That was the idea of the pre-seminary course. There was this second course that accommodated Loehe's idea of the emergency school. By contrast, people like Ottersberg and Haefner (Sigmund Fritschel's descendants), all wanted to build the colleges into good classical educational institutions which would provide the liberal arts background for studying at the seminary. They were also willing to acknowledge the importance of schools like Waverly which gave students only a two-year course but gave them Greek and a few things like that. It didn't offer as wide a background as other schools. So being accommodating to that and also being of the opinion that once doctrine is defined, almost like Rome, then all you need to do is learn it. Thus we got into the bind of not being creative theologically. We got into the bind of simply learning the dogmas.

CN: Textbook scholasticism almost.

WW: Yes, right. I think if the will of people like the Haefners and the Ottersbergs, the descendants of Fritschels, would have been the determinative voice in these kinds of emergency schools, which only had a layman's courses, they might have been more creative.

CN: Did you get courses in Bible already in college?

WW: Yes. Introduction to the Old Testament was sometimes a farce. That's where I had one of my biggest struggles, primarily I suppose because of the way the teacher taught it. I remember not liking the Bible courses because they were taught too much like Sunday School. Maybe it was still my natural disinclination against the church as such. I think I inherited a little bit of that from my Dad who was not overly enthusiastic of the church. Yet he was always there with us. I think he took great pride when I was ordained and everything. But he had not joined the mission church in town, so technically he was still on the rolls but not active in the prairie church out in the country.

CN: Do you think that was some reaction to your mother's piety?

WW: I think it was a reaction to that and especially a reaction to the pastor. And, of course, if the pastor was this highly inflated holy angel that my mother made him out to be. Well, that is the way my dad handled it.

CN: Are we talking here about Pastor Matter?

WW: Right. My younger brother, Paul, did the best job of positively integrating the Matter side. He got a Master's degree in history before he went on to study geology. He used Pastor Matter for his dissertation for his Master's degree. They were very interested in getting all this stuff at the University of Minnesota because they wanted to keep track of the very earliest records. There was this Pastor Matter who printed this little newspaper. They have a full file of that stuff. But Paul, because he was the same age as one of the great-grandsons of Franz Matter, he would go out there and play with him. They were the same age, so he enjoyed being there in the summer. Paul took a particular fascination to one of Pastor Matter's sons, a bachelor. There were four sons and one of them became a pastor. Theodor was the one who stayed home and developed the land and acquired more land. He was very well read and could give the history of things. So Paul would spend hours talking with him and so he learned a lot of things. Paul was much more positive on Matter than I ever was.

CN: He had a whole different angle to look at it through.

WW: Yes.

CN: Was theology taught at Wartburg College?

98

WW: I suppose you could say some of the things they taught about Luther were close to theology courses, but not in the sense that we had here. The closest thing is the professor who taught philosophy. He had a Ph.D. from Nebraska. Hiltner was his name and he taught philosophy. What he tried to do was teach us Christian philosophy. You know he kind of forced that. Take the arguments of Kant, for example, and show how the Christian answer is the ultimate answer for everything. There wasn't much inclination to challenge you to the edge of doubt.

CN: It sounds like the kind of philosophy they might teach at a so-called Christian college today.

WW: Yes, right.

CN: Where did Ilah come into the picture?

WW: She came into the picture the spring of '39. Again the spring event was the junior/senior banquet because there was no prom at Wartburg. They were opposed to it. Up until recently they were also opposed to coeducational dormitories because they were afraid it might lead to dancing. That's the joke they always talked about between St. Olaf and Wartburg College. The big event was the junior/senior banquet so I needed a date for that.

CN: This was your junior year.

WW: Yes. My roommate, Carlton Mall, was from Mason City and he knew Ilah from Bible camps at Clear Lake, Iowa. His dad was a pastor in Mason City and he went to these Iowa District Bible camps at Clear Lake. He took me down to meet Ilah and I asked her about it and she accepted the invitation and then it started other opportunities. I was working there that summer and saw her a number of times. I visited with her and we sort of committed ourselves to each other by the time school had begun. I remember Vivian kidding me about how I was now a senior with my little freshman.

CN: She was a freshman.

WW: Yes, here's an interesting episode. When I met Ilah the first time, as I told you I was not an aggressive personality around young ladies. I went down to meet her. She lived in an apartment house with her mother. You went in an outside door to these two apartments on the ground floor and two up above. Her apartment was there to the left, so we went in. Carlton swung open the door and said, "I'd like you to meet my friend, Bill Weiblen." And she thought Carlton was drunk or something, because I had vanished. I had stepped around the corner, as reticent I was. Then it became an occasion with a little bit of hilarity. Then we talked and it wasn't long before her mother came home. And I had to ask her mother if she could go out. And she could.

CN: You asked her mother?

WW: Yes.

CN: That took some courage.

WW: Yes, well there I was in the midst of it.

CN: What was her name?

WW: Her name was Anderson. Her father was Alvin Anderson from Northwood, Iowa. His father had come from Sweden. He was a full-blooded Swede and came over by himself. He was about seventeen but then he married a Norwegian. Her mother is descended from Scotch, Irish, and Dutch and even a little Pocahontas. So she is kind of an American mixture already. Her grandfather on her mother's side was Ulrich so I suppose the German was as much a part of her as the rest. Ilah had a Swedish grandfather, a Pennsylvania Dutch grandfather, and her grandmother's side is Scotch/Irish.

CN: So she is fully American.

WW: She is a full American. She has some Indian blood in her that's why I mentioned Pocahontas. The Swedes of that family, I don't know how many boys there were altogether, three or four came over here and each acquired land and then they brought their parents over. So the whole Swedish family was over here living in the midst of the Norwegians. It seemed like kind of a unique place. That happened more than once where there was this integration of the Norwegians and the Swedes. Her grandfather was a very gentle, very nice guy. She was baptized into the very small Shell-Rock Synod of the Lutheran Church Missouri Synod. It's the little church from which Robert Preus and Jack Preus came. Their dad was a member of that church body. Somebody told how the father of Jack Preus and Robert Preus said if you want to be active in a church (he was governor at one time), "I'll buy you a church." He probably could have. It was very conservative.

CN: And this is the church Ilah grew up in.

WW: That is where she was baptized. She didn't go there very long because she wasn't living in Northwood then. She was living in Eagle Grove near Charles City. Then her parents were divorced. That is when she came to Waverly, after that happened. Her mother got a job in Waverly and that is where she spent her most consistent years as a child.

CN: Did she ever live on a farm?

WW: Not really. Her Dad never lived on a farm. The only thing close to it would have been a little truck farm in Janesville, Iowa near Waverly when her parents were first divorced. She and her brother lived with her grandparents there for awhile and he raised watermelon and strawberries.

CN: She mostly grew up then in small towns.

WW: Yes.

CN: How did you negotiate the move to Wartburg Seminary with a betrothed, or were you engaged officially at that point?

WW: We had been officially engaged before that. By the time the fall school year had started, we had decided that we would get married. I knew that we wouldn't be getting married then, because you weren't suppose to get married when you were in seminary. The

100

only people that were already married at that time were people that had come from other vocations, like teachers. There were always a couple of those kinds of situations. But I wouldn't have wanted to get married then. We spent a lot of time driving back and forth between here and Waverly.

CN: She was continuing her college education.

WW: Yes, studying. Then she took a job with her stepfather. Her mother remarried and her stepfather was a merchant in Waverly. He ran a dry goods store and women's ready-to-wear. She took a job there running the books. He had one of these cash systems that you put it in a little device and put it on a rope and it went up to the cashier for processing. So she did that for those years I was in seminary.

CN: Where was that store?

WW: In Waverly. It got to be continual involvement with Waverly because I associated with the college people while living there during the summer. I often lived in the seminary college housing. They would rent you rooms in the dormitory where the campus crews were. So I spent the summers usually working in Waverly

CN: The seminary course was three years?

WW: Three years, yes. I debated whether to take an internship. A good friend of mine, Sig Sandrock, decided to take an internship because then he figured he could get married. His fiancée was a good friend of Ilah. They were good buddies in high school and we introduced them. So that is what he did and he was married during internship. So he was one that came back and was married on campus.

CN: That was more acceptable then.

WW: That was about the first time it was tried and he succeeded. It wasn't long then, and the war changed everything. They accepted married students when the veterans came back.

CN: Now we talked way back when we started, about the faculty at Wartburg Seminary when you were a student. Are there any particular things that you remember about your course of study or events in the student body at that time?

WW: It was a time when the war was building up and there was a great deal of concern whether you ought to be enlisting. That was one pull I felt very strongly. The dynamics of the whole cataclysm of the men at the time of World War II was so overpowering that you felt it was something you should be a part of. I wrestled with that and finally resolved it by deciding to be a chaplain. I tried to get in as a chaplain but didn't make it because they said there was something wrong with my heart. But a few years later I did get in the Air Force. They didn't catch the heart murmur.

CN: It was a murmur that they detected? Did you know you had it before that point?

WW: Yes, I had a very serious illness the summer before I began the seminary in Waverly. It was a very serious infection. I lay in bed for several weeks and that left my heart weak. I remember it pounding, so after that I think there was something. But mostly the doctors said it was a murmur that was there from the beginning.

CN: Congenital.

WW: Congenital but with no functional problems.

CN: So you would have joined as a chaplain earlier then?

WW: Yes, I tried it actually. I applied to the Navy and at that time went to Des Moines to take the physical. My blood pressure was too high from the tenseness of it. They said I'd have to wait until I could take another blood pressure check sometime later. It happened one time that there was a big recruiting bus that came through Dubuque, recruiting candidates for officer schools and things like that. It occurred to me that maybe they could check my blood pressure and send that to Des Moines. So they did and it passed. They allegedly sent it there but you can imagine the number of people involved and how things would get screwed up. So it apparently never got there. I tried to write them about it. I even called once which, of course, was a big affair. They said they had never gotten it. It was getting close to the end of the year, so I finally just got tired and figured maybe that wasn't the way it was meant to be.

CN: This was happening during the third year.

WW: Yes. Then I decided I had better get something. I told Bodensieck to put my name in for a call. That is when I got a call to the Michigan district up in northwestern Ohio. I had been trying to get in the Navy, you see, and didn't make it. My friend, who tagged along behind me, after he found out I was going to try to get in the Navy, went and didn't have any problems. He ended up going on active duty in the Navy and I didn't make it. Then after I graduated and served in Bryan, Ohio about four years, I applied and was accepted in the Air Force, which appealed to me more than the Navy.

CN: So your time as a student at the seminary was very much taken up with the beginning of U.S. involvement in the Second World War.

WW: Yes, that was a big issue. One of the things that I recall was that we regularly met with a rabbi. At that time there was an active congregation here. The rabbi would come up and he was well informed on social and political events and history. So we had many meetings and discussions with him about this whole business of World War II as it was evolving. Those are some of the things that were going on.

On another side, seminary students were kind of a favored group. You were given a 4D classification that means you were studying to be a priest. I suppose if the Catholics hadn't made a loud demand, exemption wouldn't have been offered. But if it hadn't, there wouldn't have been enough clergy to serve the people. It kind of answered my question, too. It put the emphasis on the fact that regardless of what you think and what you want to do patriotically, there is a need for pastors and we have to get you out as soon as possible.

CN: There was no acceleration of your course though?

WW: Not in mine, but the year following they started. I graduated in '43 and that was the last class that was not accelerated. After that, they had to go to school year round.

CN: Do you recall the rabbi's name?

WW: No, I don't. One of the big issues, too, was whether or not we should join the America First Committee. That was kind of Lindbergh's group. After Lindbergh went over there and looked over the situation, he wanted us feeling that the Germans had so much power that there was no way we could come anywhere close to them. Then they came out with this America First which was a petition of people joining together indicating that we should give primary consideration to ourselves here and now rather than Europe's wars.

CN: So it was kind of an isolationist policy.

WW: Yes, right. That was debated here in the refectory.

CN: Was this a student debate or a community debate?

WW: I remember some of the professors would be there, talking at the meetings. I never went along with it. I decided to stay out of it. I did not think isolation was the right position at that moment. But there were some who really took a strong position, not only for isolation but against all war.

CN: I was wondering if there was anybody representing a pacifist position?

WW: Yes, we didn't have anybody really very strong for that in our group. But I do know of one in Dubuque who was a Lutheran and is now a Presbyterian and that is Richard Drummond. He was not supported by what was then the LCA. He took the position of being a pacifist.

CN: So Drummond took a pacifist position.

WW: He refused to go into the Army. He offered to do alternative service. He left the Lutheran Church on account of this. He was a graduate of Gettysburg.

CN: I didn't know that. Is there anything else that you recall of your Wartburg Seminary time?

WW: Regarding the people of that time, we've talked about Reu and about Mattes. I think I talked a little about Augie Engelbrecht with his young grandson of Sigmund Fritschel. He lived with the students so he was very close to us. Then there was Albert Jagnow. I think I mentioned him, too.

CN: Briefly, I think.

WW: He was an Ohio Synod person. He was also American University trained. He was a graduate of Yale. He had his Ph.D. in Church History and he taught Church History. He was not very invigorating. He was an organist who could do many, many things. He did so much, I think he was always tired. About his strongest exclamation, negative or otherwise, was, "My, my." But he was a very fair person and very supportive to help you in any way that he could. He married a woman whom we had seen at the seminary and known because she was very active in the Luther League. First it was the old Wartburg League and then the Luther League. She was a very vivacious, bubbling, energetic person. I think Jagnow's mother who was keeping house for him here, also wanted him to get married. She was always talking about her Albert. She tried to encourage this relationship as much as she could and eventually they got married and had a fine family of five boys. Then he died very suddenly of a heart attack in his yard. She was left with this family. She had been a teacher, so she went back to teaching, took additional work, and lived in Iowa City for many years. She taught special education. The oldest boy had polio, so he was very crippled and had to go in a wheel chair. Nonetheless he does cave exploration. He was very strong in his upper body.

CN: Well, it was significant to have someone come with that kind of training from another church body to teach on faculty.

WW: I don't know how Reu felt about that. He also helped break down the barrier of just going to St. John's to worship and nowhere else. Seminarians were sort of expected to go to St. John's. But he was at St. Matthew's, which was an Ohio Synod church. So by his being there, that led others to go and that kind of broke down automatically this exclusiveness. It was never said that we could only go to St. John's but it was kind of an unwritten rule.

CN: It was understood.

WW: You had this coincidence of Reu's death, and the second World War and someone like Jagnow coming that marked a significant transition. Yes, that was the beginning of real transition right there with the beginning of the war. The place would be forever changed after that. It would never be the same again.

William H. Weiblen:
Pastor and Chaplain

CN: Tell me about your life as a pastor in Bryan, Ohio.

WW: The reason I got to Bryan, I suppose, was because I didn't get in the Navy. It happened to be the church which was Mrs. Bodensieck's home congregation (Henkelmann was her name). Somebody told me that somewhere along the line. One day Bodensieck called me into his office and handed me this letter of call from Bryan, Ohio. It seemed like we were going off into another part of the world because I had never been to Ohio and I didn't know much about it. There wasn't any question that we probably would accept it. But then we came to talk to Ilah about it and I accepted the call. At the end of school, I hastily graduated on Wednesday, got married on Sunday, then was ordained, and installed after a week in Bryan, Ohio on the 21st of June.

CN: Give me the dates on these various things.

WW: This was all started at the end of May in 1943. On June 13 is when I was ordained. I was married the 30th of May in 1943 and then installed the 21st of June. We came back to Waverly from our big honeymoon down in Waterloo, Iowa by bus.

CN: The big city.

WW: Ilah had an orchid for a flower and getting on the bus, she heard this woman in the bus saying in the back, "Look at that, she is wearing an iris there to make it look like she's got an orchid." Of course, Ilah was incensed. We got back within a few days and had a few things like this little dresser over here. We bought that for $3 and fixed it up. We got that ready to be shipped and a desk that I bought and we were on our way. We left Waterloo on the Illinois Central Railroad.

CN: Were you married in Waverly, then?

WW: Yes, at St. Paul's at 5:00 in the afternoon on the 30th of May. When we left Waterloo, it began to hit Ilah that she was leaving and she cried about all the way from Waterloo to Chicago. There we changed to the New York Central and the next afternoon arrived in Bryan, Ohio. We were met by two women from the congregation and they took us over to show us the parsonage where we would be living. It was spotless. The warmth with which they received us, I guess, was indicated by the way they had prepared, having the house all fixed up and spotless the day we arrived. We had a very fine relationship there and I've always felt that the people at Bryan kind of loved us into ministry. I got mad at them many times. They were very tight fisted. But overall it was a good time.

CN: It was kind of a honeymoon pastorate then.

WW: The kids were all born there.

CN: How many years were you there?

WW: Seven years. Then I entered active duty in October 1950.

CN: Did they just have one Sunday service then?

WW: I had the church in Bryan, which was St. Paul's and also Immanuel Lutheran which was near a little town by the name of Ney. It was about six miles of driving. So there were two services The church out in the country had service at 9:00 and the one in town at 11:00. So I rushed back and forth between them. I would usually stop to pick up Ilah. Then after the first year, it was Ilah and Billy. Then it was Ilah and Caroline and Bill. So it was always a big rush for her to get all those kids ready and get in the car to go over to the church. That way, however, she never had the chance to be much involved with the Sunday School because of the traveling. We just had a good time there. They had attempted to bring these two congregations together previously at other times and had not succeeded. The District leadership thought we should try it again, so we did and it did succeed.

We lost some members but then we had the fun of building our new church and we functioned as our own contractor. It was still a time of shortages of material and so forth. That was kind of an interesting process. I was even a construction worker. My skill can probably be measured from the day we put up the big beams of the church. One part of that required a big steel rod about 2 inches in diameter that went through the bottom of this A-Frame but it didn't have the dimensions on it. Since I thought I knew something about math and trigonometry and so forth, I calculated what it should be from the measure of the triangle. And so the beams were there and the rods were there that I had picked up in Toledo, Ohio, borrowing one of our member's trucks. We drove the rod through, hitting it with a sledgehammer and got it where it was suppose to be coming out the other end. It didn't appear and didn't appear and soon there was no more rod left. We soon realized it was about two feet too short. So my great calculations were all off. So we removed the rod and took it over to a fellow who did welding. He had a rod that same size, so he cut it back of the thread, inserted a piece, and welded it in. It didn't hold us up too long. It was kind of a good experience.

CN: It is still standing.

WW: Yes.

CN: The church was built at the time of the merger between these two churches?

WW: Yes. We got there in '43 and I suppose we started talking and working at this merger in '45 after the War. It was effective by '47 when we started worshipping together. The church was finished in '49. Since then it grew better, I guess.

CN: I've been there once.

WW: What was the new church at that time is now the parish hall. They just named it Weiblen Hall. So it's, "Who in the hall do you want."

CN: Yes, but the memory of that as a very significant event abides.

WW: That was a big time.

CN: For a community to have two churches join like that was very significant.

WW: We had a good time. So when we went back there we saw all these people who remembered us old timers. There's still about twenty charter members left. The very first adult confirmand I had is still a very active member of the church and was president several times. He is always doing something around the church.

CN: He may have introduced himself to me when I there.

WW: He probably did. Harold Brown.

CN: What other memories do you have of your years in Bryan?

WW: Only theological memories. There was a great deal of stirring against the lodge. There were more things you were against than you were for. And an emphasis on pure doctrine prevailed. The pastors in the area were caught in a web of pure doctrine so that they had never advanced any further. I remember I felt that they didn't take theology seriously. But while at Bryan I also had this continual desire to serve in the military. I guess that arose from the fact that everyone else was involved. I got called on active duty rather suddenly, so that took care of Bryan.

CN: You left Bryan because of the call to military duty?

WW: Right. I had joined the Reserves and then I was called to active duty. I had to agree to that when I went in. I had volunteered and was more than happy to do it.

CN: How many years were you at Bryan?

WW: I had been there seven years. When I went on active duty, it was completely ecumenical and you had to learn how to cooperate with Roman Catholics and all other kinds of churches. So that's the way I left Bryan.

CN: Well, the people were certainly appreciative of your ministry there.

WW: Oh yeah. As far as people in the congregation, there was no problem. I just want to stress it was in the relationship to the wider Church as embodied in the personage of the pastors.

CN: Where were you based in the Air Force?

WW: When I went on active duty in October 1950, I was called to duty at Otis Air Force Base in Cape Cod, Massachusetts. So my first experience was on the Cape and I served there about 16 months before I was sent to Korea. We bought a little house that was being built because it was cheaper to do that than to try to find some place to rent. There was a company building little four-room houses, no basement. And so we bought there and were very crowded with kids.

CN: Especially with four children.

WW: But, we had a good time there. You know, there were a bunch of couples. The neighbors next door became good friends that we still see to this day. And so that part, I think, was good for Ilah too, to get away from the restrictions or having to always worry about being proper and so forth in the parish.

CN: Away from the pressures of being a pastor's wife.

WW: Yeah. So we had a good time. Then I was called to Korea.

CN: Were you Chaplain to people who were involved in combat?

WW: I was Protestant Chaplain with the 67th Tactical Reconnaissance Wing. We took most of the pictures that would have been seen of the bombing on the Yolu River up along the border with China. In other words, our outfit took pictures and did the reconnaissance work to see what kind of bombing damage we had done. I found that year over there was gratifying. Often there were people standing to get in line to go to services. They had steel kind of buildings, you know, quickly made buildings. We had a Chapel in such a building. So there were Protestant and Catholic services on the hour, every hour, starting about seven in the morning until the afternoon. Most of those were pretty well filled, people waiting in line to get in the next one. That was kind of gratifying.

On the other hand, some of the things you had to do were to give character guidance lectures, to keep these guys from going out getting venereal disease and so forth. A lot depended on the various stories you could tell. This little Jewish guy came up to me after one of these character guidance lectures in which I had made the point that you should remember that each of these prostitutes that you lie with has the potential of being a mother. Think now of your mother and what she means to you and ask yourself if what you are contributing to this situation is in line with that at all. And this Jewish guy said, "Chaplain, that really got to me, making me think of my mother. It kept me from going down to that place for two weeks."

CN: I think if most people would remember a sermon for two weeks, we've really done our job. Did you have a chance to meet Koreans?

WW: Yes, we did. One of the things we did was to have an on-going program of supporting orphanages in Korean villages. Chaplains were the people who usually took the initiative to arrange to get something going between the local churches, a lot of Methodist churches and Presbyterian churches around where our base was. So we used to fan out and get to know these people. Everybody had clothing and stuff sent from home that we took to orphanages.

One time we noticed these four young kids were living under a bridge not too far from our base. And so we began to develop a relationship, stopping there and giving them some soap and candy bars. It seemed to us as good Americans that the best thing was to get them provided for. So we decided to get them in an orphanage. We went to them when they trusted us enough. We told them we would take them to get help. So they came with us. But as we drew near the orphanage, they knew very well and they all tried to jump out of the jeep. We had to round them up at the point of a gun so they wouldn't be worse off than when we had entered their life. So we took them back where they were. That taught me a good lesson that a lot of these orphanages were traps for getting supplies from Americans and then selling them on the black market. And the orphanages needed to have these well-behaved kids to show how we are helping them. It became apparent that some of the help they didn't want, like these kids who enjoyed their freedom under that bridge more than the rules of the orphanage where we were planning to take them.

CN: A lesson in contextualization.

WW: While I was in Korea, Ilah stayed in Waverly. When I came back, they were looking for an associate pastor at St. Paul's in Waverly and so they asked me. Just being home after being separated for over a year, it seemed like a nice idea. I was right at the juncture where I had to sign up for more extended active duty if I was going to stay in the Air Force. So with the congregation coming to me and asking if I would be interested, that was an easy way to go. It provided the opportunity, I suppose, that eventually brought me here.

William H. Weiblen:
Harvard and Erlangen

WW: Serving in Waverly brought regular contact with many involved in education. For example, my senior pastor was the Chairman of the Board of Theological Education.

CN: Who was that?

WW: W. F. Schmidt. He was a towering big person, about as tall as you. He was very bright young guy. His desire was to serve as a missionary. After World War I, he set out for India but the mission field in India was closed. So he had to come back and was utilized by the Board of Missions of the old Ohio Synod to start a church in Port Angeles, Washington. Then he was appointed to be one of the leaders of the seminary they were going to develop out there, but it didn't develop. So he came to St. Paul Lutheran to be in charge of the one school the Ohio Synod had outside of Columbus, at St. Paul Lutheran Church. So he had the distinction of being the last president of St. Paul Lutheran College and Seminary. He was very supportive. I told him that I really would like to utilize my G.I. bill to be able to do some graduate work. He thought that was probably a good thing if I were going to be staying in Waverly. He agreed and promoted the idea with the congregation that I get a year's leave of absence to work on a degree. That's when I went to Harvard.

CN: So they basically supported you in that effort.

WW: Yes. They gave me a leave of absence. The family continued to live in the house. The bad part of the whole thing was the separation again from the family. It was not as long a time. But nevertheless, it all adds up. When I finally got to Harvard to begin the second semester in 1956-57, I wondered what the devil I was doing. I was thrust back into living in the dormitory with all these young people again.

CN: It must have been unlike anything you had ever experienced.

WW: Yeah. But it didn't take long and I found it immensely invigorating. It opened up a whole new world.

CN: You were sitting in on lectures and seminars?

WW: Yes. I took a regular course leading to the S.T.M. It was a one-year course. I took four courses a term plus a couple seminars. You didn't have to write a thesis at that time. I took everything from Tillich I could get.

CN: How many courses with Tillich?

WW: Well, I had two full courses with him plus two seminars.

CN: So it was a big dose?

WW: Yes. I took people that were there. It was an interesting time to be at Harvard because they were just building a Divinity School. Douglas Horton was the Dean from the United Church of Christ. They not only brought in Tillich, but they had Paul Lehmann there who was a theologian and ethicist who had been at Union Seminary and Princeton. There was another young German by the name of Walter Leibrecht. Richard Niebuhr was there. And then they had some of the old standbys from Harvard itself in years past. It was a deliberate effort to make it a Christocentric seminary where it had been known as a bastion of old liberalism. So that was an invigorating time to be at Harvard. Carl Braaten was there. I used to talk to him. He was Tillich's assistant. I suppose he corrected my term paper.

CN: Carl Braaten had been the pastor at the Lutheran Church of the Messiah in Minneapolis where I interned. Who were some of the others in the student body?

WW: Well, in addition to the ones I mentioned, there was John Dillenberger who was an up and coming bright star and who also studied under Tillich at Union Seminary. Later on he left Harvard and ended his career at the Theological Union at Berkeley. So we had all those people. There were people like Georges Florovsky from the Russian Orthodox religion. And there were professors in philosophy whose lectures you could go and listen to. I know one summer I heard this one professor lecture on American philosophy. I lived with a guy in Perkins Hall. We became good friends and are to this day. He was Presbyterian by the name of Bob Walton. We used to have a lot of good discussions. Walton and I lived together that one term. The second term, I lived by myself in the Divinity Hall where Emerson had been.

CN: Did his ghost still haunt the place?

WW: His ghost was still there. I thought it was kind of unique. Here is this great Harvard, you see, and the emergency exit in case of fire was a big rope. It was hanging by the window in the room. The whole experience of being there was intellectually stimulating. I told you before I went there with the idea that I was going to reinforce myself against the heresy of this guy, Tillich. Soon some of the other students were talking about his thought and I found myself agreeing with him.

CN: How did you experience Tillich in terms of his presence?

WW: I felt kind of like the shy Dakota boy and did not make an aggressive effort to impose myself upon him. I didn't develop any personal relationship with him. I found him down-to-earth and very concerned but not accessible. He was so busy you hated to bother him. There wasn't any camaraderie like there is with us here.

CN: He would come in and lecture.

WW: In seminars, he'd be sitting there and seem to drop off. You thought he was asleep. Somebody would say something and he would immediately respond. So it shows that he was with it. But I noticed people would pay this big money to come and listen to Tillich, but they would fall asleep in the back rows, too.

CN: Listening to him?

WW: Yeah. He was not a guy who was given to dramatics at all. He lectured on in typical German style.

CN: You had to be impressed by his intellect.

WW: Yes, by what he said. Of course, he was the center of a lot of contention by the fact that the old guard was being replaced by what they considered these "Christ" people. That lead to a lot of interesting discussions. I remember once there got to be a big battle because of this crucifix that he had recommended as a very good piece of art by a young sculptor who had been in the Liberal Arts at St. Olaf College. So the university at Harvard bought it and put it up in the Chapel. But then the thing would vanish. The iconoclasts stole it and got it out of there. Then they would bring it back. In the midst of that controversy one time Tillich devoted about twenty minutes of his first lecture period to dealing with the whole issue of art in the church and so forth. There were parallels with Luther's own problems with iconoclasm at the time when he rushed back from the Wartburg because of what the people were doing, throwing statues and art out.

CN: The biggest controversy I had at St. Mark in Cape Girardeau during the building program was over what we were going to hang over the altar, because I advocated a crucifix and had to do a good job of explaining why.

WW: Did most of them want a plain cross?

CN: Yes.

WW: They call that the Easter cross. Tillich didn't like extended realism, art made so real that you could tell every drop of blood.

CN: It was too morbid.

WW: Yeah. And he preferred something that just pointed beyond itself. We called this cross an 'hupsofix' because it looked like a Greek epsilon. But you could still see there was a corpus on there. So I thought it was very nice. The last time I was at Harvard, I was wondering what they eventually did with it. So they solved the problem the way we do in churches by putting it on the rear wall. You see it when you go out.

CN: You must have really been busy to have done that much course work in one year.

WW: Yeah. It kept you moving. It was good during the summer that we still owned the house that we purchased when I was in the Air Force and were renting it out. So I could preempt that and have the house for the summer. The family was with me then. That was an interesting experience because there were still trains running from Boston down to the Cape just like they had for years. All the wealthy people would move out of the heat of Boston in the summer down to the Cape. So I experienced what it was like to be a commuter. You had to be over there to catch the train at this ungodly hour in the morning and then know exactly how to move through the train to get out at the right spot so you could catch the next one over on the other side out to Harvard Square. So that was kind of interesting and I think the family had a good time that summer. It was mostly good for Ilah and the kids, being on the beach, and with our friends who had been in the army. He had gotten out of the army and they were living there.

We renewed the friendship with them and other people around there. So that was kind of a busy year, but an interesting interruption in the middle of the year.

CN: Did you pick Harvard partly because of the location, being near Cape Cod?

WW: No, that didn't enter my mind until afterwards. It may have been partly because we liked the Cape.

CN: There were other schools you could have chosen.

WW: Yes. And I don't know what it was that drew me to Harvard. I guess having heard a little bit about Tillich, I looked at it as being something new. He seemed to be cutting quite a swath of interest in our people here at the seminary. I just thought it would be interesting. I can't deny that I wondered if I could make it at an institution like Harvard. That was kind of satisfying.

CN: To test yourself?

WW: Yeah. To find out that you could do it.

CN: I find it amazing how an encounter like that and an experience like that changes you forever. I mean the way that you have been a teacher of Tillich's theology for all these years for how many students?

WW: Yeah. And I have to realize how old that is now, talking about Tillich. I think of it as being a living moment just like when he was around.

CN: Sitting in the classroom.

WW: Yeah. And now it's all these years since.

CN: But I think there is something vital about his theology. I still think that the basic foundations have relevance for pastoral ministry in a way that scarcely any other theologian has.

WW: It never occurred to me when I was there that I would ever be here. But when I got back to Waverly, I thought we would be there for an extended period of time. But then this vacancy occurred. Matzner, who had replaced Reu, was going to retire. They advertised for nominations and someone nominated me. I wasn't even going to respond to the nomination. You had to write up all this stuff just about like you have to do now. I almost let that go by. Schmidt encouraged me to apply and so I did. Then amazingly I was elected. I well remember the evening. The trains were still running and Schmidt had been down to Dubuque here for a meeting of the Board of Regents. One of the items on the agenda was to elect the person in Systematic Theology. The Board of Theological Education did that with representatives from the Region. I don't think they had specific recommendations. You know they didn't reduce it to two like we have now.

CN: So they went through a larger list.

WW: It was a bigger list. Anyway, I was nominated and did send in some material. The night he came back I met the train in Waterloo. He said, "Well, I hope you can stand the shock. You were elected." And he just assumed that I would take it. But I wasn't that sure. I had written a letter that said it's never too late to correct a mistake as long as there is still a real possibility. I said that where I am in years of service, I don't know whether this makes sense. I realized I had many holes in my preparation. Finally, I did accept it. Then the question came, of course, what about a doctorate? During the previous summer, I had met Kuenneth, professor at Erlangen. I got the idea from my brother Paul who had studied in Europe for one year during his college time. It all seemed of interest to me and I thought it would be worth exploring. So I found out that it was a program that fit me better than going back to Harvard, or Chicago, or something like that. I'd had to take all kinds of time to prepare for the qualifying exams. So I decided to apply to Erlangen. Kuenneth accepted me as a candidate. So we went. It was a great experience.

CN: When were you there?

WW: We went to Germany in the fall of 1958.

CN: So this was prior actually to coming to teach?

WW: Yes. Because Matzner said he could still teach for a couple of years. He said I think you should go and get your Doctor's degree.

CN: Prior to beginning?

WW: They used to do that. I suppose what got me the selection in the first place was that I had a substantial block of parish experience. That's something they wanted from the person teaching Systematic Theology.

CN: You had had the seven years in Bryan.

WW: And the three years in the Air Force, and five years in Waverly. And I also had a year of graduate work.

CN: It all fit together.

WW: Yeah. And going to Germany forced me to learn German which I didn't know before. We had a great experience. Germany was good for the kids. Overall they had a good experience. I suppose that Bill, who was just in high school, lost a lot that he would have had here, playing football and stuff like that. He doesn't complain about it. For our young daughter, Faith, we would have been able to arrange for her to go one term at this girl's school the year after we left. When she was first back here, she was homesick for Germany. She wrote her little friend over there saying I wished I didn't have to write this letter. So you knew she felt at home.

CN: She put down roots.

WW: Yeah. And in Germany it seemed important to study the theological roots. I noticed in America that Tillich was studied in greater depth from a philosophical standpoint rather than from an expressly theological view. He was obviously studied theologically, but his theological roots were not probed as deeply. So that's what I went after. And because the doctrine of the Word of God as Scripture was a big issue in the Church at that time, it seemed like it should be in that area. So that's how I ended up going toward Martin Kähler's hermeneutics. I had proposed, first of all, writing a dissertation on Reu, showing how the missionary zeal of Loehe was sustained in the theological understanding of people like Reu. But my professor said Reu was not an original thinker and that the German faculty would not accept that as a dissertation topic.

CN: Not as a systematic topic. It might have gone as an historical topic.

WW: Yeah. It probably would have gone as an historical topic. Anyway they had reservations. In many ways it would have been kind of an interesting thing to have done

CN: I think today it would go as a topic.

WW: Yeah.

CN: So Kähler had this connection with Tillich.

WW: Yeah. And I learned that the systematician who influenced Tillich the most was Kähler. And so I thought I should find out something about him. It was kind of hard and frustrating to bring it all together. I discovered also that that's the very topic that Braaten had chosen.

CN: He did his on Kähler at Harvard. What other teachers did you have at Erlangen?

WW: The one that impacted me the most at Erlangen was perhaps Paul Althaus. He was still lecturing. I had a seminar with him. I remember the day I had to do my presentation. The previous student had just been severely criticized, so I was shaking in my boots. I liked Althaus. He probably didn't take as courageous a stand or distance himself from the German Christians as he could have. But he was a refined and pleasant gentleman. So I enjoyed listening to his lectures. Of course I listened to Kuenneth's lectures. Then Wilhelm Maurer was a good lecturer in the History of Thought. I listened to a lot of those people. Also there was a Jewish philosopher who gave lectures on Kierkegaard and so I listened to those. He was a lively person, something like George Forell, always having lots of jokes. So he was good to listen to. And then Wilfried Joest was the second professor of Systematic Theology and also professor of Ethics. And then there was, of course, Walter von Loewenich who wrote *The Theology of the Cross*. He was still lecturing. I listened to all of these guys as much as I could because if you get one of them examining you, you need to know where they stand. And then, of course, I had Ethelbert Stauffer for New Testament and he was a lively one. He would tell people that Jesus had blue eyes and everything like that.

CN: He was anti-Bultmann.

WW: Yes. I will never forget when we were having a kind of pastors' conference. Stauffer had written a book, which is not one of his best books, *Glaube an Jesus?* He was setting forth a different position, even claiming Jesus had blue eyes because of the part of Palestine he came from. They were having this presentation by Kuenneth on Stauffer's book. Just as Kuenneth got started lecturing, all of a sudden there was a knock on the door and there stood Stauffer with his umbrella in hand, bowing. He said, "I just learned that my name has been mentioned here and I thought I would see what it's all about." And then, of course, Kuenneth was very polite, as you can imagine. Kuenneth said I would have invited you if I had known you would be interested in coming, but I didn't think you would want to be bothered. So they were excusing each other. And all of us were sitting there waiting for these guys to get at it. And they never really did get down to any more aggressive attacks because German etiquette took over.

CN: It wasn't like the great Braaten-Forell debate.

WW: Not at all. There was this long-standing connection, simply by geography between Neuendettelsau and Erlangen. They were close enough together that there was always that connection there. And there was a connection through our professors. One of the Fritschel's sons went to study in Erlangen as well as at Leipzig. Reu seemed to have a particular affinity with the Erlangen faculty and Erlangen gave him his honorary doctor's degree for that big scientific work that he had accomplished on the catechism. So there has been a strong connection there. There haven't been a great deal of people going to Erlangen since the War, only a few. We'll talk about those. Erlangen was prominent in the 19th century and continued to be prominent, I think, at the beginning of the 20th century.

CN: They were at the heart of that Luther renaissance, weren't they?

WW: Yes. And we've talked about Zahn and von Hofmann. Then we need to mention the next generation, Elert particularly and Kuenneth. Werner Elert is the author of this book, *The Structure of Lutheranism*.

CN: Paul Althaus also?

WW: Althaus especially.

CN: You know that my doctor father, Hans Schwarz studied with Kuenneth.

WW: Yeah. He and I had the same doctor father. He was actually working on his degree when I was completing my work.

CN: I didn't realize you both worked with Kuenneth.

WW: Yeah. Although I won't say that I shared Kuenneth's point of view as closely as Schwarz indicated that he did. He later became a little more open here in the U.S. But anyway, those are the points of connection. Elert and Althaus represent solid stuff, strongly based in a biblical understanding of dogmatics. They were strongly geared to being faithful to the Lutheran heritage. And, as you know, Erlangen was not one of the theological faculties that distinguished themselves for taking early, forceful, and direct opposition to Hitler. As a matter of fact, I suppose there was, like at a lot of places, some rejoicing that Germany was recovering and making some progress. They were happy to see that. Well, they have been faulted here and there for not taking a clearer stance against the Nazis, as some other faculties tended to do. Althaus was a fine gentleman, sort of like T.I. Jensen. Do you remember him?

CN: I never met him.

WW: Althaus was a gentleman, a cultivated person, and always seeking to be friendly. To take a strong position would have been hard for him. I can see that part of his problem was that he couldn't really believe that people could be as evil as Hitler became. Well, anyway, that placed a cloud over Erlangen.

116

CN: Yeah, there was a book published by an Erickson. Have you seen that book?

WW: Yeah.

CN: Where he documents how Althaus along with Kittel and Hirsch supported Hitler. Hirsch really takes the brunt of it.

WW: Yes, and Hirsch is the one who was obviously the ringleader. There is certainly a great difference between Paul Althaus and Emmanuel Hirsch. But Althaus found himself identified as one of those who was not a collaborator, but who sort of stood in the gray area.

CN: A bystander.

WW: Yes.

CN: They make that distinction now between perpetrators, collaborators and bystanders.

WW: Yes. Bystanders stood silently by. And Elert, too. But some of the Americans started going back there to work on their degree after the war, among them Bob Schultz from Concordia, who translated Althaus's work into English.

CN: He translated the theology of Luther. Did he do the ethics, too?

WW: I think he did the ethics, also.

CN: To what degree do you think their view of the two kingdoms would have contributed to being a bystander?

WW: Why I think the general Lutheran understanding of the doctrine of the two realms, keeping the civil distinct from the spiritual, was a contributing factor in that direction. Although I don't think it can be blamed entirely, because you can go to Norway and there the Bishop of Norway with the same concepts comes to an entirely different position than being a bystander. He became an active opponent of Nazism. So right in the midst of that conflict you have contrasting views. In my mind, what gets the Germans in trouble is the strong German nationalism. That had been pushed ever since Bismarck. The whole idea of nation is not something that is there in antiquity. But the way we think of it, you know, it's pretty much an understanding from the Enlightenment on.

CN: Yes. Really from the time of the French Revolution.

WW: Yes. This drive towards nationalism, I think played as great a role as anything does. Maybe that's part of the whole two kingdoms problem that's never been fully resolved.

CN: That certainly became a prominent topic during the Luther renaissance. As an aspect of Lutheran doctrine, I don't think it had a prominent position before that time. But curiously, interest in the two kingdoms would have emerged about the same time as German nationalism.

WW: Yes, I think that's right. It became a convenient tool to justify nationalism.

CN: Yes. I had never made that connection.

117

WW: Well, all I can say is that from my own experience that I regret that I didn't get to know Elert. He died just before I got there. Some of our people worked with him a little bit. I don't know if anyone was a doctoral candidate of his, although some from Missouri Synod were. But Althaus was there. He had affection for the Americans. And he was, more so than Tillich, really a devoted participant in the life of the church. Like you, he preached every so often in the local parish. People would always say they liked to go hear Althaus preach, because he had something for everyone, little kids as well as the elderly, educated as well as the non-educated.

CN: So he was a churchman.

WW: Yes, he was a churchman and he drew support for the church. And he was really accommodating to me. In order to express the fact that forgiveness was in operation, Wartburg gave him an honorary degree. I suppose that would not be a very popular thing to do today.

CN: When would that have been?

WW: That was about 1960.

CN: Just about the time you came on faculty.

WW: Right. Krodel was here and he's the one who proposed it. Another person on the faculty at Erlangen at that time, who was very good in his resistance to the Nazis was Hermann Sasse. He was very clear cut. His only problem, as Professor Kuenneth then told me, was that Sasse had such a high and holy view of the church that in the final analysis, there was only room for Sasse and God in that church.

CN: Is this the reason he has become so popular in the Missouri Synod?

WW: Exactly. Then, of course, he went to Australia and when he first started going there, he was under the auspices of the Missouri Synod.

CN: Would that have been post-World War II?

WW: Yes. That's where he died, in Australia. The Erlangen faculty, I think, felt that he was a little too aggressive in condemning his colleagues as Nazis or as bystanders.

CN: So that may have been a strong reason why he went to Australia.

WW: Yeah, I think he made himself *persona non grata*. I don't think he could stand it and so he went to Australia. Yeah, he had quite a tragic death. I don't know if it was from smoking or what, but the apartment where he was living caught fire and he suffocated in the fire. Sasse was gone from Erlangen in the '60s.

Then there was Kuenneth, with whom I worked. And he was a follower of Karl Heim, but first became a pastor for a long time. It's interesting that the SS put a listening device on his telephone. He was never imprisoned or anything. The Bishop had enough authority that, even with Hitler's ban yet in effect at that time, he could get Kuenneth a position so that he could serve a church, even though he was forbidden to speak. He was allowed to preach sermons in the church, but he couldn't make any public utterances at all. He had been in charge of the institute in Berlin that was interested in the area of science and Christianity.

CN: That would have been the influence from Heim, then.

WW: Yes. That's why he studied with Heim.

CN: Heim wasn't at Erlangen though.

WW: No. Hein was at Tuebingen.

CN: How come Kuenneth never became more well known in the States like Elert and Althaus?

WW: I think a lot of people considered him superficial and not as a great thinker in depth. But, I don't know why, because he took up some of the popular issues. Even before the War, his writings dealt with the struggle between demons and God, dealing with those kinds of things. Then after the War, he published a great big volume on politics. So, I don't know.

CN: Well, you could argue that Althaus and Elert also were not original thinkers. They were systematizing the Lutheran tradition.

WW: I don't know. I think Kuenneth was not as involved in the pre-War ecumenical activity as Althaus was. Althaus was at the famous meeting in England where Christians came together.

CN: Faith and Order?

WW: He was one of the speakers at one of the last one of those meetings. Kuenneth wasn't as active.

CN: So maybe he didn't become as well known to the American population.

WW: I think that's it. After the War, Kuenneth became a little more involved. This is how I got to study in Erlangen. They were sending these people to the United States in connection with Lutheran World Federation meetings and so forth. They came here, at various places and various congregations, to get experience in American life. So Kuenneth ended up coming to Waverly where I was serving. And so I got to know him there. He could hardly speak English and I could speak pretty good German, so we got along quite well. So when I got the call to Wartburg, I wrote to him about coming back.

CN: You got the call to Wartburg first and then you wrote to him.

WW: Yes. That's how he ended up helping us.

CN: Had there been other Wartburg graduates who had studied at Erlangen?

WW: Yes. One distinguished one was Lowell Green. He was, last I knew, in Canada. He's one of our graduates in the '50s. He was a very bright student and a good organist. And he was, therefore, touted to go on to school. I think Salzmann was grooming him for the position that I eventually inherited. He knew his languages well, even Latin and so forth. And so he was

119

encouraged. With the connection with Elert, he went to Erlangen. But the person there, with whom most of his work was actually done, was Wilhelm Maurer.

CN: Was that the same one who wrote this book on the Augsburg Confession that was recently translated?

WW: Yeah that may be. He has now been dead for several years. It would have been an early work. But he was a very good professor. Green got his degree in the History of Doctrine on Melancthon. He's one of them. Then there's Richard Trost. He studied under Kuenneth, too. And it's interesting how he got under Kuenneth. Kuenneth is kind-hearted and has taken people like myself. Trost went over to Germany after he finished his degree here to study with Ernst Fuchs, the New Testament scholar. But he got over there and it was too far out for him.

CN: Fuchs was a strong Bultmannian.

WW: Yes. And Trost high-tailed it to Erlangen to see if Kuenneth would accept him. And he did, of course. Kuenneth would have considered that a bargain, for someone to decide not to take Fuchs and instead go with him. So that's how Trost got to Erlangen. Those are the main ones, although there are several other Lutherans. Dr. Rogness' oldest son, Mike, on the faculty at Luther, is also a graduate of Erlangen. He was over there during the last few months when I was finishing my degree.

CN: I've never put it in those terms, but Schwarz was my doctor father and he worked in Erlangen, so there is a connection there.

WW: I brought Kuenneth's book along, *Theology of the Resurrection*, as an example of how the Missouri Synod, even though they were conservative, was doing things that were helpful. To publish a book like this was useful because it brought a conservative German point of view that is distinct from crass fundamentalism here. So in it's better days, Missouri was doing all of us a service by giving an entree for these kinds of people into our dialogue. It's too bad that it ended as it did. But I think of it as a great day when you had people like Arthur Carl Piepkorn, who was not only a great historian of the early church but one who could have taught liturgy for the teachers of liturgy. He brought a lot of Loehe's emphasis for high church liturgical practice. But there were all kinds of good people from Missouri.

CN: I didn't realize this book had been translated ever. The only book I've seen by Kuenneth in translation was a book of sermons. This was a book that he wrote after the War.

WW: We came home from Germany in August of '60 and then I went back in the spring of '61 to finish it up. I was hoping to be able to do it before Christmas. One day I saw the Dean there and asked whether I could still get it in or not. I went up to the place where I was working and had everything laid out and wrote a couple of paragraphs and that was the conclusion. I wanted to be finished by Christmas. With a few changes and some minor additions, they approved it and then I had the exam. During the exam somebody asked me a question. The answer should have been Marcion, something about who influenced the development of the Canon. And I didn't seem to be getting it. So Stauffer lifted up his New Testament. The other professor couldn't see him doing that. He waved it like that and I knew that he was supporting me because it was a clue.

CN: That was kind.

WW: He saw they were asking what was it that kept Marcion from being a complete Gnostic. And, of course, it was the New Testament. Stauffer helped me with that question.

So afterwards I was able to telephone home. Ilah and the kids were down at St. John's. They were having a pastors' conference meeting with the seminary faculty. They always used to attend. So they were all there and they learned the good news that I had finished.

Professor William H. Weiblen

WW: I came back here by Christmas and started being involved and soon was taken up with all kinds of additional duties. I had the position of Registrar. That was similar to being Dean or maybe Dean of Students.

CN: You were appointed to that fairly early on?

WW: Yeah. Salzmann was retiring from that. They asked me if I would do it. I did it and kept doing it until Kent Knutson was here. So that kept me busy, writing all these letters to students.

CN: You had a lot of administration in addition to teaching.

WW: That included Admissions and academic advising as well.

CN: Now there are six or eight different positions to do those tasks.

WW: Well, we didn't do as much then as we do now. But it was enough to keep one active and busy. The good thing about it, I suppose, was it brought me in special close contact with all the students. It was always interesting to be working with all these files and then see them embodied in a person at school here.

CN: Yes.

WW: A whole lot of tragedies there, too. The biggest heartache in Admissions is having to say no. That usually leads us as church people to be, in the end, quite cruel. We keep postponing that no. One young fellow, who had a very tragic life, was abandoned by his parents and raised by all different kinds of people. You wondered how he survived, but he had gotten through college. There was a lot of talk about whether he could be a pastor or not. But they left it up to us to decide. It was one of those times when the faculty was a little more determined to say no than it had been in other times. So that's what we did. The guy left here, went home, walked out into the river, and drowned. I've often thought of that, the sadness of it. We tried to be there with him, but in the end I'm sure he looked upon it as the final blow. I always was the one who was probably too generous with the yes's.

And then we had another student one time who was failing Greek. It got to be that perennial thing. He just couldn't get Greek. And he came to visit about Greek one Friday afternoon. And I, of course, being in the position where was required to do so said that it was not likely that we could make exceptions because it's agreed upon by the whole group of colleges and seminaries. So he left and that night one of our blustering guys from Texas walked through Mendota. At that time we rented out rooms to students who lived in these little trailers so they could have a place to study. And there this kid was hanging from the transom to the window in the door above. He cut him down and he survived.

122

CN: He got there fairly early then.

WW: Yeah. Whether it just happened that they were coming through or whether the kid wanted to make a display, I don't know.

CN: He succeeded at that, in any case.

WW: Yes, he did that very well. The kid was taken over to Mercy Hospital and given some treatment there. It ended up that he didn't study for ministry, which was probably a good thing. So we have those kinds of things.

CN: Well, I worry about the repercussions of some of the decisions I'm making. It's really awesome.

WW: It is. It affects the entire life. We can talk about them, realize that there are certain things about them, sometimes even humorous or tragically funny, you know. But it isn't a funny business.

CN: No. It's far more awesome than I ever realized when I came here.

WW: Yeah. That's a very crucial position. You know it's probably as crucial as any because it's a place where we do find a way to say no.

CN: The whole church looks at internship that way, not just the seminary.

WW: And it is true that some people are not cut out for parish ministry. On the other hand, if people want to prepare themselves with theological education and not necessarily serve in the parish, being a minister in some other sense, they should have the opportunity to do that.

CN: Yes.

WW: In our understanding about ordination, we're so bound to the parish, unlike the Roman Catholics who have a whole different view of what it's all about.

CN: If we only had a little more breadth to our notion of ordained ministry.

WW: Yeah. There are a number of cases like this guy from Texas. Couldn't he have learned to work in a library or an archives, rendering lifelong service?

CN: What were you teaching as you began your ministry here?

WW: When I came here we had a lot of different courses. We had three and two and one hour courses. The three-hour courses were the required ones. It was assumed that you had one each in the various sections of Dogmatics. A three-hour course in the Doctrine of God, Creation and Humanity; a three-hour course in Christology; and a three-hour course in church and the Means of Grace. T.I. Jensen was the other person in Systematic Theology. But the year after I came here, he went on sabbatical. So I was teaching the whole load, all the required courses in Systematic Theology. It meant at least twelve hours in the classroom in one term, plus doing the Registrar work.

CN: Let me never complain in your presence about my workload.

WW: That was too much. I just lived from one lecture to the next. I considered it a great thing to rejoice if I could get to the next lecture, get through it, and know it didn't come up again until Friday.

CN: You taught using Reu's *Dogmatics* at first?

WW: We still had Reu's *Dogmatics* the first year or two. Before too long I switched over to use Brunner as a main text.

CN: The three volumes of Emil Brunner?

WW: Yeah. He's Reformed but fairly close to Lutheran. At least it had the advantage of being a little more contemporary.

CN: Where did you work Tillich in?

WW: I don't think I did the first year or so. I started working Tillich in about a year after I was here. We started graduate school again and began the S.T.M. program in the summer courses and things like that. That's where I worked Tillich in. But also then I started introducing Tillich in the required Dogmatics course.

CN: In your lectures?

WW: In my lectures and some other readings that the students were asked to do.

CN: How was your teaching different than Matzner?

WW: Well, Matzner was a straight repetition of Reu's *Dogmatics*.

CN: So that just continued with Matzner?

WW: Yes. That's what Matzner did. I tried to bring a different approach in having a lecture, but always raising some questions for discussion, trying to stimulate some dialogue, because they had had hardly any class discussion at all. And so we would break up some of those classes into discussion groups. That, of course, made more work for you, but it provided an opportunity to get a little more discussion, particularly in relation to the first year course, talking about what dogmatics was. I remember very shortly after I came here in trying that approach, having the students come down to our house. Our first house was the second brick one where students now live. A lot of different student groups came down for coffee and cookies and theological discussion. That developed later into beer over at Mulgrew's, with cheese and chilidogs.

CN: All the fine things of life, one of them being theology.

WW: Yeah.

CN: Was T.I. Jensen also using Reu or was he using other things?

WW: He didn't use Reu. I guess he assigned Reu to read. He had his own lectures. He had them all written out and went through them thoroughly. I'll never forget in the blustering of the '60s, at about '65-'66, he was teaching Ethics. One student simply interrupted the class and said, "We don't want to hear any more about that. We would like to discuss certain questions like ..." That was so devastating to T.I. that he asked Kent Knutson if he couldn't find some way to get him out of the classroom, that he couldn't take it any more. And so T.I. became Kent Knutson's administrative assistant for a term.

CN: This was the beginning of a kind of student uprising?

WW: That's right, in the '60s. Students thought they knew it all. This guy was a bright young student who had studied Psychology and Philosophy at Luther College. He didn't want this dull stuff, what Kierkegaard said or what T.I. Jensen thought.

CN: So Jensen retreated?

WW: Yeah. It was too bad. He could have waited and maybe stayed another year or two and he would have experienced a kind of different kind of response.

CN: So he was at retirement then?

WW: Yes, that's where he ended his teaching and went into retirement.

CN: He translated Prenter's dogmatics, I think?

WW: Yes. That book was never used as it might have been. Maybe it's because it was printed in such ponderous, small type.

CN: Well, it was published during that same time of ferment and didn't find its audience.

CN: Tell me about Kent Knutson becoming President of Wartburg. What was it like when he was President and you were on the faculty here?

WW: Well, when Kent Knutson was elected that turned out to be quite an exciting time. I remember when the nominees were named. Naturally because Kent was from Luther Seminary, there was a great division between Wartburg and Luther. A lot of people thought in the merger that Wartburg should have been merged some place because we didn't need that many seminaries.

CN: They were saying that already in 1960 at the beginning of the American Lutheran Church?

WW: They said that before we even started in the '60s. I don't know as a faculty what some of them thought of Kent. But I don't think most of us were particularly looking for some new exciting development. Ewald had been president. He was important for the opening to do a lot of things, even though sometimes he had to be pushed. Nevertheless I think he deserves credit for the opening of the ecumenical age, simply because he worked with it and did a lot for it. It was in that kind of context that the election was held, including people like Richard Salzmann, who was Dr. Reu's grandson, a capable guy who had the misfortune of divorce. We thought he might be a good president. Obviously, he wasn't in the running. The way the election was held at that time was that the Board called for nominations and nominations were presented and they were announced. Then in a joint meeting of the Board of Theological Education, the seminary's president was elected. That night when he was elected, an exciting moment afterwards, was a surprise at first.

CN: Was it known that he was one who was being considered?

WW: Yes, he was on the list there. But I never really personally gave him much thought. I suppose I was hoping that Salzmann would find his way in but as things turned out, I can see in retrospect, it was much better the way it went. So Kent was elected pretty unanimously.

CN: He was a professor at that time?

WW: He was a professor of Systematic Theology at Luther. Carl Braaten always told me afterwards that it came to be an advantage for Kent that he was here. He became better known in the whole church when he became president. Carl Braaten would tell me that, "Well, you guys should know that this was a calculated move on the part of Kent. He wanted to become President of the Church and knew the way to be in with the constituency would be in a position of importance in one of the other seminaries." So he was open to that, but according to Carl he was desirous of it and planning for it. I don't think that's ever been proven.

CN: That's Braaten's take.

WW: That Braaten's take all right. So when Kent came, he opened a whole new era. I think he gave excitement and determination and vitality to the faculty. But it was a very short-lived time.

CN: Was it about two years?

WW: He came here in '69 and left in '71. When he came as president, he created a very exciting climate.

CN: His reputation as theologian was pretty strong?

WW: I think he was recognized as one of the most important systematicians, but more balanced and more churchly oriented than some of the others.

CN: His books give that impression. They are more for the whole church, pastors and lay people.

WW: Yes. So then he was hardly elected and he was called away. That was an exciting time, too, when we were involved in the whole election of the President of the ALC. It gave us here at Wartburg that much more pride and vitality and gusto for the task to know that the President had come from Wartburg.

CN: So he really made his mark in the short time he was here and won the confidence of people.

WW: Yeah. Those little houses were constructed, a genuine effort toward getting a more adequate facility, instead of those little trailers we had up until that time. The night he was elected, he called the faculty and later we talked to Streng. One or the other told us the story of when Kent called his Dad up in Goldfield, Iowa, who was a farmer. Kent said to his Dad, "Dad, I was elected President of the Church." His Dad said, " Well, that's nice. How's the weather down there?" And Kent said that put it all in perspective for him.

CN: Now his presidency in the ALC didn't last long either because of his illness. The diagnosis of his disease came when?

WW: The diagnosis came I suppose sometime in the summer of that same year.

CN: So just shortly thereafter?

WW: Well, it must have been '72 because they did the Church convention every two years. That's when he first noticed the signs. I think the diagnosis of Jacob Creutsfeldt syndrome was established probably in winter sometime. He went through that whole Convention and he already must have been suffering some symptoms. For example, at the Convention in October '72, they were expecting the president from the Lutheran Church in Indonesia. He was scheduled to be at the Convention and couldn't come all at the last minute. Kent took it upon himself to give a lecture on evangelism, which he sort of shook out of his sleeve and gave it on Sunday night at the Convention, without an indication of any problems. He conducted the business meeting, intricate parliamentary procedures, without difficulty. A few weeks after that he was already sick, checked into the hospital, and they soon determined it was this disease.

CN: Rapid deterioration?

WW: Yeah. So he went from being a person who was articulate to a person who couldn't speak or walk. Very devastating.

CN: How large was the faculty here at that time?

WW: It would have included Holm, T.I. Jensen, Bill Streng, myself, Schick, Kjeseth, Poovey, Pirner, and Benz.

CN: So the Danish people were still here at that time?

WW: Yes, I think so. Nyholm was leaving shortly thereafter, but I think he was also still here. I guess Ralph Quere came during Kent's administration. At that time when someone retired, the president had the authority to appoint. So often it happened that someone was appointed and then the election process was started and this person was called and that's the way it was. A lot simpler than it is these days.

CN: So the president would appoint and then that person would be in the running.

WW: Yes. It often was that he was the only one. Later the procedures were sharpened into a more comprehensive procedure.

CN: So was there an Interim President after he left to be President of the Church?

WW: Yes. Poovey was appointed by the Board to act as Interim President.

President William H. Weiblen

CN: Tell me about your election to become president of Wartburg Theological Seminary.

WW: I don't know how many were nominated in all, amongst them myself. I was asked if I would be open to it by some of the faculty. When Kent was elected, they asked me the same thing, but I said no. But at the time after Kent left, then I was open to the idea. I entered the process and was elected at the meeting of the seminary's Board of Theological education at the Lutheran Seminary in Columbus.

CN: Were you at that meeting?

WW: Yes. I waited around up in the dormitory where I had a room and thought somebody would come and let me know. I could see the meeting must have broken up already, so I came down and asked somebody.

CN: Real formal.

WW: Yeah. I asked somebody what had happened. They said, "Well, you were elected." It was both exciting anticipation as well as anxiety about the job, but it was a happy time. There was a nice installation service.

CN: What was the transition like as you became president?

WW: In my inaugural address, I'd spoken about the theme of dedication and direction. I emphasized that this was a time in which we, like all the forbearers of the Wartburg tradition, have to dedicate ourselves to the task of theological education. One thing I emphasized strongly was the idea of the international expansion and also the importance of paying attention to the community where we are located. Looking back now. I can see we were starting to think those things that have now come to expression, the whole emphasis on mission in a world scope.

CN: Was there an increase then in the international student population?

WW: Well, I think we worked at that. Right about that time Rueben Pederson, who was from the old Augustana Synod, had a position with the Lutheran Council. He had a number of Tanzanians come here. We were open to it. He seemed to be quite open to us and we talked several times. We agreed that if our faculty would agree to accept Tanzanian students—particularly he was taking about Tanzania, but also from other countries in Africa—that if they studied a year and everything went well, at the end of another year, we would bring their family over. We would award them a B.D, what is now a M.Div.

CN: After two years?

WW: Yeah, recognizing that their previous education was worth something. I think that's what helped us to be able to get a number of international students, particularly at that time. So it kind of perpetuates itself. Wartburg became known as a place where it's good for international students to go. And so I was pleased about that.

CN: Then Namibia and other countries came into the picture, too.

WW: Yes. Namibia came in a particular way when Abisai Shejavali came here in '76. That was our first contact with Namibian students. We all took an interest in the situation, and identified with his plight of living under apartheid, being deprived of independence. It had been mandated to them by the United Nations so that became a big part of the struggle.

CN: Had there been international students from Germany all along?

WW: Yes, that program had been going already when I came here. We regularized it so that every year there would be an exchange both ways.

CN: This was with Neuendettelsau?

WW: Yes. We did the same thing with Norway, with the Menighetsfakultet in Oslo.

CN: That was regularized.

WW: We assured that we had at least one of those each year. And we kind of adopted that as a principle to get an exchange going to the extent that we were able. Financing was always the biggest problem. But we could raise money a little bit more easily for bringing international students here, because people looked upon that as mission work. In the old ALC, there was as strong a zeal for mission work as there is in the ELCA. So people loved to have them in their congregations.

CN: For mission festivals and preachers. Were there other countries that also are worth mentioning?

WW: We had a pretty continuous exchange with Brazil, one that still continues. There were students that came from there and people from here that went down there. There wasn't as much traffic from here to there as there was the other way around. You could count on the coming of a Brazilian student even as they come now.

CN: What about Papua New Guinea?

WW: Yes, that too. There was this historically close tie of Wartburg with Papua New Guinea, so that was automatic. It has continued, mostly without interruption. Sometimes we didn't have a student from there.

CN: Did that begin when you became president?

WW: I think it was started during that time. Over the course of time we also had little flirtations with China and Hong Kong, Taiwan and Japan, though not much.

CN: It never developed in the same way.

WW: No.

CN: What was it like at the seminary when you were president, in light of the end of the Vietnam War and the student protest movement, to be here in that particular climate?

WW: We were immersed in the whole excitement of the much-involved Vietnam War crisis. There were a lot of student protests, even prior to when I was elected president. There was a lot of identification with Martin Luther King, Jr. Students from here went down to Selma in 1965. It was also the year we had the flood, so for a week or more practically all the students at the seminary were working with the flood. But in the engagement with church and society, there developed a continuing interest that came to a boil during the early years of my presidency. You would have students who were getting very bold. We had encouraged student participation. I had emphasized the uniqueness of Wartburg all along, with its own sense of community flowing from Loehe's idea.

In the process of that, the students felt themselves very open to speak very candidly about things. I can remember when Kent Knutson was still president and T.I. Jensen went to him and said, "Would you please give me something else to do until I retire?" It was just within a year of his retirement. He said, "I can't take this rejection by the students." Because he was a person who gave very carefully constructed lectures and expected a certain amount of reading. And he would come to class and the students would say, "We don't want to listen to what you have prepared. These are the issues we'd like to talk about."

CN: Similar to what happened to Pannenberg in Germany, I think.

WW: Yeah. So Kent very generously made him his assistant. He took care of the management of the grounds. That's just one kind of an example. There was another group of students who were getting all excited about the inter-seminary connections. Union Seminary in New York was doing a lot of protesting. There were four students here, all wrought up about this, who transferred because we were too far behind the times and not close enough to the action, like they would be in New York City. And so they transferred and went to New York. Well, then the next year they wanted to come back and instruct the seminary students.

CN: On what they had learned?

WW: Yes. So I agreed with them that they could have one classroom and put up all their signs and provocative, dirty language.

CN: Saul Alinsky type tactics?

WW: Yes. "The church sucks", you know. But they discovered the students kind of isolated them because they were going on with their own focus. But that was the kind of wild atmosphere in which you were living. There was a lot of good that came with that, but it was hard to keep people's nose to the grindstone.

CN: What did it mean for the curriculum then?

WW: Well, the curriculum had gone through a major revision just a few years before. Prior to the revision in 1967, the curriculum consisted of major courses of four hours, some three-hour courses, and some two, with a number of one-hour courses. Every student had a lot of little dinky courses and they wanted consolidation. Out of that developed the 4-1-4 academic year. St. Olaf had started experimenting with that. Students seemed to like the idea, so we put that into practice in '67. Then along with the concern for social justice that was demanded, eventually we ended up calling a person on the faculty to handle that focus, Nile Harper.

CN: He was called to the Schools of Theology in Dubuque?

WW: Yeah. We were all affected by that and became intentionally involved together in the community here in Dubuque. Specific activities were integrated into the curriculum. It began to stimulate the idea that we could do things as Wartburg that were not limited to Dubuque. So we had conversations with people in the Denver community and found great willingness and leadership, suggesting that we have a branch of our life in Denver. So we applied for and received a grant from Lutheran Brotherhood to start the Denver House of Studies and decided to go with it for a couple of years. It was sort of like sending Peter Kjeseth with a few students out on the Mormon Trail with a load of material: beds and things they would need, books for a library, and a moving van and cars. We started with the idea that Denver would be a place where they would be involved in inner-city activity and engaged in the issues with the Blacks and American Indians also. Then a couple of years later, the need in the Southwest, in Texas, for Hispanic Ministry became an issue. So it was during those years, so full of protest and social justice issues and community action that the curriculum began to include that program. We provided opportunities during the January Interim. Still today some of those things continue. People still take the Rural Plunge and Inner City plunges, too, like Milwaukee and Detroit. We had some great ones in Detroit, working with pastors in challenging ministry. In that respect, Wartburg has always felt kind of vulnerable, that it's out here in little old Dubuque, a Roman Catholic community. But nevertheless in a way, being weak in that sense, being vulnerable, provided it the freedom to be and become creative.

CN: So there was quite a bit of ferment coming out of that period to think about issues of church and society.

WW: Yes. One of the other things I wanted to relate to you, in the early years of my presidency, not the ALC Board but the Lutheran Council Board had been meeting in New York. They had run a study, as they always do, about theological education. This guy dreamed a little how it might be if seminaries were moved around a little and consolidated, so they would be more efficient in meeting the needs of the church. So they naturally talked about how Wartburg could be moved. So I got back to Dubuque. The Telegraph Herald came in the evening at that time and here on the front page was, "Wartburg May Move."

CN: You hadn't anticipated that.

WW: No. I hadn't anticipated it being on the front page. So that got everybody stirred up. We had Walt Wietzke down here from the ALC.

CN: That was when I was here as a student. I recall that big day.

WW: But that's kind of the churn in which things were moving.

131

CN: But actually the recommendation about Wartburg came from a study by the Lutheran Council?

WW: Yes. There were some creative ideas. I proposed the idea, there is a copy of that somewhere, that we didn't have to concede that theological education could be done exclusively in these fortress enclosures. You could have Wartburg in Denver, Wartburg in Austin, Texas, many other places.

CN: To think about multiple campuses.

WW: Yes. And along with that, we had purchased the house in Denver and had quite a bit going on there. The program was constructed in such a way that we had a well-established visible witness there. Of course, that was the case in Texas too. It consumed a lot of energy and eventually we had the Seminary Appeal.

CN: Do you think this idea of seminary on several campuses still has merit today?

WW: I think it does, very much. I'd like to see there be more along those lines. It would be great to see them trying. It's too bad that we had to lose the place in Denver because we had a physical house there. It does something to have a committed place that was yours.

CN: With the ELCA, it had to close because it wasn't in our Region.

WW: It wasn't in our Region and PLTS didn't have the money to sustain it. We don't hear much about multiple campuses any more. At that time, this was going on in the state colleges, to conceive of themselves as the University of Wisconsin, with campuses at Platteville, Eau Claire, Whitewater, and so forth. They function as their own in many ways but are still ultimately part of a bigger university. I would think coming into the computer age more and more, as we are now, this would be increasingly viable. The exchange we thought about, now communicating with one another over television and computers, has begun to show a good result, so that you make it available to various places as part of the educational system.

CN: That's the way it seems to me. I think theological education has to think more about taking education outward instead of only bringing people inward.

WW: It'll be interesting to see.

CN: Did you continue to teach during those years?

WW: Yeah, I usually taught one course.

CN: Each semester.

WW: Yeah, usually Tillich. Poovey and I used to teach a course on the correlation of theology and preaching. We'd take a number of great preachers. Poovey called it a Seminar on Great Preachers. I thought of it as a correlation of theology and preaching. But we got along well and had a lot of fun doing that together.

CN: Preachers throughout history?

WW: Yeah. We took some further back in history but mostly contemporary ones. I recall one particularly exciting incident was a fellow had Harry Emerson Fosdick from Riverside Church in New York as the one that he was presenting. He wrote to Fosdick and told him what he was doing in this course. Fosdick wrote him back a nice two-paged handwritten letter in which he said I envy you the opportunity of being able to be entering the ministry at this time. As I come to my end, I think of you beginning. He had some marvelous things to say. It just confirmed to me what often has been the case, that it is sometimes the liberals who are much more genuine, pleasant people, kind and considerate, who took the time to write such notes of encouragement.

CN: Something that was above and beyond the call of duty.

WW: Yeah. Art Cochrane and I did a course together on Confessions. There were also some others. I thought it was a good thing to bring in some people from the larger church to share in a course. Fred Schoitz came down here some weekends. He simply related his own experience. He had a lot that we could learn something about.

CN: I remember the famous Forell-Braaten debates.

WW: Yes. That was one of our better achievements.

CN: Could you say something about the significance of Tillich for you, not only as President, but in your career?

WW: My connection with Tillich came about in this way. I had the opportunity of doing graduate work under the G.I. Bill and the church at Waverly where I was serving gave me the opportunity to go to Harvard and do that. The reason I had chosen Harvard was that I had heard all about this Tillich and the wonderful creative things he was bringing to theology. And so my first thought was, "Well, I can't believe that. It sounds like just another one of these liberals." So I chose Harvard because Tillich was there and I wanted to go and find out about him, mainly to disprove his ideas and show that they were wrong. But it came to be a life-changing experience for me. I sat in his class the first day and it just seemed like he expressed things that I had been wanting to say and he said them the way that I could understand them. You know, I had the same problem as most people first hearing him did, that he's very abstract, sometimes hard to comprehend. Nevertheless I found him fully exciting for that and to be at Harvard at that time was equally exciting. Douglas Horton was the Dean of the Seminary and he was from the UCC and he was a good follower of Barth and Tillich both. He was at the Divinity School, really building it up. Before the war, I suppose Harvard was known as a place where old-time liberalism might have prevailed. But now he was bringing in people to Harvard that were either from the dialectic theology line or the contemporary line. Paul Lehmann came from Union Seminary, and Krister Stendahl was a young New Testament professor from Sweden, a Lutheran. And then Paul Tillich was called to the highest office of a professor that you could get at Harvard. So it was interesting to be there when all this was coming about. So I found Tillich not only speaking to me the way I wanted to say something into the theological milieu of that day but also as an exciting challenge of the new times. In that sense it was like Kant said, it awakened me out of my systematic slumbers. Tillich drew out the meaning of being Lutheran in its most extended completeness. So that was a great time both to be at Harvard and to be with the other students.

CN: When did you first teach Tillich's theology?

WW: I don't think I did it right away when I first came here.

CN: You said before that they were still using Reu's dogmatics.

WW: Yes, they were still using Reu's dogmatics and it shows you how intimidated I was. I still used it for a number of years too. But I used others also, like Brunner. So it was only really as we revived the graduate school. Dr. Reu had had an S.T.M. program. What it amounted to was studying with him, which a number of famous people did, Presidents from Missouri Synod and so forth came to work with Reu. Krodel was here when we revived that, a friend of his. And so I started by teaching Martin Kähler and so-called historical Jesus. Krodel got a translation through Braaten and had that duplicated. That was the first development. That would have been long before I was president.

CN: In the 1960s?

WW: Yeah. It would have been in 1963. And I got involved in that. Later I began teaching graduate courses and decided to teach Tillich. So when I became president, the course I usually taught had something to do with Tillich. By then it became something of an annual event.

CN: Which it has remained up until now.

WW: Yeah.

CN: What difference do you think Tillich has had for the pastors who have come out of Wartburg?

WW: I hope for one thing that they have grasped the unqualified meaning of grace. I think through his basic fundamental understanding of grace, he has helped us Lutherans immeasurably. Like Carl Braaten said, "Paul Tillich is the gift that the Lutheran Church never received." We received him in many ways and used him but didn't explicitly welcome him as a Lutheran theologian.

CN: So we never claimed him as Lutheran?

WW: When he said I am a Lutheran, he always had to make sure he didn't mean the Lutheran Church here. He wanted to distinguish between Lutheranism and Lutheran. But he was very clear that he was a Lutheran and his position was utterly Lutheran in the meaning of grace. So I think that's where he has had a lasting identity. And I think he has a contribution to make there still today. I think one of our problems as theologians is that we are all so ready for new things. We hardly digest the last motif that has worked its way up before we are grabbing for something else. And we never really totally exploited all the possibilities. We just accept whatever is new.

CN: And that would be true of Tillich's theology in many ways.

WW: Yes, I think so. There is no doubt that Tillich had a problem with his own personal life. In many ways he was like Clinton. As soon as that is known by some people, that's the best reason of all to throw him aside. I feel affinity for him, recognizing who I am as a sinner. We need to think not only about how theology affects our preaching but about how life affects the decisions we make theologically. You can't really write a sermon in the sanctity of the seminary. You have to be involved in a congregation because they help to write the sermon. I think of the congregational members who came together and I would come once a week from the seminary and at night we would study the text the pastor was going to preach on for the next week. One week he had the text of the miracle at the wedding of Canaan. Waiting for a response after reading the text, a lady said, "I wished he wouldn't have done that." And there's a lot of things I wished Tillich had not done, but I have a feeling that sexuality was a demon for him, maybe out of the piety in which he grew up. I think his theology was valid nonetheless.

CN: Are there other aspects of his theology that you think have been important for pastors?

WW: I think another important one, for pastors particularly, is his way of analyzing the political, social situation, in finding a clear way for participating in the human struggles of the time in society. His little known writings on political expectations show you how genuine real participation needs to be. I think he has a lot of good stuff there. It would be good to have a course dealing with those things in the very year we have a presidential election. He got into all kinds of trouble with his socialist politics.

CN: The whole idea of paying attention to the culture and political situation to see what theology needs to be addressing.

WW: Yeah. I think his ways of pointing out how we engage culture or relate to culture is a lasting contribution.

CN: Are there other things that come to your mind when you think about your years as president?

WW: Well, I suppose the tough one is the ending of that time. There is some pain and ambiguity connected to it. As I had always said, there are different kinds of crisis always threatening a place like Wartburg. There's always the concern that you make sure you have got enough students, that enrollment's going to keep up. And then there are the finances. And if they come one at a time, they usually can be managed. God forbid that they would ever come together. We had never really had that because all the years I was around, we had good enrollment. Some of those years, it was extremely high, in 1976, 218 or something like that. But at the very time we were doing all the work with the Seminary Appeal, we were involved here at Wartburg with making use of Aquinas. It took a year to do our building renovation. It led to the time when we were going to have a deficit.

CN: You used the word "ambiguity" to describe the presidency.

WW: There were good days, happy days, painful days. I always felt that I could bring a lot to the meaning of grace in the community. Being there for people and stuff. I felt good about the years, but sometimes I felt what we should have done most of all was focus on building up the endowment. Endowment was added later. The seminary presidents, Svendsbye and Meuser and myself, made clear that unless we increased the endowments by millions and millions of dollars, it would be a disaster because you have to provide endowments in the future to maintain these buildings.

CN: Buildings always have to be a means to an end, not an end in themselves.

WW: Yeah. In retrospect, what I wished I would have done when the Seminary Appeal was being lined up, was to have said, "We won't build any buildings until we get enough money from the total in-gathering from the Seminary Appeal, until we get income that is big enough to pay for the remodeling we want to do." Then we would have always had a bigger and more adequate endowment.

CN: I think that we all would have been terribly impoverished if you hadn't given your life so fully to Wartburg.

William Weiblen and the Wartburg Seminary Class of 1943 (above
and below left). Preaching at Trinity Lutheran Church in Miller,
South Dakota in 1942 (below right).

With his parents and siblings (ca. 1942; left to right): Don,
Dorothy, Anna (mother), George (father), Rich, Bill, and Paul.

Lieutenant William Weiblen,
Chaplain, U.S. Air Force.

Professor William Weiblen, at his installation in 1960 with Henry Schuh, after returning from his doctoral studies at Erlangen, Germany. As a professor of systematic theology, Bill also served the seminary as its Registrar and helped with Admissions.

President William Weiblen, at his installation on May 10, 1971. Serving until 1984, Bill would see the seminary admit and graduate women to pastoral ministry, expand with the Denver House of Studies, add faculty at the Episcopal Seminary of the Southwest and Austin Presbyterian Seminary (the precursor to today's Lutheran Seminary Program of the Southwest), and go through a major renovation and expansion of the seminary buildings. (Photograph courtesy of Dubuque Telegraph-Herald.)

Wartburg's new president speaks at installation

Wartburg installs William Weiblen as 10th president

Bill and Ilah Weiblen (above), friends since 1939 and married since 1943, together they have raised 3 children. They are still regular participants to chapel services on campus. Seen below (2001) seated in Weiblen Commons, a room at Wartburg Seminary named in their honor.

A proud Weiblen family on the occasion of their 50th Wedding Anniversary, May 30, 1993!

Next to Bill (left side of photograph): Laura Weiblen (granddaughter; front, seated in chair), Jon Olson (grandson; far left on chair) and Faith Trapp (daughter, next to Bill on chair), with Don Trapp (son-in-law; standing).

Next to Ilah (right side of photograph): Barbara Weiblen (daughter-in-law; front, seated in chair), Carolyn Gelpke (daugher; next to Ilah on chair) and Charlie Weiblen (grandson; far right on chair), with Erik Olson (grandson; standing) and Bill Weiblen (son; standing).

Part Three:

Theological Articles and Papers

Introduction to Part Three

The following articles and papers document Dr. Weiblen's engagement with the theological currents of his generation. "Disguised in Simplicity" was first published in the December 3, 1974 issue of *The Lutheran Standard*. The editor invited Bill to address the meaning of Holy Communion, particularly in view of debate around the question of the proper age for admitting children to the table. His testimony to the grace of God in the Eucharist is characteristic of his theology.

The essay, "Black Theology in America as a Question of Christian Existence," was written for the publication of a *Festschrift* in honor of Weiblen's *Doktorvater*, Walter Kuenneth. The original essay was published in German in the volume, *Christsein in einer pluralistischen Gesellschaft* (Hamburg: Friedrich Wittig, 1971, pp. 203-217). Bill offers appreciative comments about the theology of Kuenneth in the earlier chapter of this book where he comments on his time in Erlangen. For his contribution to the *Festschrift*, Bill had been asked to reflect on vital aspects of U.S. theology in the present. One of the new sources that was shaping his teaching of systematic theology at the seminary was the Black Theology of James Cone. This essay was one of the earliest commentaries on the significance of Black Theology published in Germany. It demonstrates how Dr. Weiblen had his finger on the theological pulse of the time. I am grateful to Erik Breddin for an original draft of the essay in English, upon which this translation is based.

The next three pieces derive from Weiblen's service on the Commission on Fellowship between the Lutheran Church—Missouri Synod and The American Lutheran Church in the 1970s. The two church bodies had only recently agreed to enter into pulpit and altar fellowship in 1968. However, the election of new leadership in the Missouri Synod together with the A.L.C. decision to begin ordaining women in 1971 placed this agreement in serious jeopardy. These papers, presented at meetings of the Commission over the decade of the 70s, document the state of the discussion during this time of turmoil in the Missouri Synod. Of particular interest is Weiblen's insight into matters of biblical and confessional hermeneutics.

In September 1989 Wartburg Theological Seminary celebrated the 100th anniversary of its return to the city of Dubuque. This year also marked the 120th anniversary of the birth of J. Michael Reu. Weiblen prepared the essay, "J. Michael Reu—A Self-Made Theologian," first as spoken remarks and then for publication in *Currents in Theology and Mission* (volume 16: 341-345). It offers a wonderful interpretation of the contribution of Dr. Reu to the history of the seminary and the church.

In both Part Three and Part Four of this book, the decision was made, in consultation with Dr. Weiblen, to incorporate inclusive language into the text. This is fully consistent with his commitment to a theology that continues to adapt to new circumstances and challenges.

Disguised in Simplicity:

The Lord' Supper is an Ordinary Meal with Extraordinary Meaning for People on their Way to the Future

The Lutheran Standard
December 3, 1974, Vol. 14, No. 23

Celebration of the Lord's Supper has always been at the center of worship life of the people of God.

Sometimes its importance has been stressed by the practice of such frequent celebration that Communion has tended to become a magical act. At other times the holy significance of the Sacrament of the Altar has been expressed by an attitude of such awe and reverence that people have felt they should receive Communion only on rare occasions.

But God's people always have understood one thing about partaking of the Lord's Supper. They have realized God continues to come to meet people in a real and forceful way. This seems to be true from the earliest times, when Christians first began to celebrate the new life they had found in Christ.

In Baptism God claims the individual and recovers each one as "lost" property, so to speak. God removes the barriers that keep the sinner separate. Likewise in Holy Communion, the believer hears the blessed promise that God belongs together with God's people.

The central act of worship

No wonder, then, the Eucharist has become the central act of Christian worship. God through God's Son, Jesus Christ, serves as our host at this table and declares we have been made God's children and are called to be God's people. "This is my blood of the covenant, which is poured out for many for the forgiveness of sins" (Matt. 26:28). As Luther emphasizes in the Catechism, "Where there is forgiveness of sin, there is life and salvation."

The fact our Lord invites us to come to him brings us the needed assurance that God is truly present with us in all of life. That is why our church has always emphasized the point that we receive the real body and blood of Christ with the bread and wine.

Celebration of the Lord's Supper is a declaration of our conviction that God deals with us through what we call "Word and Sacrament." We believe God uses means to come to us. God comes to us where we are in this world, in our own bodily lives, in our own specific times and places. We do not have to look for some high-powered "spiritual" withdrawal from this world in order to receive the grace of God.

We confess that God comes to us rather than that we have to seek after God. So the Lord's Supper shows us how God and human beings belong together and reminds us God has taken the initiative. God has acted decisively in Christ to restore us back into a life-giving relationship.

Leading to discipleship
The Lord's Supper is also a commission to discipleship and service. Sometimes we have tended to forget the close relationship of Holy Communion to Baptism.

Without Baptism, the Lord's Supper would be meaningless. And without the Lord's Supper, Baptism would have no place. When our Lord sent the apostles to make disciples of all the world and to baptize people in the name of the Father, Son, and Holy Spirit, he declared his intention to recover all people for the God who created them out of love and destined them for intimate fellowship.

Our Lord also declared that the people of God were to become instruments of God's desire to bring others into a living relationship. Many people have made the point in our day that Baptism is our commission to be servants. We are to be servants of our Lord to bring the Gospel to all the world.

Baptism, then, is the commission of every Christian to be a minister of the Gospel. The regular celebration of the Lord's Supper is a renewal of God's call to us to be God's people. It also enables us to respond that we want to be God's servants and that we want to follow Christ as his disciple.

Understanding sacrifice.
The Lord's Supper therefore is the event in which Christians may come to a Gospel-oriented understanding of sacrifice. Probably this view was distorted when the Lord's Supper was turned into a sacrifice Christian people thought they offered to God through their priest. Making the Sacrament of the Alter a sacrifice for our sins instead of the communication of forgiveness has created many difficulties.

When we come together to receive the body and blood of Christ, it is important that we remember not only that Christ completed the perfect sacrifice for us, but also that we sacrifice ourselves to live sacrificially for others.

Just as Jesus was the man for others, so we are promised that in some small, broken way we can live not only for ourselves. But by the power of the Spirit we can live for others and experience the true meaning of thanksgiving to God through our lives. "I appeal to you therefore, brothers and sisters, by the mercies of God, to present your bodies as a living sacrifice, holy and acceptable to God, which is your spiritual worship" (Rom. 12:1).

Our Lord's sacrifice removed the guilt of our sins and granted us forgiveness once for all. He now brings into being the community of forgiven sinners – the church. The Lord's Supper is a continuing affirmation of the church as a community of faith, hope, and love created by God's power.

Community of the forgiven

There is a tendency to turn the church into a "society of the good people." When we think of the church in that way, we lose sight of the saving fact that the church is the fellowship in which sinners can be together with each and above all with God, and know that they belong together. To this extent we ought constantly to seek forms and expressions of worship in the Lord's Supper which highlight the church as the community of forgiven sinners.

The Lord's Supper also is the event in which God invites us to hear in a unique way the unbelievable news that the future of our own personal lives and the future of the world are both in the hands of God. Each time we celebrate Holy Communion, God repeats the unconditional promise that Christ will come again and bring everything to fulfillment.

As Paul tells us, "As often as you eat this bread and drink the cup, you proclaim the Lord's death until he comes" (1 Cor. 11:26). The Lord's Supper therefore looks backward, looks to the present, but above all, looks to the future. "Blessed be the God and Father of our Lord Jesus Christ. By God's great mercy we have been born anew to living hope" (1 Peter 1:3).

Christ, our gracious host, comes in Holy Communion to give us courage to accept the present world in which we live, knowing this is not the final conclusion to either the events of history or our lives. The Lord's Supper is a statement to each one of us that we can live with confidence, even in the midst of sickness and death.

Shaped by the future

Our lives, in the final analysis, are shaped by the future God has prepared for us in Jesus Christ. We know that the future is one which has been recreated by the resurrection. It is a future in which the boundary of death in this existence has been breached by the ultimate victory of life eternal!

Through this gift of life we receive strength to fight all the forces of evil in our world today. The Lord's Supper is the amazing means of grace through which we are refreshed to struggle against death and destruction and to affirm the powers of liberation, life, and love in God.

Indeed, the Lord's Supper is a simple meal. But disguised in its simplicity is the power and presence of our Lord for us.

Black Theology in America:
Christian Existence in Question

First published as
"Black Theology in Amerika als Frage an die Christliche Existenz,"
pp. 203-217 in *Christsein in einer pluralistischen Gesellschaft,*
Edited by Hans Schultz and Hans Schwarz.
Hamburg: Friedrich Wittig Verlag, 1971.

In a pluralistic society, life is regulated through differing political ideologies, economic philosophies, pedagogical concepts and religious experiences. The necessity of diverse, coexisting religious convictions is generally taken for granted.

The attitude required for religious coexistence raises a basic question for the Christian self-understanding: to what extent can a Christian community adopt the unique claim of the Christian faith, the radically different claim and position taken relating to lifestyle and thought? Naturally, this is not a new question. In every generation the Christian community has in its own way dealt with and discussed this question. Categories such as apologetics, the relationship between Christianity and culture, the two kingdoms, the sacred and secular have always played an important role in the problematic of Christian theology. Lastly, the question regarding the understanding of the gospel itself has always been present, and is not based solely on the methodological question of how the gospel should be interpreted.

Today the question regarding coexistence within the Christian community itself has become acute. One part of the problem is the question of how one can remain true to the gospel of Jesus Christ in the face of the multiplicity of theological opinions that have developed within each community's own confession. The battle between those who hold to the traditional confessional understandings of the church and those who feel that a more timely and context specific understanding is necessary only leads to an intensification of the problem. The increasing tension between those who claim a specific location for the relevance of Christianity and those who are convinced that being a Christian consists in a personal piety and in a true exercise of ecclesial practices reveals the tragic possibility of not paying attention to the problem.

Moreover, the point of intersection of these tragic, demonic, and promising possibilities, all of which involve the problem of pluralism, is located, at least in America, in the racial problem. It is the question of race, with its significance for true Christian tolerance, that has emerged during the 1970s in America. In the Christian community, this problem has presented itself through black theology.[1]

This essay presents a short discussion of the basic theological principles of black theology and thereby a brief report on the possibilities for the Christian faith in a pluralistic society. The complicated sociological and historical contexts out of which this theology emerges cannot be adequately dealt with in such a short paper. The result will therefore be provisional and fragmentary. In addition, black theology is in the beginning stages of its theological self understanding and the form it will eventually take is unknown. Nevertheless an unmistakable 'newness' in its current development must be taken seriously. It is to this 'newness' that we will turn our attention.

The term 'black theology' has come to the forefront of theological consideration through a statement of the National Council of Black Churchmen from June 1969 and in the epoch making book, *Black Theology & Black Power*, by James H. Cone, Professor of theology at Union Theological Seminary in New York.[2] It should be made clear in a wider sense that black theology has deep roots in the black preachers of the pre-civil war era. Without the representative statement of freedom for blacks which Dr. Martin Luther King presented, it would have never come to historical realization. King himself supposedly never used the term black theology. Based on his dislike of the slogan, black power, he would most probably not be approving of its present day glorification. Nevertheless, King had to a large degree promoted the message of liberation, awakened self-confidence, and risked the daring path of change; these are the heartbeat of black theology. In terms that honor the uniqueness of each, one could say that in Martin Luther King the soul of this theology came into being, whereas a theology such as that of James Cone describes its form and interprets its meaning.[3]

There are people who react strongly to the terminology and insist that Christian theology can be neither black nor white. This opinion is related to the idea that being true to the gospel means the decisive and categorical rejection of every interpretation that is inclined to use the gospel to reach its own goals, regardless of how noble those goals may be. Thus an acknowledgement of black theology is finally a denial of the gospel itself. Even when one agrees that these attempts agree with the liberating nature of the gospel and are not an intentionally violent, nationalistic interpretation of the gospel, such as the "Deutsche Christen" of the 1930s, those who hold this opinion would point out that the Christian message must have precedence over the historical situation into which it is being applied. (I wish at this point to emphasize that my teacher, Professor Walter Künneth, was one of the perspicacious and bravest interpreters of the gospel during the difficult times of the 1930s. Künneth daringly exposed the German Christian interpretation of the gospel and resisted its

---

[1] Black Theology; A Statement of the National Committee of Black Churchmen; Prepared by the Committee on Theological Prospectus; presented on June 13, 1969 at the Interdenominational Theological Center, Atlanta Georgia, printed in *The Christian Century*, October 15, 1969, p. 1310. Also see the commentary to this statement from Preston N. Williams, chairman of this committee, in the same edition of the publication, pp. 1311f.
[2] James H. Cone. *Black Theology & Black Power*. (New York: Seabury Press, 1969).
[3] See especially chapter 2 in Martin Luther King's *Where Do We Go From Here?: Chaos or Community*, (New York: Bantam Book, 1968).

153

temptation.)[4] Nevertheless, would it be consistent with a carefully considered description of Christian theological existence to simply dismiss it? Even when one regrets the basic formula, that a particular historical experience can never be allowed to function as the authoritative norm for theological deliberation, it appears that such a rejection of black theology has never really grasped or understood what it means.

While it is not possible to fully bring the uninitiated reader to a proper understanding of the issues, at the very least an attempt should be made to give a non-partisan overview, and that is based on the conviction that particular historical occurrences must be understood historically before theological verdict can be made.

In a statement of the National Committee of Black Churchmen, the question, "Why black theology?," was answered in a paragraph that traces the development of black reality back to the oppression of the black slave: "Black theology already existed in the spirituals and slave songs and the admonitions of the slave preachers and their followers." In light of these facts we must say that the *kairos* of black theology has come from the popularity of the term black power.

All non-black theologians are called therefore to face the challenge of the present historical manifestation that is contained in the expression, black power.[5] Advocates of black theology call this the most important development in American life in the 20th century. Blacks understand black power as a healthy, long missing, humanizing power through which oppressed black victims can affirm their own black identity. From their own black resources they can strengthen their own power and thereby overcome the oppression of a white racist society. As James H. Cone states, "Black power is the black man's seeking justice on the basis of his own initiative, using the method necessary for his situation and employing his own timetable....Black power, in short, is an *attitude*, an inward affirmation of the essential worth of blackness."[6]

In fact, this term has developed a positive use since it was first used by Stokely Carmichael in 1966. Martin Luther King raised basic objections against it at an important meeting of the black civil rights leaders in June 1966, after which James Meredith was shot, during the freedom march from Memphis to Mississippi.[7] King felt that this term, regardless of its many positive aspects, was to a certain degree nihilistic, and missed its purpose. However, especially since King's assassination, the term has become among blacks a general expression of the way in which the blacks think of themselves and the strongest symbol through which the political social struggle for justice can arrive at success.[8] In order to

---

[4] Walter Künneth's reflective analysis of the interaction between Christian faith and National Socialism, *Der große Abfall* (Hamburg: Friedrich Wittig, 1947), is still recommended as a clear analysis of the situation of that time.

[5] "Black Theology," *The Christian Century*, 1310.

[6] Cone, *Black Theology and Black Power*, 8.

[7] Martin Luther King, *Where Do We Go From Here?*, 27ff.

[8] For a short overview of the history and meaning of the term 'Black Power', see C. Freeman Sleeper's *Black Power and Christian Responsibility* (Nashville: Abingdon Press, 1969), especially 24-52. It may also be helpful to see the "Black Manifesto" to the White Christian Churches and the Jewish Synagogues in the United States of America and all other Racial Institutions, presented by James Forman and adopted by the National Black

arrive at only a general and initial understanding of the soul of black theology, it is thus necessary to grasp the religious and revolutionary enthusiasm which is connected to the expression black power. Within this expression is concentrated 300 years of oppression and poverty that the blacks have suffered under the whites. The term is basically an expression of the newly discovered confidence, which is grounded in God, of how blacks are convinced they are standing on the side of truth and are being driven by the hope of their own dignity.

We will consider black theology from the perspective that James Cone clearly represents. Cone is convinced that "[c]ontemporary theology from Karl Barth to Jürgen Moltmann conceives of the theological task as one which speaks from within the covenant community with the sole purpose of making the gospel meaningful to the times in which men live." [9] Cone therefore is concerned to bring together black power and Christian theology and to see the unchangeable gospel of Jesus Christ in light of black power. He recognizes that there is "a desperate need for a *black theology*...whose sole purpose is to apply the freeing power of the gospel to black people under white oppression." [10] Cone, believing that even black theologians usually have considered the problem from the white point-of-view, provides an interpretation of the Christian message which has the sole purpose of freeing the gospel from its 'whiteness' and thus bringing blacks into a situation where in Christ they can rightly affirm themselves. [11]

Beginning with these basic presuppositions, Cone gives some readers the impression that he believes that God is black, following Maulana Ron Karenga, who said, "The fact that I am black is my ultimate reality." [12] This impulse awakens the passion of black theology both in the face of its own historical reality as well as in the face of the unchangeableness of the gospel. Cone is far from denying the universal character of this ultimate reality. He appears to pose the basic question whether blacks must deny their identity in order to be able to accept Christian faith. [13]

Black theology is a concrete expression of the basic problem that Christian theology has wrestled with during its entire history: What is the relationship between the Christian faith and culture? Does it come down to a choice: either the gospel or the world?

The recently emerging movement, 'No Other Gospel', has urgently brought the attention of parishioners and theologians to this question. It is in fact true that from the earliest times, as the statements from early para-Christian Gnostic groups show, that the content of Christianity can be lost when the all consuming concern and motive is to bring Christianity into agreement with the basic statements of foreign ideologies and philosophies. Is there a similar danger in the desire to write a black theology?

Whenever one does theology, there is always this danger. However, perhaps the danger is even greater on the other side when, in the name of staying true to the Christian message,

---

Economic Conference in Detroit, Michigan on April 26, 1969. Also Charles E. Fager, *White Reflections on Black Power* (Grand Rapids: Eerdmans, 1967).
[9] Cone, *Black Theology and Black Power*, 31.
[10] Cone, 31.
[11] Cf. Cone, 31f.
[12] Quoted by Cone, 32.
[13] Cf. Cone, 33.

they go no further than a revelational positivism which proclaims no gospel, but only recite ancient ideologies using pious phrases and correct sounding dogmatic formulations.

To what extent a theological expression brings the Christian message into correlation with the human situation depends on the historical context in which the particular ideas of gospel and the human situation are located. Thus the method of correlation, developed by Paul Tillich, appears to be as effective as any other method in insuring the integration of the gospel with the situation in which the gospel speaks. The key expression according to Tillich's view is 'mutual dependency'. It is never only an either/or, a both/and, or a new synthesis. It is the realization that theology cannot take place in a vacuum, but that it occurs in a special situation. It is an awareness that the uniqueness of the gospel must be retained and that the gospel, understood theologically, determines the personal standpoint within the human situation. Cone appears to advocate this when he emphasizes the necessity of a black theology. This tendency is strengthened in that Cone begins his theological treatise with the biblical view of Jesus of Nazareth. He desires his black theology to be Christ centered. He presents Schleiermacher, Barth and Pannenberg as advocates of his thesis, that Christ is the core of Christian faith. As evidence that the Christian faith begins and ends with the human Jesus—with his life, his death and his resurrection—Cone stresses the decisive point that Jesus' message is essentially one of liberation, and that, "In Christ, God enters human affairs and take sides with the oppressed."[14]

After Cone has unequivocally given evidence that the concrete historical work of God is based in Jesus as the Christ, he deals with the correlation of this message to black power. It appears to me that one must grasp this point if one wishes to correctly understand Cone's claim: "Christianity is not alien to Black Power; it is a Black Power."[15] "...Black power is the spirit of Christ himself in the black-white dialogue which makes possible the emancipation of blacks from self hatred and frees whites from their racism....The gospel of Christ is consistent with Black Power and the freedom Christ brings."[16]

Black power, as a living symbol of the situation of blacks, provides the frame for the answer of the gospel, which is made clear in black theology. One should, however, not forget that for advocates of black power, like Cone, the liberating gospel determines not only the answer of black Christians to the gospel but also has much to do with the ways and means that the problem and questions are themselves formed. In other words, the creative power of the great joy in Christ not only permits but demands that black theology display its own integrity. The call goes out to the non-blacks, the ones listening to what is said and to those in repentence and faith, not just as one more voice to be answered in a pluralistic society but perhaps as *the* voice in which God in Christ can most clearly be heard today.

Now, what is the primary claim of black theology, if one acknowledges its claim to authority? The first and most important claim is the proclamation that Christ is the liberator and that the liberating presence of Christ can be seen in the world in no clearer way than in the battle of the blacks for freedom. "Black theology is based on the concept that Christ's current fight for the black, also frees the white oppressor, in that it forces the white to refer to blacks as a 'you' not an 'it'."[17] Christ gives the oppressed courage to dialogue with the

---

[14] Cone, 36.
[15] Cone, 38.
[16] Cone, 62ff.
[17] Cone, 62.

oppressor, in spite of the possibility of pain. In this time of dialogue blacks are not only able to grasp their own self-identity but whites are also brought to recognize the 'un-Christianness' of racism, out of which whites have operated and demonically enslaved blacks who have lived under the power and control of the white thumb. In other words, Christ's liberating presence, the power of God in the world today, means *freedom now*.

So that no error in understanding occurs, Cone explains that no teaching is acceptable that contradicts the claim of blacks for freedom. Black theology must say, "If the doctrine is compatible with or enhances the drive for black freedom, then it is the gospel of Jesus Christ. If the doctrine is against or indifferent to the essence as expressed in Black Power, then it is the work of the Antichrist."[18]

We have firmly established that the departure point for black theology is the proclamation of the liberating power of Christ and have identified this power to be currently manifest as black power. The meaning of this theological formulation for blacks is enlightening: the acknowledgement of their own blackness, respect for their own identity, the courage for a victorious life to overcome oppression, and motivation to risk suffering in the revolutionary power of Christ for the liberation of humanity. All of these are aspects of the justifying and merciful actions of God in Jesus Christ. When one observes the modern black, especially the young student generation, one cannot help but admire their optimistic hunger for life which they have received as a gift for participating in the liberating presence of Christ though black power. If one overlooks some of the exaggerated revolutionary rhetoric of these young blacks, one must be convinced that their new self-understanding and way of life are valid and astonishingly exciting.

It is exactly in the difference, between black theology's interpretation of the gospel as blacks perceive it and the way it affects the non-black and whites, that we must accordingly question the adequacy of such a theology in a pluralistic society. Should not black theology as the bearer of a liberating, empowering message of the gospel also be viable for white, racist America if it is a valid expression of the Christian message? Does not the gospel itself judge inadequate every expression of theology that does not proclaim the all encompassing justice of the merciful God in Christ? These are questions with which one must in all seriousness and honesty deal. At the very least, the first impression that one gains from a study of black theology is that the solitary message that it has for whites is that they are racist and oppressors and that in their theology, especially in the church, they have distorted the message of Jesus into one of self-justification for whites.

Cone's point in unmasking the sins of the white church and the failure of American theology is to show that they supported the oppression of blacks. A comparison can even be made between the situation during the Third Reich in the church in Germany and the situation in white American churches, brought on by the failure of American theology, in order to show the true extent of the revolutionary implications of the gospel.[19] Cone, who appears to have no message of forgiveness, righteousness and liberation for the non-white, ends this section with the statement that the only valid theological assertion is one that makes clear that "black revolution is the work of Christ."

---

[18] Cone, 121.
[19] Cone, 82. The following quote is on 89.

It is on this point that white parishioners and theologians usually pose their questions to the defenders of black theology: "How much of your theology is merely rhetoric, and to what degree do you believe it yourself?" "We understand that you must exaggerate your position so that you might be heard, but please tell us what is the common ground for whites and blacks on which theology may move forward?" Questions such as these demonstrate the degree to which we have fallen into complacency. Even the manner of the questions betrays our satisfaction with our self-understanding and, moreover, our disinclination to hear a prophetic voice when it arises in our midst. Such questions have the tendency to condemn black theology as being unChristian because it has no message of liberation for the non-black.

However, the problem that we non-black American Christians seem to have forgotten is that the gospel of freedom in Christ must come to us in an authentic and real way, in the same way the word of freedom has come to blacks. The gospel can only come to us as good news when we realize our own mistaken position. The message of black theology for white American Christians is a word that unmasks their white situation. The message of the gospel as 'freedom now' is received by blacks and whites differently in the black-white struggle.

Whoever has grown up within the Lutheran tradition of law and gospel should be able to understand this easily. To proclaim the word of God according to the law-gospel method means that what is law to you may be a joyful message for another; and what for one is gospel may be law for another. The effect of the one and same word of God depends on the situation into which it is directed. The result of the word in the case of black theology is that it is a liberating message for blacks, just as it is a message of exposure and burden for the other. Should we expect anything else? The word of God occurs as a specific message for a specific need. In black theology the word of God is a message of freedom for blacks and a message of judgment for whites. The word of judgment will reach its climax as a forgiving and freeing message when it is heard so as to bring repentance and faith. In other words, the white theological analysis of black theology should direct its attention to the meaning of repentance for the context of the fundamentally racist attitude of whites, before it attempts to serve as judge over the adequacy of black theology as an expression of the Christian message. If this position becomes the starting point for the criterion of black theology, the question should be asked about its consistency with evangelical theology.

Evangelical theology has always stressed the importance of repentance in understanding the relationship of God in Christ to humans. Thus it is noteworthy that we have said nothing regarding the nature of repentance up to now. If repentance, including recognition, confession and contrition, are all parts of the process in which the Holy Spirit leads us into a personal faith relationship with God, why then is such repentance not necessary in reference to our theological formulations? Such a concession at this time could help theology in the 70s to come to grips with the proposals of black theology. If the theologians who belong to churches were to make a unified statement of the inadequacy of their theological statements, they would soon be in a position of listening to the message of Christ's presence that can also occur in the formulations of black theology.

If the starting point of black theology is the condition of blacks and the proclamation of their liberation through Christ, here are some fundamental perspectives of this theology:

1)   Black theology takes the suffering and humiliation in the lives of blacks seriously and takes up the task of analyzing the condition of

blacks "in the light of God's revelation in Jesus Christ with the purpose of creating a new understanding of black dignity among black people, and providing the necessary soul in that people, to destroy white racism."[20]

2) Black theology attempts to free the discussion over religious authority from the calm academic quarters of theologians (regardless if they are fundamentalist, liberal, neo-orthodox or another), and puts in the central place a discussion regarding the world, particularly the black world. It makes the experience of the oppressed blacks the highest authority, for it is through their oppression that blacks have come to a special knowledge of Christ. Therefore, the teachings of God, humanity, Christ or the Scriptures will only be declared valid if they are in agreement with black freedom or further its cause. "[A]ll Christian doctrines must be interpreted in such a manner that they unreservedly say something to black people who are living under unbearable oppression."[21]

3) Black theology reorients eschatology from the beyond to the now. "It is not concerned with the 'last things' but with the 'white thing'....The appeal to the next life is a lack of hope....It refuses to accept any concept of God which makes black suffering the will of God....Black theology refuses to embrace an interpretation of eschatology which would divert attention from injustice now."

4) Black theology encourages a new value system which is influenced by the spirit of black self-determination and brings blacks to a sense of awareness. In this Cone quotes Nietzsche, "There was only *one* Christian, and he died on the cross."[22] Thereby he makes reference to Malcolm Boyd on the underground church, moving toward an entirely new method of Christian existence in which blacks break forth from non-being into being, and affirm black self-identity.

Black theology finds an almost ready-to-use, pre-existing foundational principle for the attainment of its goal in the currently popular theology of revolution. As one could expect, Cone quotes Moltmann more often than any other contemporary theologian. The author of black theology walks the same path as Moltmann, who expresses more frequently than any other contemporary theologian, that "[p]eace with God means conflict with the world" and that hope is senseless when it "does not change the thought action of men."[23] He concludes his exposition with a moving chapter about "Revolution, Violence, and Reconciliation in Black Theology".[24] Here he makes a blunt observation: "The debate is over. There will be no more meetings between liberal religious whites and middle-class Negros to discuss the status of race relations in their communities. Black Theology believes that the problem of racism will not be solved through talk but through *action*. Therefore, its task is to carve out a revolutionary theology based on relevant involvement in the world of racism."[25] Simply said, black theology is a theology of revolution.

---

[20] Cone, 117.
[21] For this quote and the following, see Cone, 121-127.
[22] Cone, 128.
[23] Cone, 102.
[24] Cone, 135-152.
[25] Cone, 135.

The true meaning of revolution cannot be allowed to be equated with mere protest. For black theology revolution means a radical encounter with the structure of white racism, with the intention of destroying its menacing power. Simultaneously, the absolute rule of God over creation is emphasized. Convinced that the argued case rests on a solid biblical framework, the advocacy of revolution closes with the statement, that "the Christian...is obligated by a freedom grounded in the Creator to break all laws which contradict human dignity."[26] That means, in the words of Camilo Torres, "Revolutionary action is a Christian, a priestly struggle."[27]

At first glance this appears to be in opposition to the position represented in Walter Künneth's well-known work, *Politik zwischen Dämon und Gott*, (Politics between Demon and God) in which he states: "The Christian as solitary citizen as well as the Christian community, even as subjects to an 'unjust state' (as occurs in a totalitarian state), are summoned not to active opposition but to patience and prayer."[28] In reality, however, Künneth and black theology appear to be in agreement on the basics. Künneth adds the following explanation: "In concrete circumstances in which the authority's dealings go against God's command, the individual Christian must obey 'God more' than humans and be prepared for suffering disobedience."[29]

This appears to be precisely the context in which black theology is based. It is the situation in which humans are being oppressed by other humans. This characterizes the unique context of blacks in the 1970s of the 20th century in America, from which this theology has originated. It is this historical context in which we exist by which the worth of black theology is to be judged, and especially its revolutionary character must be evaluated. We do not presume to make any judgment concerning the political tactics and legitimacy of revolutionary black power movements such as the Black Panthers. We only seek to emphasize that the basic theological principles that black theology make for revolution are nourished by the biblical conviction that the highest calling of every disciple of Christ is faithfulness to God, and not to the maintenance of an alleged Christianized status quo of law and order.

What black theology has to say concerning violence should also be evaluated within this context. "In dealing with the question of violence and black people, Black Theology does not begin by assuming that this question can be answered merely by looking at the Western distinction between right and wrong. It begins by looking at the *face* of black America in the light of Jesus Christ."[30]

In this light, the problem of violence has a totally other appearance. From the perspective of black theology in America, it is not a question of violence or non-violence, of evil or good. It is much more a choice between the lesser of two evils. It means that it is the responsibility of the followers of Jesus in the 70s to explore: "What is Jesus doing?" and "Where is Jesus today at work?" rather than asking, "What would Jesus do in this

---

[26] Cone, 137.
[27] Quoted by Cone, 137.
[28] Walter Künneth, *Politik zwischen Dämon und Gott* (Berlin: Lutherisches Verlagshaus, 1954), 316.
[29] Künneth, 316.
[30] Cone, 141.

situation?" To recognize the presence of Christ in human affairs today means that there are no absolute rules by which a person can discern an answer whether or not one should join in revolutionary violence or participate in nonviolence; whether one should tolerate the violence a structural system seeks to perpetuate.[31] The answer can only be found in surrender to God and thereby in the freedom which God gives to humans through Christ.

This appears to agree with what Künneth says concerning the limits of obedience.[32] Künneth's three-fold limit regarding obedience consists of an uncompromising and complete loyalty to God alone. That is exactly what the proponents of black theology say. The difference between the limits of civil obedience, which Künneth presents, and those that are defended by black theology is enormous. However, the basic starting point of ultimate loyalty in both positions appears to be the same. So we have now reached the critical point in our reflection of the Christian faith in a pluralistic society. The basic question with which our reflection began appears once more in a penetrating way. There is a point at which assimilation and tolerance in a pluralistic society must cease for Christians. That is the point at which the basic affirmation of God in Christ is denied. Black theology summons the conscience of those who call themselves Christian to accountability. We are forcefully reminded that we cannot deny to our black brothers and sisters the human dignity which God provided in creation and for which God has freed them in Christ. In the last section from *Black Theology & Black Power*, Cone asks the question about the Christian concept of reconciliation. Reconciliation is indeed the sovereign and exclusive work of God through which God in Jesus Christ became human so that humanity might be saved.[33] What 'wholeness' for the blacks in America means is obviously not an easily manufactured harmony between whites and blacks in the sense of 'white values'; instead it means a radical self-affirmation for blacks and a radical change of understanding for whites. The radical change of understanding for whites is the recognition that one cannot have God without "being black." One cannot have "Christ without obedience, love without death....Whiteness, as revealed in the history of America, is the expression of what is wrong with man."[34]

Many would label this as 'black' arrogance and 'black' pride. However, when one looks at it from the correct perspective, one recognizes that, "Being black in America has very little to do with skin color. To be black means that your heart, your soul, your mind, and your body are where the dispossessed are."[35] One recognizes, when one truly listens to the message of black theology, that this message calls non-blacks to repentance, to recognize that we have turned our Christian self-affirmation into a self-serving, self-preserving, self-justifying understanding of ourselves. The message brought by this theology forces us to find our identity in God's faithfulness to *all* people and to gain a new understanding of our black brothers and sisters whom we all have so gravely wronged.

Black theology shows us the decisive problem of the uniqueness of the gospel in a pluralistic society with reference to the American situation. We believe that some of the new paths that have been opened to us are also of significance to the German reader. We believe it could be of service not only in relationship to the question of faithfulness to the

---

[31] Cf. Cone, 143.
[32] Cf. Künneth, 385ff.
[33] Cf. Cone, 148.
[34] Cone, 150.
[35] Cone, 151.

gospel of Jesus Christ, which arose from black theology at every point in this essay, but also as the center of Walter Künneth's productive lifelong theological work.

Reflections on
the Theological Basis
for Church Fellowship

Presented at the Meeting of the Commission on Fellowship,
Lutheran Church—Missouri Synod/
The American Lutheran Church
February 24 and 25, 1972

Ever since the Council of Constantinople in 381, Christians in every age and from every part of the globe have affirmed their conviction that the church of Jesus Christ is one. Both of our churches, in the acceptance of the ancient ecumenical creeds of Christendom, affirm this fundamental unity of the church. We believe in one holy catholic and apostolic church. Through affirmations of faith like the one in our common creeds, we attempt to give expression to the fact that the basic unity of the church rests in God's own integrity and in the unqualified grace which God has shown to humanity in sending the Son, Jesus Christ, to reconcile us with God and bring us into the reality of the people of God. The confession of faith in which we affirm our basic unity in spite of our alienation and separation from one another, is primarily an affirmation of God's faithfulness to us. It is not essentially a proclamation of our unquestioned faithfulness to God. The unity of the church is greater than the divisions which human beings maintain within the church. It is in this context that churches like ours (LCMS and ALC) concerned with church fellowship drew near to each other, negotiated with each other, and under God's blessing and grace, established fellowship with one another.

The process which preceded the establishment of fellowship brought together commissioners of the LCMS and ALC. They were given the task of writing several essays to demonstrate the fundamental agreement, existing between their churches in their understanding of the gospel. The documents which this Commission produced and which our churches discussed individually and together demonstrated this unity. The statements on "What Commitment to the 'Sola Gratia' of the Lutheran Confession Involves," "The Lutheran Confessions and 'Sola Scriptura'," and "The Doctrine of the Church in the Lutheran Confessions," concluded with a joint statement by the members of the Commission which said,

> The members of the Committee are unanimous in asserting that where Lutheran bodies have been granted and have discovered a consensus in the preaching of the Gospel in conformity with "a pure understanding of it," and in the administration of the sacraments, "in accordance with the Divine Word (AC VII), they not only may, but should enter into pulpit and altar fellowship."

163

This statement expresses the same basic thought of the Augsburg Confession, namely, that basic agreement in the gospel is the essential matter in establishing fellowship between churches. Subsequent synodical resolutions of the LCMS and ALC stressed the point that there was indeed agreement on what the basis of fellowship should be. In establishing pulpit and altar fellowship at its convention in Denver, Colorado, the LCMS concluded by saying:

> We, the members of the Lutheran Church–Missouri Synod, rejoice over the existing unity of faith and confession, as stated in the doctrinal position of The American Lutheran Church and The Lutheran Church–Missouri Synod, and we embrace the opportunities and assume the obligations of altar and pulpit fellowship. Recognizing that because of our sinfulness and human frailties there remain imperfections in faith and understanding of the riches of God's grace, as well as failing in life and practice consistent with the Gospel, we pledge ourselves to draw these and all other problems affecting our relationships into the perspective of God's grace as revealed in the divine Word and deal with them within that framework. We pledge ourselves always to have a tender regard for each others' consciences and to stand by each other in mutual sympathy and understanding, forbearance and love. As members of The Lutheran Church—Missouri Synod, committed to the Holy Gospel, we obligate ourselves to continued study and discussion, always remembering that we, in the love of Christ, must bear one another's burdens and so fulfill the law of Christ. (Gal. 6:62).

The American Lutheran Church expressed itself similarly when it affirmed at Omaha, Nebraska, October, 1968, that point of view about church fellowship which it had previously affirmed in the Minneapolis Theses, the United Testimony, and the resolution on fellowship of its Constituting Convention in 1960.

From these facts and sequence of events it is evident that there was a common understanding about the basis of fellowship,

If we are asked to elaborate some of the implications of our (ALC) concentration on the gospel, the following are some of the points that should be considered:

1. Fellowship between churches is primarily a gift of God. Pulpit and altar fellowship is created by the working of God's Spirit in the midst of God's people. When the people of God allow the Spirit to move in their midst, we have the conviction, that God will lead to an understanding and awareness of divine grace that will enable God's people to extend genuine fellowship to each other.

2. Churches who embrace the same fundamental understanding of the gospel by their common confessions of faith, yet who are not in pulpit and altar fellowship with each other, would be hard put to justify their separations. The LCMS and ALC found compelling reasons on basis of their understanding of the gospel to establish pulpit and altar fellowship.

3. Members of the ALC Commission and the ALC are genuinely convinced that the Confessions of the Lutheran Church provide a significant and comprehensive confessional expression of the unity which our church shares with the LCMS in the gospel of Jesus Christ.

4. We (ALC) affirm without equivocation that the Holy Scriptures are a completely reliable means, together with the sacraments, through which the Holy Spirit evokes and maintains faith in Jesus Christ as Lord and Savior. It is in this faith that the people who comprise the membership of our two churches, with their common roots as the people of God, who, therefore, were led to acknowledge each other in pulpit and altar fellowship. The Bishop of The American Lutheran Church, Dr. Kent S. Knutson, expressed this poignantly in his address to the Convention of the Lutheran Church–Missouri Synod in Milwaukee and it is reaffirmed in the statement from the Church Council in October, 1971.

5. We believe that the good news about God's saving grace in Jesus Christ elicits this kind of response of faith in which members of churches with common confessions accept each other with integrity even when there are certain divergences and variations in their theological understanding, ecclesiastical practice, and life. By listening and submitting to the Word of God penitently and expectantly, God's people are able to give highest priority to the meaning of the gospel. In establishing this priority, the way is provided to allow for certain variations of understanding.

6. The Scriptures of the church expressly teach that common agreement on the meaning of the gospel indicates an awareness of both the freedom which the gospel implies, as well as sensitivity to the binding discipline which the gospel rightly expects from those who respond in faith to it.

    If we allow the Holy Spirit to reform and renew the church by the creative power of the gospel, we ought to, in our common understanding of the gospel, find the possibility for affirming both faithfulness to the whole gospel, as well as freedom in the gospel. It is not an "either/or," but a "both/and." In accordance with the whole tenor and direction of the Augsburg Confession, the call of our church today is to a revitalized proclamation and living of the gospel. The emphasis expressed in 1 Corinthians 12:14, 13:3; Galatians 5:1; and Ephesians 4:1-17 point in this direction.

7. Fellowship between churches based upon agreement in the gospel, stressed throughout the Augsburg Confession, is especially enunciated in Articles I and VII. In accordance with this way of thinking, however, it is not consensus that is to be the judge over the church in matters of doctrine, church fellowship and Christian activity. It is, rather, Holy Scripture which is to be the guide and norm for all matters of fellowship.

8. The gospel is the central point of the Scriptures which must guide and direct our common understanding in remaining true to an evangelical exposition of the Old and New Testament Scriptures, as Articles I and V of the Formula of Concord so clearly specify.

165

9. An evangelical interpretation of the Scriptures recognizes that the Scriptures themselves must be interpreted from their center in Jesus Christ. From this perspective, it becomes clear that there is a great deal of diversity within the Scriptural documents themselves. There are many ways that this can be demonstrated. Some examples: a.) The variety of presentation of the life of Jesus in the four gospels; b.) The differences in the theology of Paul and James where the issue on the surface is precisely the gospel of justification by grace alone apart from works; c.) In 1 Corinthians 11:5 we have statement of women prophesying with heads covered and in I Corinthians 14:34 there is the statement that women are not to speak at all.

In conclusion, it seems appropriate to highlight the urgent need there is for the LCMS and ALC to formulate a new and clear statement of the gospel to our contemporary world. While the old structures and forms of life are crumbling around us and all kinds of strange and demonic ideologies, as well as pagan religions, new and old, are seductively seeking to attract the hearts of people everywhere, we dare not come with warmed-over formulations about the meaning of the gospel.

The need of the hour is for all who find their unquestioned loyalty focused in the gospel of Jesus Christ to come forth with statements of the gospel that are faithful to the adequacy of the gospel as the answer to the need of human beings today. In the midst of all the death, destruction, and defeat of people, the gospel must be allowed to shine as the only star and ray of living hope. Let us, as people committed to the gospel, devote all of our theological and confessional energies to an expression of God's saving grace in Christ that will call all people to faith.

Repentance has always been the beginning point of new life in the church. Perhaps the point at which we are most seriously being called to repentance in our ecclesiastical life today, so that this new life of hope in Christ can begin, is precisely at the point of our treasured theological formulations. Just maybe, if we will allow the Holy Spirit to lead us in repentance together at the point of theology, we could arise in forgiveness and renewal with a new direction of hope in Christ for ourselves, our churches, and for our mission to the world.

A Statement
on Confessional Subscription,
Scriptures, Gospel, and Church Fellowship

Presented at the Meeting of the Commission on Fellowship,
Lutheran Church—Missouri Synod/
The American Lutheran Church
St. Louis, Missouri, ca. 1974

1.   We have often stressed the point that fellowship between churches is primarily a gift of God. Pulpit and altar fellowship is created by the working of God's Spirit in the midst of God's people. When the people of God allow the Holy Spirit to move in their midst, we believe that the Holy Spirit will lead to the kind of understanding and awareness of God's grace that will enable God's people to extend genuine fellowship to each other. This we affirm together in our mutual confession of the ecumenical creeds. It means that churches who embrace the same fundamental understanding of the gospel by their common confessions of faith, yet who are not in pulpit and altar fellowship with each other, would be hard put to justify their separations. The LCMS and ALC found compelling reasons on basis of their understanding of the Gospel to establish pulpit and altar fellowship. It is hard for us to come to any other conclusion but that the whole testimony of Scripture, and in turn the Lutheran Confessions, lead us to confess the catholic character of our understanding of the gospel. We confess our unworthiness of such a great gift but in thanksgiving can only accept the generous gift that we believe comes from God, and not in the first instance from our negotiations and writing of doctrinal statements. Confessional subscription means the declaration of this catholic truth: the Lutheran Confessions are a repudiation of sectarianism.

2.   Members of the ALC Commission and the ALC are genuinely convinced that the Confessions of the Lutheran Church provide a significant and comprehensive confessional expression of the unity which our church shares with the LCMS in the gospel of Jesus Christ. We subscribe to the Confessions of the Lutheran Church without equivocation. We believe the Confessions are necessary expressions of who the people of God are.   We believe that the Confessions of the Lutheran Church are binding and are comprehensive expressions of what the Holy Scriptures teach. However, the Scriptures alone are the final and ultimate authority in all matters of faith and life. In our understanding, the Confessions have a significant place, but not the primary place of authority. Confessions have derivative significance.   We believe that because the Confessions of the Church are genuine expositions of the gospel, they have universal significance. In other words, we do not look to our Confessions as a mere catalog or list of our unique doctrines. We subscribe to them

167

because they are an integral expression of what the Gospel is all about. It can not be better stated than as Dr. Reu put it:

> Just as symbols cannot be considered a necessity in the sense that Scriptures are, so they also lack the authority accorded to Scriptures. While the authority accorded to Scriptures is absolute, that accorded to symbols is conditioned and relative. Their authority depends on the measure of their agreement with Scriptures, that only infallible source and norm of all matters pertaining to our salvation. In whatever measure symbols correspond to Scriptures in that same measure, but only in that measure, do they also share their authority. That imposes upon the church the duty to continually study both and thus to assure itself ever anew of such agreement. New generations should not accept as their own the symbols set up by former generations without having themselves gained the joyous assurance that such agreement exists. Especially the prospective ministers and teachers in the church must be faithfully instructed in the Scriptures and the symbols. For when they are asked to assent to them as the *norma docendi* and to pledge themselves to abide by them in the entire conduct of their office, they should be able to do so in all sincerity and for no other reason than they have by personal study been convinced of the perfect agreement between them (and the Scriptures).

3. We believe that creeds and confessions are the result of a historical development within the Church. Confessions of the Church came into being out of a particular situation. All of us recall that our Augsburg Confession developed when accused of heresy, our forebearers were anxious to make a statement to the authorities of the time and show them that they were true to the gospel, and true members of the one, holy, catholic church.

Since Confessions have developed in a particular historic situation and are historical documents they must be understood historically. That does not mean that they are irrelevant or insignificant. We do not believe that they are timeless statements. We do believe that they are statements made at a particular time about a gospel which is always relevant and always contemporary. One of the problems that arises at this point is that in seeking to be confessional Lutherans we can refuse to allow for any growth of experience in understanding the history out of which the Confessions have come, to say nothing of the history in which we live now. Sometimes it is assumed that thoughts and ideas expressed in words or formulas in one period of history remains eternally the same. When we do this we forget the fact that statements themselves want to grow, just as truly as plants and animals want to grow. Growth is simply a sign of life. If the Confessions have a living relationship to the life-giving gospel, then the Confessions will continuously participate in the life and growth of the church's experience down through the years.

4. If we look upon the Confessions historically, then the question immediately arises, "Doesn't that make them relative and subject to our own interpretation more than having lasting significance?" Not so! When we say that we believe that the Lutheran Confessions are true and completely reliable exposition of the truth of the gospel, we want to declare without any equivocation, that we are convinced that the Confessions of our

Church correctly answer the issues which were at stake at the time the Confessions were made. But it just doesn't stay there. We are not just talking about past things. We also want to declare that we believe that the issues which were raised and the issues which were answered at that time will always be at the center of what the gospel has to say to humanity. At the same time, we certainly do not want to ignore the experience of Lutheran confessors of the faith from the time our confessions were made down to the present time. We believe that the same spirit who led our forebearers to make their confession in their time has continued to be present in the life and history of our church today. We believe the historical situation is important. A good illustration of what we are talking about is the lesson that can be learned from the parable of the pounds in the gospel. There we learn how you can bury your money in the ground and leave it there and four centuries later descendents can dig it up and find it intact just as it was when it was put there. But it also teaches us that you can invest the money and have it increase in value. You can find the essence of Lutheranism buried in the Confessions just as the writer put it there 400 years ago or you can study the thoughts and experiences of Lutherans in the last four centuries and rejoice over the growth of understanding and meaning of what the Confessions are saying about the gospel. So, in my mind, between the Scylla of confessional indifference and the Charybdis of confessional absolutistic arrogance, there has to be a place where the gospel bids us all to take our common stand so that we can say with Luther, "Here I stand, in firm conviction of my faith." The issue is more thorough-going and significant than a debate between narrow confessionalism and "devil may care" non-confessionalism. The issue is whether we will submit to the apostolic witness of Jesus Christ and recognize that this witness continues to live in every new historical situation and was not frozen in one particular historical time.

5.   We believe there is no such thing as a perfect subscription to the Confessions of the Church. I think it is important that we recognize that there is a consensus about what genuine subscription to the Confessions means, but we do have to be aware that we cannot come up with the perfect assent to the teachings of the church – so the debate between whether we subscribe to the Confessions because they are a genuine exposition of the gospel or insofar as they are genuine expositions of the gospel – it seems to me is an exercise in futility. We need to recognize the difference between being sectarian and being catholic. I believe that to be sectarian means to follow a particular leader with a particular point of view that is being promoted. If we follow a particular exposition of some leader within our group, it seems to me we have surrendered our catholic understanding of the gospel and have become sectarian and there is always the tendency toward sectarianism in the church. It must be resisted and combated with every ounce of energy because the gospel is for all people in all time.

We believe that the fundamental confession of the church is that Jesus is the Christ, that Jesus is Lord, God is our Father, the Holy Spirit is active in bringing us to acknowledge Jesus as Lord and maintaining the church. Our basic confession is that as God is one in Christ by the Spirit, so God is effective as one Lord, in one faith, in one baptism. It seems to me, therefore, that we can rejoice in the universal character of our Confessions which point to this fundamental unity. We can refuse to look at our life as confessional churches in a way that would tend to divide us from other people. We can identify with all of God's people and seek to affirm the fundamental unity of humanity recreated by love in God's grace in Jesus Christ, even while we strongly acknowledge that in confessing our faith we will express many dissents from the world and from those who distort the clear gospel.

6.   We affirm without equivocation that the Holy Scriptures are a completely reliable means, together with the sacraments, through which the Holy Spirit evokes and maintains faith in Jesus Christ as Lord and Savior and gives us our unity. It is in this faith that the people who comprise the membership of our two churches, in their common roots as the people of God, were led to acknowledge each other in pulpit and altar fellowship.

7.   We believe that the good news about God's saving grace in Jesus Christ elicits this kind of response of faith in which members of churches with common confessions accept each other with integrity even when there are certain divergences and variations in their theological understanding, ecclesiastical practice, and life.   By listening and submitting to the Word of God penitently and expectantly, God's people are able to give highest priority to the meaning of the gospel. In establishing this priority, the way is provided to allow for certain variations of understanding in non-essentials.

8.   The Scriptures of the church expressly teach that common agreement on the meaning of the gospel indicates an awareness of both the freedom which the gospel implies, as well as sensitivity to the binding discipline which the gospel rightly expects from those who respond in faith to it.

If we allow the Holy Spirit to reform and renew the church by the creative power of the gospel, we ought to, in our common understanding of the gospel, find the possibility for affirming both faithfulness to the whole gospel, as well as freedom in the gospel. It is not an "either/or," but a "both/and." In accordance with the whole tenor and direction of the Augsburg Confession, the call of our church today is to a revitalized proclamation and living of the Gospel. The emphasis expressed in 1 Corinthians 12:14, 13:3; Galatians 5:1; and Ephesians 4:1-17 point in this direction.

9.   Fellowship between churches based upon agreement in the gospel, stressed throughout the Augsburg Confession, is especially enunciated in Articles I and VII. In accordance with this way of thinking, however, it is not consensus that is to be the judge over the church in matters of doctrine, church fellowship and Christian activity. It is, rather, Holy Scripture which is to be the guide and norm for all matters of fellowship.

10.   The gospel is the central point of the Scriptures which must guide and direct our common understanding in remaining true to an evangelical exposition of the Old and New Testament Scriptures, as Articles I and V of the Formula of Concord so clearly specify.

11.   An evangelical interpretation of the Scriptures recognizes that the Scriptures themselves must be interpreted from their center in Jesus Christ. From this perspective, it becomes clear that there is a great deal of diversity within the scriptural documents themselves. There are many ways that this can be demonstrated. Some examples: a.) The variety of presentation of the life of Jesus in the four gospels; b.) The differences in the theology of Paul and James where the issue on the surface is precisely the gospel of justification by grace alone apart from works; c.) In 1 Corinthians 11:5 we have a

statement of women prophesying with heads covered and 1 Corinthians 14:34 there is the statement that women are not to speak at all.

12.   In its statement of October 1971, the Church Council of The American Lutheran Church expressed the conviction (and the church in convention has twice sustained this conviction), that an evangelical interpretation of the New Testament allows some issues like the ordination of women to be placed in the freedom of the Church precisely because the New Testament allows such great variety. If, according to the Augsburg Confession, Article VII, "human traditions or rites and ceremonies instituted by men" need not be "alike everywhere" for the unity of the Church, then ordination, whether of women or men, can't constitute a barrier. (Tappert BC, p. 32, Latin text translation) Melanchthon also argues that women covering their heads is a temporary rule in an area that is basically under Christian liberty, so also speakers in church (See Augsburg Confession, Article XXVIII, Ecclesiastical Power – Tappert BC, pp. 89f and 50-56).

Toward Understanding One Another

Presented at the Meeting of the Commission on Fellowship,
Lutheran Church – Missouri Synod/
The American Lutheran Church
St. Louis, Missouri, 29 February 1980

At the last meeting of the Commission on Fellowship of LCMS-ALC it was suggested that an effort be made to identify a few of the important points of difference that seem to keep the two Church bodies from being able to fully and honestly embrace each other in full Christian fellowship. It may be beneficial for us to state such differences in all candor and forthrightness so that we can find ways to remove barriers to unity. Christian sisters and brothers should be able to be honest and direct with each other. In the delineation that follows such an attempt is made. Hopefully the effort will not appear judgmental.

The presentation simply attempts to raise a few points. There probably are issues at every point of doctrine that could be disputed and debated. The points that are discussed are prefaced with a general statement about the wide basis of agreement out of which the difference grew.

In accord with the above procedure it is important to recognize that we come from a common confessional background. We are of the same Lutheran lineage. There, of course, are historical factors that have made us what we are and some of the historical conditioning factors are:

ALC	LCMS

Ethnic/Historical Conditioning Factors

The ALC is a merger of churches coming from Lutheran origins of different ethnic and ecclesiastical/confessional backgrounds. Therefore its synodical loyalties are seen in light of wider ecumenical possibilities.	The LCMS is a church that comes from a rather homogenous German ethnic background and has experienced a consistent, strong ecclesiastical/confessional loyalty of over 125 years and therefore has an intense synodical consciousness.

Understanding of Authority

Both ALC and LCMS affirm that they accept the Holy Scriptures as the only and true authority in all matters of Christian faith and life. But it is obvious in inter-synodical relations that there is a definite difference in the way authority itself is understood by each church.

Before we describe the differences between the ALC/LCMS, it probably will be helpful to quickly review what the phenomenon expressed by the word authority actually means.

From the viewpoint of religion in general and Christian theology in particular, authority is quite generally understood as the right and power to declare what is obligatory in doctrine and practice. This idea of the right and power to determine ultimate beliefs has traditionally been coupled with the presupposition that there must be one voice through which supreme authority is expressed. The papacy is built upon this concept of authority.

One of the main points of the Reformation protest was against the above concept of papal authority. Luther and subsequently the Lutheran Confessions, however, not only disavowed the legitimacy of papal authority but more importantly came out clear and strong for the final and exclusive authority of the gospel. The right and power to determine matters of Christian faith and life is the gospel as the preached and living word.

There is some difficulty with this understanding of authority in that such a view of authority does not satisfy people who want clear and definite external order as well as a quick and easy way to solve doctrinal disputes. Obviously it will make a difference in a person's as well as a church's concept of the gospel, scriptural authority, and hermeneutics, as to the presuppositions that are subsumed about authority. The following is an attempt to isolate the over-arching similarities and then to state some of the significant differences of the ALC and LCMS

Both ALC and LCMS are obviously and totally committed to an evangelical understanding of authority. Neither church body would like to be thought of as a narrow, exclusivistic, authoritarian church body. But in spite of the pervasive commitment to a gospel-centered understanding of authority, clear differences are apparent:

The ALC tends to understand religious and doctrinal authority as something that can only be exercised in a broken human manner. ALC does not believe that such a stance leads to relativism but that it does demand a posture of certain open questions.	The LCMS tends to understand religious and doctrinal authority as something that is perfect and absolute. This stand tends to lead LCMS people to a posture that requires total consensus on all issues.

Holy Scriptures

The LCMS and the ALC both stress, with great emphasis, that the Holy Scriptures are truly the Word of God and the only infallible authority in all matters of faith and life. When one remembers the many discussions representatives of these two church bodies have had with each other (during the past two decades alone) about the Word of God and Scripture, it becomes obvious that both church bodies are genuinely committed to a rigorous biblical basis to all of their theology. A reflection on developments since pulpit and altar fellowship was first declared in 1969 also makes clear that there are great differences about the church bodies view of the Holy Scriptures:

To the ALC, it is important to comprehend the Word of God as means of grace as well as ultimate authority. The ALC looks upon the Holy Scriptures as the Word of God of divine origin, but likewise the scriptures are human documents coming out of a variety of identifiable historical circumstances. Consequently the scriptures are to be studied, translated, and interpreted as divinely inspired, as well as historically written records and testimony of God's living, revealing Word.	LCMS has a tendency to subordinate the Word of God as means of grace to Word of God as ultimate authority. The LCMS stresses the identity of the words of the Holy Scriptures and Word of God. Indeed recognizing the human, historical dimension to the sacred scriptures are the inspired Word of God and without error, they convey only accurate information in all areas of human history and knowledge.

The Gospel

The ALC and LCMS both claim that the gospel is the center of the Old and New Testament Scriptures and that the message of Jesus Christ is the heart of the gospel. However, when it comes to the articulation of what the gospel is, it is obvious there are differences of emphasis:

The ALC stresses the gospel as the *viva vox evangelii* and concentrates on the kerygma. No doubt this emphasis tends to appear to the LCMS people as though the gospel is reduced to a rather subjective message. Fear of LCMS about ALC's use in the historical/critical approach in biblical studies probably stems from this perception.	The LCMS lays emphasis upon the gospel in all its doctrinal articles. To the ALC people it appears that this LCMS emphasis tends to reduce the gospel o an extended set of doctrinal propositions. It at times appears to ALC people that in its strong emphasis on doctrinal purity, LCMS comes very close to subordinating the love principle to the truth principle.

Hermeneutics

Both ALC and LCMS would insist that they follow the historic Lutheran hermeneutical method. Both churches insist that the Scriptures should, first of all, be interpreted from their center –Jesus Christ. Likewise, both insist that Scripture be interpreted by Scriptures. ALC and LCMS both have statements about inspiration as being very essential in their whole understanding of Scripture and the word inerrancy, which seems to cause so much problem between the two churches, is used by both. There is no doubt that both ALC and

LCMS have been influenced by the fundamentalism of the first half of this century with regard to the use of such terms as inerrancy.

The ALC does not advocate an easy transition from inspiration to inerrancy. From an ALC perspective, it appears that many LCMS teachers have, themselves, qualified what they mean by the term "inerrancy." However, it appears to the ALC that these qualifications mean very little in inter-church discussions.	The LCMS proceeds from the axia that Scripture should be interpreted by Scripture; that inspiration and inerrancy of Scripture needs to be recognized for an adequate understanding of Scripture; that other interpretative tools, functions and methods are not useful in the interpretation of Scripture .

In the area of hermeneutics, the most crucial point of difference lies in the use of other interpretive tools, assumptions and methods. This can be illustrated most clearly by reference to the word "liberal" and what that connotes in the two churches.

The ALC cannot conscientiously construe liberal as always meaning something negative. The ALC distinguishes between liberal theology and liberal scholarship. ALC people tend to conclude that liberal scholarship means using all historical and ethnological and archeological tools to understand texts. ALC scholars do not attribute evil, or maliciousness, to the tools per se or to the methods per se. ALC people, therefore, without deviousness or apology understand themselves to be liberal scholars.	In the LCMS, liberal is used usually in a pejorative, monolithic way. To the LCMS liberal theology proceeds from certain presuppositions like these: 1. Jesus was only a man like others. 2. What theologians must do is get behind the heterogeneity in all religious expression down to the psychological elements basic to all religious expression and there discover the unifying factos and accessible common denominators. Naturally LCMS representatives rightly conclude from these presuppositions that liberal theology would be destructive to the clear definite historical reality of the gospel.

Ordination

Both the ALC and the LCMS regard the office of the ministry as having a divine institution and that there is a distinction between the pastoral vocation and the universal priesthood of all believers. Neither the ALC or the LCMS believe that the pastoral office is a continuation of the priesthood of the Old Testament, nor that it consists of certain rights and powers vested in the apostles which only the apostles and their successors can confer on others. Neither church believes that an indelible character is conferred upon the candidates by ordination. Both church bodies exhibit a strong sense of the vocation of the pastor being that of shepherd. Both churches stress the point that pastors are called by congregations and that it is on the basis of the call from the congregations that candidates are ordained.

| In the ALC there is a lot of emphasis that when one is called into the holy ministry, we are talking about the ministry of the whole church. ALC people tend to emphasize the functional nature of the pastoral office and lay stress upon the fact that the pastoral vocation is one that exists only in the context of the universal priesthood. | In the actual exercise of the pastoral vocation, it seems to ALC people that the LCMS draws a more rigid difference between clergy and laity than prevails in the ALC It may be that the consciousness of difference is in terms of expression rather than essence, but it does appear to ALC people that there is more of a priestly caste concern and mentality in the LCMS than there is amongst the ALC clergy and laity. |

Conclusion

Lutheran Self-Criticism

Another area that deserves consideration expressing some of the differences between the ALC and LCMS is that of how we are able to critically look at ourselves. Each of us legitimately proceeds from our own confessional self-understanding and identification, but ALC people believe there is a sharp divergence either in the willingness or capacity of the LCMS rigorously to be self-critical.

It is the mark of totalitarianism in both religion and politics to insist on monolithic understanding, to suppress dissent, to discredit premises which undergirds the lives of others, to protect constituents from other points of view, to entrust guidance to an oligarchy, and to be fearful of religion. When ALC teachers use language patterns suggesting that repentance encompasses the whole of life, that means ruing not only moral infidelity but doctrinal inflexibility. ALC people are not seeking thereby to destroy the truth, they only want to say that all human formulations have a tentativeness within them. They do not want Christian doctrine to become the occasion for idolatry. Our trust is in God not in human formulation about God.

Lutherans have freely criticized others. They have postured themselves as 'guardians' of the truth – but they err on two counts; they have been loveless in their relationships and they have used truth as a dividing rather than a uniting tool.

Criticism from without will always have some effect. It may reinforce prejudices already in control or it can generate honest review which eventuates in change. But the desired condition is that critical self-analysis emerge from within. To have that, a church must not only believe in the Reformation, but carry through the continuing reformation of the body of Christ. Without this, churches become sects. While conscious of our own flaws, we would charitably suggest that the LCMS has much to learn in this respect. The best of both worlds would bear much fruit if we would have vigorous evangelical, academically rigorous self-analysis as a natural part of each church.

J. Michael Reu – A Self-Made Theologian

Currents in Theology in Mission 16 (1989): 341-345

On September 20, 1989, Wartburg Seminary celebrated the l00th Anniversary of its second beginning in Dubuque, Iowa. Wartburg first began its life in Dubuque in 1854 as a direct result of the missionary efforts of Wilhelm Loehe from Neuendettelsau, Germany. After three precarious years in Dubuque, the seminary was moved to St. Sebald, Clayton, Iowa. Having outgrown the facility at St. Sebald, the seminary was moved to an empty building in Mendota, Illinois in 1875. By 1889 still more space was needed, and a number of cities on the American frontier made offers of sites to attract the seminary to make its home with them.

Dubuque, Iowa made the offer of a beautiful, vacant Victorian mansion, set on 30 acres, on one of the limestone ridges of the southwest part of the city. The offer was accepted, and so the seminary found its permanent home.

The fall of 1989 also marks the 120th anniversary of the birth of one of Wartburg's renowned theologians and educators, Johan Michael Reu (1869-1943). September 1989 is also the 90th anniversary of Professor Reu's call to teach at Wartburg Seminary.

For nearly the first fifty years of its life, the faculty of Wartburg Seminary consisted of the brothers Fritschel, Sigmund and Gottfried, and Director Georg Grossmann. The second phase of Wartburg's life in Dubuque was dominated by the second generation of Fritschels, Maximilian (son of Sigmund) and George (son of Gottfried), and Johan Michael Reu.

Sigmund and Gottfried Fritschel were prepared for their calling as teachers of future pastors by Loehe and his associates in Neuendettelsau. Professor Reu was the last of the faculty sent from Loehe's emergency seminary. Reu stands at the intersection of Wartburg faculty roots in Neuendettelsau and from the wider circles of the Lutheran Church in Europe and America.

Recognizing that any academic institution is ultimately judged by the quality of its faculty and graduates, the Centennial Committee has planned a theological festival to celebrate the contribution of its faculty in the past and present but specifically to focus on new directions for the future. This event will be November 9 and 10, 1989.

It seemed natural to the committee to highlight Professor Reu as the center of that festival. Indeed, Professor Reu is by far Wartburg's most extensive and widely-published scholar. Although Reu would not have wanted to have been extolled above his predecessors or successors, he was chosen as the centerpiece of the festival because of his pivotal historical position. Looking at Professor Reu's contribution to scholarship in the church should give all who aspire to serve in the church encouragement and challenge. Professor Reu came out of modest beginnings and very limited formal academic preparation to become a dedicated scholar, faithful theologian, committed educator, and confessional negotiator for Lutheran unity.

Reu's life is also a remarkable testimony to the validity of Wilhelm Loehe's idea to provide another route to prepare people for the parish ministry. Loehe's emergency arrangement, which provided hundreds of pastors for the Lutheran church on the frontier in America, Papua New Guinea, Brazil, and other places, reminds us that the way to learning and creative service need not be bound to established models. Professor Reu stands as a superb example of Loehe's idea that you could take a bright young student with eight to ten years of basic education, teach that student how to study and think, and the student could become a life-long learner and scholar. That is what happened to Professor Reu, for if there ever was a self-made scholar, Reu was certainly that person.

The scholarly output of Reu in quantity and quality is simply amazing. It required 55 typewritten pages just to list the books, mimeographed scripts, and articles that flowed from Dr. Reu's productive pen. Reu wrote no less than 3600 book reviews, as well as substantial articles for the *Kirchliche Zeitschrift*, which he edited for nearly 40 years. Reu's monumental nine-volume (sometimes referred to as 11-volume) work on the history and use of Luther's Catechism from 1530 to 1600 (which brought him a Doctor of Theology degree from Friedrich Alexander University in Erlangen, Germany, even before the last volumes were printed), remains the exhaustive and definitive work on that subject.

How was it possible for Professor Reu to achieve what he did? The answer lies primarily in the genius and discipline of Reu himself. Reu, it seems, was not only gifted with a near photographic memory, but he seems to have been born with a scientific, computer-like method of classifying and organizing whatever subject he chose to research.

Some credit for recognizing and channeling the young Reu's gifts goes to the pastor of the congregation in which Reu grew up. Pfarrer Bop tutored Reu in Latin, Greek, and probably Hebrew during the years of Reu's catechetical instruction. He thus may have been the most significant teacher Reu ever had. By teaching Reu the classical languages, Pfarrer Bop helped Reu discover the foundation for a valid epistemology.

The key components of that epistemology were history and language. Reu came to understand (and stressed in all his teaching) that the historical dimension of the human spirit is its most unique dimension. Human language is the crucial factor in the development of historical consciousness and the greatest facilitator of preserving the record of history. Out of this matrix of history and language Reu was able to absorb the scholarly methods of his historical group, the German Confessional Lutherans, simply by reading the appropriate records.

Reu mastered English very well but did most of his writing in German. During the last years of his teaching he acknowledged to some of his students that he might have made a greater impact with his scholarly efforts if he had forced himself to make the transition to English early in his career.

There are two areas of Reu's scholarship for which he became world renowned: 1) Luther research, and 2) the history and use of Luther's Catechism. In both areas he debunked many popular misconceptions. By going back to long-neglected original sources Reu was able to present a more accurate picture of Luther's great contributions. For example, in his work, *Luther's German Bible*, Reu demonstrated that though hymnody was sorely neglected during the years before Luther, it was not totally non-existent, as some popular notions seem to have indicated by extolling Luther as the sole creator of hymnody. Reu wanted to show the great contribution of Luther, but he wanted the estimate of Luther to be enhanced by being accurate.

Similarly, Reu showed that indeed Luther opened up a whole new world for the church and Germany by what he did in getting the Bible into the language of the people. Reu pointed out that Luther's was not the first German Bible, as sometimes excessive praise of Luther might have indicated. By his careful scholarship, Reu demonstrated the uniqueness of the contribution of Luther in regard to the Bible and Catechism. Reu demonstrated how Luther opened the Bible to the people and how Luther developed the Catechism for the home, the school, and the church.

Just as Luther's scholarship was directed to making the eternal message of the Bible come alive with all its power to the people in his (Luther's) time, so also Professor Reu directed his scholarship to helping the pastors and teachers of the church bring the liberating message of the Bible and Reformation to people of today. In other words, Reu's scholarship was pastorally centered. Scholarship, he believed, served the task of theology only if it was practical and applicable to the contemporary life of the people of God.

Reu was called to Wartburg to teach systematic theology. However, during his years of teaching he at one time or another taught every subject in the curriculum. In an article in the *Wartburg Seminary Quarterly*, Dr. Bodensieck provided a summary of what Professor Reu had taught:

> Dr. Reu taught the following subjects: Hebrew, two years; Greek, six years; Introduction to the New Testament, four years; Introduction to the Greek Text, one year; Introduction to the Old Testament, four years; Hebrew exegesis, two years; Old Testament Exegesis on the basis of the translated text, two years; Greek Exegesis: Romans, seventeen years; Galatians, seventeen years; Philippians, twelve years; Ephesians, ten years, and James, ten years; Symbolics, nine years; Life of Luther, three years; Dogmatics, thirty-seven years; Introduction to Theology, two years; for sixteen years he taught Religious Education and for another ten years he taught a one hour course in practical methods; Liturgics, eight years; Homiletics (Theory), twenty-three years; and Homiletical Exercises, thirty years.[1]

This review of Reu's comprehensive teaching experience also makes clear that Reu's particular area of competence was systematic theology. It was in dogmatics, ethics, and apologetics that Reu excelled as a faithful theologian of the church.

It is not only in his formal treatment of dogmatics, ethics, and apologetics in the respective textbooks (which Reu developed for the classes he taught) that one should look to understand the thrust of his theological thought, but also in the various monographs like *Two Treatises on the Means of Grace* which he wrote. Likewise, a careful study of his

---

[1] Dr. Julius Bodensieck, *Wartburg Seminary Quarterly*, December 15, 1943.

many articles, editorial comments, and especially the book reviews which appeared in *Kirchliche Zeitschrift* during the 40 years of his editorship manifests Reu's consistent position in systematic theology.

It was Reu's position that sound theological understanding proceeds from solid exegetical and historical study. Eventually all scholarly efforts in such study came to a focus. Like many before him, Reu found this focus in the Reformation doctrine of justification by grace through faith. This was the material principle that guided Reu in his doctrinal, ethical, and apologetic formulations. The indisputable formal principle of Reu's theology was that of all self- conscious Protestant theologians, namely, the ultimate authority of Scripture. Reu also made the point that he was a confessional theologian and distinguished himself from theologians (with whom he otherwise enthusiastically agreed) like Martin Kähler and Karl Heim.

One could not say that Michael Reu was a creative systematic theologian in the sense of someone like Paul Tillich. Reu was rather a masterful organizer and synthesizer of the vast material from the Bible, the history of doctrine, the Confessions, and the human situation.

Thus Reu's *Dogmatics* is organized around the basic theme of communion between God and humanity. The *Dogmatics* is developed in six main parts as follows:

> Part 1: "The Communion of God with Man Grounded in God and His
> Eternal Decree of Salvation"
> Part 2: "Established Through Creation"
> Part 3: "Disrupted Through Sin"
> Part 4: "Restored in the Person and Work of Jesus Christ"
> Part 5: "Appropriated Through the Agency of the Holy Spirit"
> Part 6: "Consummated in Eternity"

Clearly, Reu was convinced that the overarching concept of communion between God and humanity brought together the divine/human encounter, and this most appropriately expressed the meaning of justification by grace through faith.

The objective phase of this material principle (the accomplishment of redemption through Christ's death and resurrection) and its subjective phase (its appropriation through faith alone) may be comprised in the one expression – Communion of God with Man.[2]

What Reu did in taking this relational approach is what many of his contemporaries in Germany were doing. Systematicians, like Christoph Luthardt and Martin Kähler sought to incorporate the human, experiential side which Luther had integrated so well and which Schleiermacher had reemphasized after great neglect in the time of orthodox rationalism. It is the same motif to which Paul Tillich has given unique emphasis in modern times through his method of correlation.

Reu proceeded to develop his dogmatics by showing how each particular statement of faith was derived from Scripture. He then went on to define the substance of each doctrine and

---

[2] Reu's role as educator is explored by Paul Johnson in "An Assessment of the Education Philosophy of J. M. Reu Using the Hermeneutic Paradigms of J. F. Herbart and of J. C. K. Hofmann and the Erlangen School." 1989 doctoral dissertation at the University of Illinois.

its inner connection with the total of Christian doctrine. Following a review of each doctrine's historical development, Reu concluded by showing how the doctrine was reflected in the experience of the Christian. In other words, what one believes expresses itself in what one understands about oneself and what one does – Christian faith and life belong together. In this way Reu thought of himself as a "practical theologian," and he was not displeased when he was so called by the famous Leipzig, Germany University as Professor of Practical Theology. Reu considered the title an honor and an affirmation of his strong conviction that systematic theology was at the center of pastoral or practical theology.

Some of Reu's most important books were written in practical theology. His *Catechetics* and *Homiletics* are two examples. They are not "how to" books but rather scholarly theologies of catechetics and homiletics.

Mention was made earlier that in addition to his work as a scholar and theologian Reu also contributed to the seminary and the church as an educator and as a negotiator of Lutheran unity. His contributions in these areas will also be given attention during the festival.

As an educator Reu initiated the first graduate studies program at Wartburg in the 1930s. People like O. P. Kretzmann and Martin Scharlemann studied with him at that time. Reu also initiated what is one of the oldest (if not the oldest) continuing education programs for pastors in America, the Luther Academy. Now known as the Luther Academy of the Rockies, the program was begun by Reu in 1937.

The part Reu played in merger negotiations among Lutherans during the twenties and thirties will be the final area assessed in the November event. As a merger negotiator, Reu was often not as effective as he was as a scholar. It will be interesting to see this side of the self-made scholar and theologian explored now that a half century has passed.

It will also be interesting to see how extensively the assessment of Reu made at the time of his death, by the President of the Lutheran Free Church, has come true:

> He will be remembered as one of the great theologians the Lutheran Church in this country has possessed, and through his books he will continue to teach and witness as a father in the church.[3]

---

[3] T. O. Burnvedt in *Kirchliche Zeitschrift*, Reu Memorial No. (1945):127.

Part Four:

Addresses and Sermons

Introduction to Part Four

William Weiblen was inaugurated as Wartburg Theological Seminary's 10th president on May 10, 1971. "Dedication and Direction" is the address offered on that festive occasion. President Weiblen deeply grounded the seminary in its historic past, while at the same time charting a course for the future. His message resonates with confidence about the resources brought to the seminary both by students and by the congregations of the church. The theme of death and resurrection links the life of the seminary to the way of Jesus Christ. With the exception of this address, all the selections in Part Four have never before been published.

"Forward to Our Heritage" is the provocative title of Dr. Weiblen's address delivered on the occasion of the Confirmation Reunion held at the 100th anniversary of St. Paul's Lutheran Church in Waverly, Iowa on July 16, 1972. Bill chose this topic through inspiration from the Bavarian Lutheran Church that had recently employed a similar theme, "Forward to Loehe." Pastor Weiblen returned to the St. Paul's congregation for this occasion as their former pastor. Without becoming preoccupied with how it was in the "good old days," he summoned the church to take up its mission task anew. The guiding text for the address is Philippians 3:7-14.

The Iowa District of the American Lutheran Church invited President Weiblen to address its convention in the mid-1970s. President Bruno Schlachtenhaufen offered Mark 4:28-29 as the theme verses: "The earth produces of itself, first the blade, then the ear, then the full grain in the ear. But when the grain is ripe, at once he puts in the sickle, because the harvest has come." (RSV). "Ministry and Grace" is the title of this address.

At the 1980 convention of the American Lutheran Church, Dr. Weiblen was one of the final nominees for President of the church body. While it was clear that David Preus would be re-elected to that office (which proved to be the case), some who heard the candidate speeches have commented that this was William Weiblen's finest hour as a churchman and an orator. "A New Day" is a transcription of that speech, taken from audio tape of the convention and stored in the archives of the ELCA.

The book concludes with representative selections from Dr. Weiblen's career at the seminary: a commencement address from May 1996, four sermons delivered at chapel, and a message of farewell. Although there were many such occasions at which Bill was the speaker, not many are extant. These provide a delightful sampling of his creative use of the text for the sake of addressing the issues of the day.

Dedication and Direction

Inaugural Address as President of Wartburg Theological Seminary
May 10, 1971

This seminary was given the name Wartburg in 1857. The seminary had already been operating for three years in Dubuque on Garfield Avenue and was now moving to new quarters at St. Sebald, west and north of Strawberry Point. The founding fathers were confident that the seminary would have a better chance for life and growth on the open land, where fertile soil could provide adequate food and abundant trees would guarantee fuel for warmth. It was, of course, to be the first of three moves before it came back to Dubuque, after 18 years at St. Sebald and 14 years in Mendota, Illinois.

In naming the seminary Wartburg, the founders expressed the fervent hope that this little school (atop a valley knoll with prairie as far as one could see spreading to the west and south and woods verdantly green and thick carpeting the north and east expanses) would become a mighty fortress, a secure training place for ministry just like its namesake, the Wartburg fortress near Eisenach had been a secure refuge for Luther at the beginning of the Reformation. The fathers prayed that this new Wartburg on the prairie might become a place where men could be formed in the freedom of the gospel! A place where men would learn and develop competence in serving. A place where men would be equipped to bring the good news of Christ to the settlers on the land and to the native Americans, those strangers in the land, who wanted only to be left alone! Our fathers prayed that Christ might be made to increase in healing and power through the establishment of a fortress of learning.

Since that time, Wartburg, as you know, has been joined by Trinity Seminary and Luther of Afton and St. Paul, Minnesota and has been a part of two major ecclesiastical consolidations of Lutherans. In its history of over a century, I suppose its supporters, its students, its teachers, and leaders have all striven to make it a mighty fortress of training for ministry. It is my prayer tonight, that all of us might share in this same kind of vision and devotion to the ministry of God's grace in Christ.

This occasion then, seems a particularly appropriate time to dedicate our energies and efforts to the exciting, and ever new task of preparing for the ministry of God's people.

Dedication to the educational activity known as theological training first of all means that Wartburg Theological Seminary is not a self-perpetuating institution. It has no automatic right to life. It has life because life has been given to it. Life has been given to it for a purpose — to prepare people for the ministry of the church.

The Scope of our Ministry

Ministry is the name we give to what the church does. Ministry intends to describe those activities and actions by which the church could be seen to have a meaningful connection to what has happened for humanity and the world in Jesus Christ. If the church is wherever Jesus is acknowledged as the Christ and confessed as Lord by people, then ministry is simply the people of God giving active expression to what they declare themselves to be — a community of faith, hope and love - a people committed to the Lordship of Jesus as the Christ.

Down through the centuries Christians have understood the central focus of this ministry to be the apostolic ministry of Word and sacrament. Today we are going through a far-reaching redefinition of the shape and identity of this basic focus of the church's life. Priests and pastors have identity problems. Some have real doubts as to whether they can function meaningfully in the role of the ordained clergy if they are to carry out an authentic ministry. I believe that many new and different forms of participating in the ministry of Word and sacrament will be the wave of the future. The awareness that the pastoral ministry is more a matter of a function of all of us than it is the privilege of a few of us will increase so that the sharp clergy/laity division will diminish. I believe however, that the central significance of the apostolic ministry of God's people will continue. It seems to me that it is part of the arrangement that is included in the way God relates to people in time and space.

Since each person is uniquely human; one who communicates through language; an intellectual, emotional, and volitional person, uniquely individual and socially interrelated; word and language will always be important. A ministry of Word and sacrament will always be crucial if we are to be addressed by the Word of God. It may indeed, and surely will happen, that preparation for ministry will go through radical revision. But this is not new. Each generation of God's people has been called upon to respond to the particular needs of its time and develop a formation of persons for ministry that would edify the whole body of Christ. Naturally, according to the judgment we make, some generations have performed this task better than others. Our concern, it seems to me, should be that we may remain open and responsive to the peculiar needs and opportunities of our time. Today we are not so much called to judge and discern the past as we are called to be faithful to the need of the hour and open to the challenge of the future.

Emerging Unity

In their understanding of what faithfulness to this ministry of God's presence in Christ to his church and the world *meant*, Christians in the past often separated themselves from one another. Over their different ideas about how the whole people of God fitted into this ministry of the means of grace, charge and counter-charge of heresy have been thrown. We are thankful that today there is emerging a universal recognition by God's people, in many denominations, of the fundamental fact that the whole ministry of God's people is the ministry of all the people of God. There is a growing ecumenism which portends that the recognition of the validity of the apostolic ministry of one another may eventually be possible. So it is a joy for me today to call for dedication to Wartburg's purpose of preparing for the church's ministry in unity with brothers and sisters from many other churches than my own! Especially in close association with our nearest and closest allies and neighbors in The Association of Theological Faculties in Iowa, we can celebrate the joy of ministry. With humility and gratitude we can dedicate ourselves to the task of educating for ministry, recognizing that such an affirmation always involves confessional integrity but that such confessional faithfulness also means a recognition of the unity of faith wherever and whenever it comes to expression.

Dedication to Ministry

Our dedication to the ministry of the church gives direction to the thing the church tries to do in its theological seminaries. The specific ministry of Wartburg gets its direction from a basic dedication to ministry. The direction of everything we propose and plan must be grounded in the substance of the gospel of Jesus Christ from which we live. Our confessional statement, which says that it is enough to agree concerning the teaching of the gospel, makes it clear that the direction of all we do proceeds from the center of the message of Christ. The question becomes, "How do we relate the authentic insights of the Christian message to revolutionary social change? How do we allow the gospel to speak to the environmental and other crises with which we are faced, without distorting or diluting the message itself?"

As important as any other factor in carrying out this task, it seems to me, is to be *aware* of some of the limits and possibilities contained in decisions that one makes about how to do theology. The way you put the whole theological enterprise together makes a big difference. You know, you can put theological study together in a demonically distorting, authoritarian manner in the name of faithful obedience to the authority of Scripture. The fine line between radical Christian obedience to the Word of God and blind religious fanaticism is not always easy to discern. At the other end of the spectrum is the anything-goes, permissive attitude which sometimes in seeking instant relevance for everything, has nothing to say about anything.

To be guided by a desire for confessional integrity, and a quest for ecumenical openness may be what is needed in the effort to put it all together in a way that does justice to the legitimate rights of all the participants in theological training — students, faculty, boards, congregations, and society as they seek to interpret God's message to themselves and our times! A reverent devotion to the ultimate authority of God's message to us in Jesus the Christ will, I believe, make it possible to do precisely that!

Flexibility

I believe that one of the clear directions that comes to us today from the converging heritages from which Wartburg draws its strength is stated in the principle of flexibility which we are seeking to embody in curricular changes, as well as educational methods. The Iowa Synod heritage stresses the importance of distinguishing between ultimate and preliminary concerns. The Trinity UELC motif will never let us forget the freedom, as well as the faithfulness that the gospel implies. My point is that the innovative position which has come to be associated with Wartburg Seminary is simply drawing out the possibilities of the roots from which we have come.

Pioneers

All of the seminaries which are now united in Wartburg were pioneer ventures. To be a pioneer meant that one would be ready to risk. It meant the adaptability and readiness to shift to meet emergency were part of life. *Resourceful* and *flexible*, in the midst of a changing environment, is a direction we can follow as we look to our mission in the 70s. We can make a commitment to a philosophy of education which is more of a quest for freedom and independence in grace, than a search for security and identification in institutional strength and power.

During the coming months and years, I envision ourselves encouraging freedom and individual creativity on the part of all participants in the learning process so that beginning where the student is in ability, previous preparation, and motivation, we can develop the kind of support systems of intellectual, emotional, and volitional self-discipline which make for mature and useful scholarship.

Partnership in Learning

It is my hope that our learning activity here would more and more become a total enterprise involving the parish, parish pastor, worker priests, and seminary professors, and regard the student as a contributor and developer as well as a receiver. The future I await is one in which our common task is viewed as an engagement in which board of regents, board of theological education, and administration in addition to evaluating and approving recommendations, setting and adjusting budgets, become integrally involved in the ongoing life of theological learning itself.

Seminary Training A Transitional Activity

The entire activity ought to help a person make the transition from preparation for study to the permanent vocation of being a theologian, more accurately, a pastor-theologian. By this I do not mean student or theologian in any sophisticated, narrow, arid, strictly bookish, academic sense. I mean student in its original sense of seeker of wisdom. I mean academic in devotion to search for truth and openness to insight. I mean theologian in the sense of a follower of the knowledge and wisdom of God. I mean a person open to new possibilities but grounded in the meaning of the gospel. I mean a person looking for ways to serve and continue an endless quest. A person, who in a time when instant relevance seems to be the test for truth, will not settle for superficial utilitarianism in making theological interpretations, but will work patiently to square conclusions with the way the gospel lays out reality. One who will strive for understanding the total implications of issues and in seeing the extended completeness of individual theological formulations will find relevance squared with truth. A pastor, scholar, theologian, or should we say, a servant of communicating the message of reconstruction, renewal and hope that God is addressing to humanity in the midst of our own plunge to self-destruction. Hopefully, theological training would help the growth and development of a person following the quest.

Our Resources

To begin to accomplish such a training effort will mean that the seminary will have to increasingly direct its attention and efforts to all the resources available. And there are many resources that we need and that are waiting to be fully utilized.

In my way of thinking, the faculty remains the crucial component of all the several parts that make up the kind of total theological engagement we have been talking about. I do not mean that the faculty stands at the top of hierarchical structure of authority, or even wisdom. I mean crucial in the sense of most necessary catalyst to release the training process. I mean important in the sense of sacrificial service and providing stability and continuity. I believe that our faculty, as well as friends and allies here tonight, representing a host of schools, view their ministry as such a sacred trust. Our own faculty is a healthy combination of various theological stances, traditions and trainings that should enable us to enrich each other in a community of learning that can, in turn, be enriching and stimulating to all whom they are privileged to serve. I hope we can strengthen even more the trust and respect we have for each other, expand the relation to church and community resources we already now enjoy, and in so doing, find ever-enlarging satisfaction of participating in the miracle of learning and the expanding interaction between our three faculties here in Dubuque as a particularly vital part of our continued professional growth.

We are just beginning to make use of our students' untapped resources of ingenuity, energy, and motivation. There seems to be a positive law of learning that students today are imposing upon us, namely: learning expands according to the seriousness with which teachers and their programs of education take the students' quest for truth.

I am also convinced that the congregation, the parish, i.e., people gathered in their confession of Jesus the Christ is a vast, barely tapped resource of theological preparation. Oh, it's true we all know that field experience is necessary and we are quite sure that every candidate recommended for ordination should have had an internship during which the study of theology could be related to the actual practice of ministry. Above all, we know that the parishes are important for providing the funds to keep our doors open — we rightfully remind all visitors to our campus from the congregations that Wartburg belongs to them. The contributors in our parishes pay the bills. We are thankful that the congregations of The ALC have supported their seminaries so well and indicated their intention to continue their support with particular concern. The church's decision at San Antonio concerning budget for theological training demonstrated this.

But beyond all these resources of the parish, I am thinking particularly of the direct contribution which congregations and places of ministry can make when we begin to see that insight, wisdom, and direction for the future can flow to theological centers of learning as well as from the centers to the congregation.

In recognizing this, we will increase the amount of involvement and engagement in theological training that is just waiting to be done on the vast and varied campuses which the seminary can utilize by plugging into the thousands of parishes of our church. The parish is the arena for living theology today. The life of the church beats with all kinds of intriguing possibilities in the congregation.

Many times the established patterns of what congregational life is must experience death before the power of the resurrection — the ever new life of Christ — can emerge. During the coming year, we, for example, will have some of our most interesting internships in eastern South Dakota, a state which has experienced a continuing decline of population and an even more pronounced rural to town drift so that congregations established by our grandparents are experiencing death in all its agonizing features of the pain of struggle to survive, resentment, faded glory, etc. Precisely out of such death, new life for ministry is emerging. For example, a ministry to the Indian, (the first Americans), which our founding fathers wanted to carry out is being taken up by the learning an intern will get for ministry to the Indian with the guidance of a Catholic Jesuit father. Another intern will be learning this ministry through an experience in Oklahoma.

The way of life in the church has always been by death and resurrection. In this kind of understanding we can indeed hope, not merely to revive, but to bring the fully new, the completely unexpected, the possibility of a new synthesis for our divided culture — a hope beyond the dissolution which seems to lie ahead.

Above all there are all the communities of people — the so-called secular world. We can join the efforts for peace, for justice, and necessary social change in the awareness that wherever the forces of love, life, and liberation are contending against the forces of death, destruction, and oppression, there the power of Christ and the Spirit are at work. The classroom, and the street join in the place of preparation for the ministry of the means of grace in today's world.

At this point, I would like to address a special word to the City of Dubuque. We look to you not primarily for money, although we know how dependent we are on each other. Wartburg brings over a half-million dollars into the Dubuque economy every year. And we and our students receive probably more than that in turn through employment and services. Beyond such considerations, however, we will look to you for helping us in our task. We ask you to join us in trying to understand the socio-political and economic forces by probing the structures of life in community together. We will come not as fully enlightened experts to tell you what is wrong and how injustices can and must be eradicated, but we come to join with all of you as concerned citizens for the growth and development in community affairs which will help our youth, our aged, the dispossessed, the affluent, and the big group of most of us, the middle-class, find ways to help each other.

I believe the call of God today to you and me is to dedicate ourselves to this mission and the promise of God's Spirit is to give us the direction to remain faithful to our calling. Will you join me in asking God to grant us all joy in remembering this day, but even more, to await every day with expectation in God's guiding presence and blessing?

Our Prayer

O, God, our vows of obedience to be your disciples is an aspiration which only your grace can fulfill.

We remember that your grace is made real in human weaknesses and so we ask you to give us all the temperament to place our weaknesses in your hands and not to despise what you have redeemed and can use. In the experience of your generous acceptance of us, we ask for help in being genuinely alert and open to the weaknesses and needs of all those around us.

For our common task we ask for strength to escape the pitfall of ecclesiastical pride and presumption. When we are tempted to talk, in God's name, the nonsense which often will attract and excite but rarely direct bleeding hearts to the crucible of the cross and the restoration of the resurrection, we pray for wisdom to see the way of folly.

May we never substitute tarnished moral codes for the good word our Lord would like us to speak. May we never parade superficial religiosity in the place where our Master looks for honest humanity. May we be able to discern the difference between emotional intoxication and the celebration of our Lord's presence and victory.

Theological education, preparation for ministry, is a humble task but precisely because it is so, its complexity increases a hundredfold. It is not the complexity which demands our devotion. Rather your grace which is hidden in the complex affairs of life together! The possibility of the reunification of life into a unity of love and meaning is the goal we follow.

John 3:30 - He must increase, but I must decrease. This can be our dedication today and our direction for tomorrow.

Forward to our Heritage

Sermon on the Occasion of the 100th Anniversary (1872-1972)
of St. Paul's Lutheran Church, Waverly, Iowa
Confirmation Reunion Service, July 16, 1972
Text: Philippians 3:7-14

Prayer:

God, our loving almighty Father, you have made us your own. On this day we remember in
a particular way your goodness to us in the ministry and life of St. Paul's Lutheran Church.
We thank you for your grace manifesting itself in spite of weaknesses and foibles during the
past 100 years. We thank you in a particular way for the enrichment we have received in
our preparation for confirmation here in the bosom of this church.

Above all, we thank you that you have given us the rich gift of life in your Son, Jesus Christ
our Lord. Help us never to despise the unique gift of life and personality which you have
given to each one of us. As we think about celebrating your grace in our midst, help us to
see that you have opened all fullness of life to us in the world in which we live. May we
never despise what you have redeemed and created, namely, our own individual lives.

As we think of 100 years, we remember not only successes, but failures. We ask you to
help us see how you can be present, and have been present in our failures. Give us the
strength to accept our heritage with its weaknesses, its strengths, and its unlimited
possibilities. Give us the courage and insight to use your grace so that you can work
through our weaknesses to achieve new things.

Help us to see that your mission of new hope and new life moves mightily through all the
broken forms of congregations like St. Paul's. Make us in relation to all people everywhere,
catalysts of healing and reconciliation. Help us to become instruments who will enable
others to celebrate life and grace made alive by your Son and the power of your Holy Spirit.
By your Spirit of life and love, impel us to the tasks which lie before us with our eyes wide
open to the reality of needs and imperfections in our church, but even more, our eyes open
and sensitive to the resources of faith, hope, and love which you provide for us. Help us by
your power to rejoice in our calling to go forward in faith.   Amen.

Dear Friends in Christ:

It is a real joy to be in this pulpit again. I have a host of happy memories from my years as
your servant in the ministry of St. Paul's congregation. I look back to those years, when I
was your servant, as "golden years". I rejoice with you in your celebration of God's grace
for 100 years.

It is an interesting coincidence that the very year that St. Paul's was formally organized as a congregation, after several years of being a preaching place, was the very year that the man from Germany, who perhaps more than any other individual was uniquely responsible for the mission of the church reaching out to us, came to the end of his ministry here on earth. Pastor Wilhelm Loehe from Neuendettelsau, Germany, died January 2, 1872. During this year that you are celebrating your 100th anniversary, people throughout the world are commemorating the life and ministry of Loehe, looking back to this death 100 years ago. In Germany, they are commemorating Loehe's life, as they remember the 100th anniversary of his death, with the theme, "Forward to Loehe." It was out of that coincidence that the theme for my sermon and the selection of the text was suggested to me. I would suggest that in remembering our heritage from Luther, Loehe, and above all our heritage from the New Testament in the words of our text from Paul, that we take as the word for our reflections today the theme: "Forward to Our Heritage." This, it seems to me, is the message and burden of our text.

At the end of 100 years of history and after 4,346 people have stood before this altar and its predecessors to confirm their faith, we feel the weight of the past pressing upon us. There is a perpetual human tendency to glorify that portion of the past, which has been significant for us, and to forget those portions of the past which have not been good and helpful. On this day of reunion, it would be easy for us to dwell long and nostalgically upon our past together as a people of God here at St. Paul's. We could recount many great and glorious things. We could savor the beauty of having rested in the everlasting arms of God's grace in the midst of this congregation. We could point to the strength and power which has emerged from the life we have enjoyed. We could think particularly of the magnificent program of preparation leading to confirmation. We could think of the unhappy memories about confirmation and preparation for it. We could think of those disturbing days when a member felt estranged from the congregation for a lifetime because of failing to meet an appointment with the pastor regarding an announcement for communion in preparation for confirmation. It would be easy to dwell on the past in this way.

I believe, however, Paul shows us a better way to deal with the past. Recognizing that the past can be either a burden or a blessing, depending upon how we deal with it, he shows us how to deal with the past as a gift of grace. The burdens of guilt and sin from any past can be placed at the throne of God's mercy. Then one can see from the past with thanksgiving. Then one can move away from the past in repentance and courage. Paul surrendered everything that was past which might be inclined to make him be proud. He relegated to the background everything which would enable him to be secure in what he had done. This is the way we too, during this year of celebration of God's grace, must deal with the glorious past that is ours. We can make a decisive judgment that our security before God will not be built upon past accomplishments or grandeur.

The celebration of God's grace should enable us to look back and make a judgment that we will take confidence for the future not in the experiences, as such, that we have had, but in only one thing and that is the thing that Paul does not forget about the past. Paul does not forget the experience by which he found a new life in Christ. He remembers vividly how Christ changed his life. Paul always celebrated that experience in which his sense of self-security was forever shattered. Paul thanked God for the experience in which he was torn away from all that he called his own. Paul rejoiced in the experience by which he was freed from the fetters of self to live for Christ, so that he could say, "For me to live is Christ and to die is gain." Paul remains true and faithful to this great liberation in Christ.

This crisis in his past which liberated him from simply glorying in a heritage and made him open to the boundless horizons of the future, is the same experience that we can participate in today. As we remember 100 years of the experience of God's grace, and particularly the good things that we have enjoyed here together, as well as some of the unpleasant (but yet things that we can thank God for today), we shall not glory in them. We shall thank God for them and repent of our failures and guilt in the past that we may face the future with courage.

If we are able to receive everything that has come to us in our life and history with gratitude and thanksgiving, then we will be able to realize how the power of God's Spirit has been operative in our life and history. We will be able to see the Holy Spirit as a creative presence and power constantly coming into our lives to release us from self-concern, showering sustaining power and grace upon us. Then in repentance and faith, we will be open to the future. In this experience of grace, we can understand that what has been given to us was not given us to linger over, but to make us look forward, that it might bear fruit in the future.

By grace we can see that the gifts that St. Paul's has enjoyed for 100 years were gifts to make the congregation more mature and capable for carrying out the mission it will have in the next 100 years. Above all, let us realize that what we have and are is a gift of God and all that we can and shall become is God's gift too. In the celebration of this gift is the fullness of the joy of life itself. Our readiness for action and sacrifice for the future can only be maintained and come to good effect if this willingness involves a commitment to live by the gift of God's grace. We will want to allow God's grace to act upon us, within us, as God desires and not as it seems appropriate to us. This means a readiness, like Paul, to abandon ourselves to the void in which there is no support and security which the future seems to hold out. A void and lack of support in which we are sustained only by the grip of Jesus Christ, who during the past 100 years, has thrust his power and his direction into every corner of our life and history. So much then for the acknowledgement and celebration of what has gone before. Now, what about the future?

We have said that we should center our thoughts on "Forward to Our Heritage." This, too, it seems to me, is what St. Paul was stressing in our text. He was pointing out that the lives of all of us are governed by this motif of 'that which has not yet happened'. Paul said, "Brothers and sisters, I do not consider that I have made it on my own, but one thing I do, forgetting what lies behind and straining forward to what lies ahead, I press on to the prize of the upward call of God in Christ Jesus." In other words, our heritage is to be with Christ. Our heritage is the celebration of God's goodness which accepts us in spite of ourselves, in spite of our failures. God continues to be faithful to us. We cannot begin to recite or count all of the blessings which pertain to our heritage to which we constantly ought to move forward. We isolate only a few of them to magnify the total.

One of the great things in our tradition, it seems to me, is the fact that God has made it clear to us that redemption in Christ includes all of life and history. Our new life in Christ is not some rarified dislodgement from this real world, but it is being given strength and the resources to experience in the midst of everything that comes in life, the forward pull of

God to see that life consists out of that force which has been manifest in Jesus Christ in his death and resurrection. This is a great liberation.

There are not some bad things about us and some good things, in the sense that one can be separated from the other, but all life is a mixture. All life and all history in this mixture can be accepted as the arena through which the grace of God works. There is not some domain up above the world where God operates with us, but God comes close and operates clearly with us here and now. This view, that God is present through all the things of life and history, has been a consistent *strong point of our tradition*. May we face the future with this kind of an awareness.

Preparation for making our confirmation vows in such awareness has always been an integral and important part of our tradition. Now it is true that such confirmation instruction can become a promotion for the preservation of the system. Consistent reappropriation and induction into the substance of what the Christian faith is, is a vital part of our ongoing preparation for commitment to Jesus Christ. Such instruction, however, dare never be focused on preservation alone. Our preparation for confirmation must be more than commitment to previous statements of faith.

There are many people who sound ominous notes about the future. There are those who say that all the good values of the past are being lost. There are even those who are saying the Christians and the church are on their way out! These prophets of despair and doom are not new in human history. In a way, each generation has had to listen to such declarations of despair. Christianity was born in a time of expectation about the end of the world and uncertainty of the future. In the midst of all that, Christ arose from the dead and Christians went about proclaiming that the end would come, the consummation would take place in Christ, and that in him, *all life would be wrapped together in a new and meaningful way*. It is particularly important for us today then, too, to realize that we are called to a mission of moving forward to our heritage, to meet the needs of our time.

It is very clear to us that the future will require courage, calm, and confidence. We know that the future will demand sacrifices. Can we move out into that future as those who have been set free from the bondage of themselves and the world around them? Are we ready to move forward to the real treasure of our heritage, that is, God's grace which sets us free by constantly breaking into our lives with new power and meaning? Are we willing to let the freeing power of God in Christ shatter the sinful self which constantly arises in our hearts, tempting us to believe that life really consists in finding security in the way we have found it from the life we have lived in the past? Are we today prepared to let God's Holy Spirit shatter our pride, our unconcern, and our frivolity, so that we can respond to the demand for changing the quality of life in a way that more adequately squares with the profession we make about the meaning of life in Jesus Christ?

I believe that we are ready to make this kind of commitment. All around we sense that Christians are anxiously striving to find ways to live out that which they profess to be. One way that we can do this is to acknowledge with new force the fact that God is alive in all of life and history today. We can assure the distraught and depressed people around us that God has not abandoned our time. We can declare God's promises as Paul did, that to live is Christ. When people ask what life is all about, we can tell them that life is all about what has happened in the Cross, in the surrender of everything that seeks to preserve life, and everything that seeks to define the meaning of life as consisting in nothing more than keeping what we have. We can show and tell them that there awaits a new future in God!

Another of the great things of our heritage is the insistence that Christian hope is not glorified optimism. The New Testament stresses realism! Our heritage stresses realism! To hope in Christ is not to participate in the establishment of the ultimate "optimist club." To look forward in hope and to move out to our heritage of hope in the Christian faith, is not closing one's eyes to the hard brutal facts of life. It is not particularly being blind to the suffering which is the lot of so many human beings. When Paul says, "I strain forward to the future," it was not an idea of escapism. In other places Paul indicates, as he does in Romans 8, that hope is always contrary to what is seen. The Christian hope is based in the cross and resurrection of Christ. Through participation in the cross and the resurrection of Christ, the Christian can set his hope on the impossible!

To trust in the Crucified One is to be able to surrender everything in this life which would define life in nothing more than being secure. Continual self-giving in love has life as both its source and its achievement. The Christian faith, it seems to me, therefore, in our time, can be a declaration that the future never belongs to those who will seize it, but really only can be shared by those who will be open for it. The Christian is convinced that openness to the future is openness to the God who is the future.

We do not believe that the past and present cause the future. We are convinced that there awaits everyone in Christ always something completely new. We are convinced that God, the Holy One, and the One who comes to us as the One completely different and the One totally beyond us, is also the *entirely New One*. Paul said it in these words to the Corinthians, "If anyone is in Christ, there is a new creation." Without Christ human hope does tend to become a pipe dream. In Christ, however, it becomes specific! We can reach the conclusion like Paul where we are willing to die with Christ, confident that we shall also rise with him. To be a Christian today then, means that we must be willing to recognize that if necessary, we should follow Christ into death knowing that it is only through death and resurrection that the new can emerge.

Like Paul, we can be inspired to the kind of heroic living that our times demand, summarized in the words of G. A. Studdert-Kennedy:

The Unutterable Beauty

> It isn't proved, you fool. It can't be proved.
> How can you prove a victory before it's won?
> How can you prove a man who leads
> To be a leader worth the following?
> Unless you follow to the death.
> Well, God's my leader, and I hold that He
> Is good and strong enough to work his plan
> And purpose out to its appointed end.

Paul has shown us that all that is past is indeed prologue to the great future that lies before us and so with those who remember their heritage in gratitude and remembering our involvement with great people of the past, we too can join today in saying, "Forward to Our Heritage." Forward to the acceptance of the wholeness of life! Forward to an unlimited future of participation in the grace of God! We say to you at St. Paul's on this occasion, "Forward to the faith, hope, and love in Christ your Lord which gives you a great future. Launch out into the uncharted days ahead with courage, confidence, and great excitement! Abandon yourselves in happiness over what you already have become in Christ, looking forward to what you yet shall be." Forward, then, to life in God through Christ! We look back in thanksgiving and repentance, but our gaze is directed to what lies ahead!

Ministry and Grace

Message to the Iowa District
of The American Lutheran Church
(ca. 1975)

We want to talk to you about the pastoral vocation and the meaning of grace. In other words let's think about ministry and grace. First we will try to define what we understand by the concepts ministry and grace and in so doing ask the question as to whether or not concepts like ministry and grace convey the kind of meaning we wish.

There, of course, are many people who would insist that terms like ministry and grace are remnants of a religious past that no longer exists and that if we want to say anything meaningful to women and men today we had best get off our antiquated rhetoric and on to the job of creating some new language that will communicate what we might want to say about Jesus Christ and his church, particularly the life and mission of the church.

Now it is certainly true that a lot of our theological concepts have become either so inflated through many interpretations or so deflated of any specific content that they convey nothing but the sound of a very weak tinkling cymbal, at the very best. However, most of the substantial theological concepts like grace, justification, faith, reconciliation, redemption, sin, judgment, need only to be freed from some of the ecclesiastical and liturgical overlay with which we have burdened them to again be useful and powerful in communicating the Christian message.

In many ways, that is one of the primary tasks of theology—to untangle the web of misconception, distortions, and, yes, even deceptions which have bound up some of our most sacred concepts like those that we have under consideration in this discussion—ministry and grace.

Take the concept grace. If you would take a random sampling of what is understood by this important theological term by the person on the street today, I am sure that you would find most everything but that which is at the root of this great biblical idea: God's favorable disposition to humanity and the world in spite of the abandonment and rejection which we properly deserve for our deliberate turning away from the Father who is the source of all life and goodness!

Probably ministry would make a little better showing. But is this really the case? If my very limited observations are correct, generally ministry would be understood as the vocation of the pastor or preacher. At the outset let us then attempt to state what these two concepts have usually been expected to convey in Christian theological communication.

In line with the biblical understanding of that great truth which came to focus in the New Testament, by the term *charis* we think of God's friendly attitude to us, how the almighty, powerful Creator relates to the ungrateful, rebellious creature. I think particularly of the so-called parable of the prodigal son—more appropriately expounded as "the waiting father" by Helmut Thielicke. God's attitude toward the sinner is the opposite of the tendency to strike back in revenge, which so readily engulfs us when we have been insulted or ignored. In other words, the source of all life in the depths of the divine being is favorably disposed toward the created universe which seems bent on a course of denying God as the source and basis of life. Jesus Christ: For in the cross and resurrection is the full and offensive expression of this.

By ministry we understand what the New Testament means when it talks about what the people of God do when they live out of this grace which has given them life. In other words, ministry is the name that we give to what the people of God do.

I take it that what we are about in our day to day life as people in congregations, and in the districts, conferences and national synod of the American Lutheran Church, for example, is seeking to let God the Holy Spirit make a vital and integral relationship between ministry and grace.

It is not just the way we are led to put the concepts themselves together in theological formulations that is important (God knows this is indeed essential) but it is the entire understanding, the affirmation and negations, the ethical actions and non-actions, that result from the way we put our vocation as the servant people together with God that is important.

The longer I look at my own proclivity to put it all together in some sure-fire methods for achieving God's good cause (yet which do not help real renewal to emerge from crisis, to say nothing of keeping me on a course of celebrating God's grace), the more I am convinced that the theological decisions we make (or do not make) about our pastoral vocation and the parish (or community of God's people) are far more important than the decisions we make about strategy or structure. Now it is obviously true that decisions about strategy and structure are tremendously important questions in the life of pastor and people.

For example, one of the big theological decisions which every pastor has to keep on making is to ask the question: How does God work in the world and particularly in human beings? Various groups of Christians have answered this question as did the enthusiasts in Luther's time with the decision that God works immediately on the human spirit and therefore some inner core of the human spirit is the place to look for the impingement of God in life and history.

Luther, as you will recall, insisted on basis of a broad and profound understanding of the biblical view of human beings and their world, that God can work through all of life and history and that God's most salient work occurs through the means of Word and sacrament. It was the old question as to whether the finite can be a medium through which the infinite can come.

Now if you are led to decide that the life and history of humankind in this present age cannot be used by God to come to us in the message of the cross and resurrection, you tend to divide reality into extreme poles of sacred and secular. Then you tend to extol the sacred at the expense of the secular so that what is important is to enhance the sacred. This means then that if you carry this to extremes you are on the road to monasticism. Recognizing the proper truth of the Christian affirmation, the important fact is that God is at the heart of the universe. The individualistic view tends to neglect the fact that all of creation, even this broken world, is still God's. Sometimes in trying to applaud what God has done in Christ and is still doing by the power of the Spirit, we almost negate (at least distort) what God the loving Creator has done and is doing with humanity and the rest of nature. Thereby we tend (by such theological decisions) to so separate the dimensions of nature that we end up seeing human beings neither as divinely created celebrants of God's grace nor as a broken and alienated sinners, but basically as arrogant emperors of nature, tyrants and despots who constantly rape and plunder all of nature and, worst of all, who think that they are secure in their own destiny and position, while actually destroying themselves by destroying nature.

A very small example of this would be the usual attitude we take to some of the more secular aspects of our pastoral vocation. For example, consider administration. We often look at administration as a necessary evil, rather than viewing it as a genuine opportunity to serve God within the structures of this world. We Lutherans stress this incarnational ministry as the theology of the cross or, translated into a method for reaching theological decisions, as the proper distinction between law and gospel.

It is the same thing Dietrich Bonhoeffer was talking about when he stressed the this–worldliness of the Christian faith. In highlighting Jesus as the "man for others" and the this-worldliness of Christian faith, Bonhoeffer was drawing out the implications of a theology of the cross!

A New Day

Nominee's Speech for General President
The American Lutheran Church Convention
October 2, 1980

Dear Sisters and Beloved Brothers in Jesus Christ:

Two decades and five months ago, in Minneapolis, representatives of three bodies of Lutheranism met to form the American Lutheran Church which we know today. Dr. Henry Schuh, almost overpowering in presence, tough minded yet tender hearted, led the members of the former American Lutheran Church. Fred Schiotz, patient, gentle and strong at the same time, led the Evangelical Lutheran Church. William Larsen, quiet, calm, competent, led the United Evangelical Lutheran Church. Dr. John Stensvaag stood in the wings and waited for a couple years, in his patience and persistent, to lead the Lutheran Free Church, under the theme, "We United, Thine is the Glory."

United! Danes, Norwegians, Germans – coming together, because we were convinced that we belonged together. United – coming together, then as now, from the far reaches of the East, across the strength of Ohio, in the heartland of this nation, to the far West, in all its vast opportunity in the South, because we were certain we had a common faith. United – coming together because we were assured that we were held by the same love in Jesus Christ that would not let us go. We embraced one another in vibrant, expectant hope, convinced that pooling resources, in diversity alike, we could more adequately fulfill God's special mission for us in this world. Together we were determined to be God's servant people in this, the latter half, of the twentieth century. We were open to new challenges, challenges in our cities and opportunities to be with our Black, Hispanic, and Native American sisters and brothers. The challenge is to become a church to all people, to all the world. Especially we were open to the challenge to accept each other in our sexuality as we looked forward to greater discovery about being man and woman.

Now, at the beginning of the Eighties, we come together again. It is a new day. We are painfully and penitently aware that we have not met very many of the expectations we had in coming together twenty years ago. We indeed have discovered the blessings of change as we have permitted the ordination of women, but we have not discovered much exhilaration in being together with our Black brothers and sisters, and the Hispanics. We have come to know at least that we don't know how, and now at least we are asking so that we can learn to be with them. But we are still united in one faith, still held by the love of Jesus Christ, still excited about what we can do together to fulfill our mission, still seeking to be the servant people of God, for we have a call to announce God's "Good News" for the eighties.

As we come together for this convention, I think it is important to remember how it happened that each one of us got here. Yes, it is certainly true that we were elected by some delegates back home. But I think it is even more true that we are here to do the work of our church and convention because we were baptized, and because in baptism we have been commissioned to do the work of the church. And we have to make tough decisions in this convention, and in the years ahead. It will help us to remember that our commission also carries with it God's promise to be with us and to empower us.

We come together now to get our bearings for being the church in the eighties. We are very conscious that we live in perilous days. It is not an easy time to exercise our total ministry. Everywhere we turn there are unparalleled decisions to make. How do we make our way through the maze of choices before us, choices about science, technology, genetic control, energy, political and economic decisions? How do we find our way through this maze? But most of all, I think, how do we make our choices and decisions responsibly from the perspective of faith, love and hope in Jesus Christ our Lord? That has never been easy, and certainly is not easy now.

There are those who come with quick and easy solutions, but obviously we certainly want no part of that. At this point, I think, the heart of our confessional heritage can guide and help us. Each of our confessional commitments, that we have in our Confessions, guide us to give our allegiance only to one, namely to God. Each of the confessions of the church in their own way point us to this great fact – we should fear, love, and trust in God above all things! The unfinished Reformation means, it seems to me also, that neither ideology nor power, neither affluence nor poverty, not even the church itself, dare intrude between God and people in this world, and the power of God to remake God's people, and free them for love and ministry.

In the midst of changing times, the church must indeed be reforming. Just like baptism means that the old Adam in us, together with all sins and evils, should be drowned by daily sorrow and repentance, and be put to death, so that the new Adam should daily come forth and rise to live before God, in righteous and holiness forever. So, also, the church must daily repent and come forth new. Cleansed through the waters of baptism, we have been incorporated into the body of Christ, into the new people of God. For if anyone is in Christ, that person is a new creation and shares new life, the life of the servant people of God.

And so our church must order and reorder, make difficult changes and adjustments, so that its reason for being, to be God's servant people through faith active in love, moved by hope, may indeed happen, and that we will find the appropriate message to speak to a society in transition.

How will we stand in these times? I believe here our pioneer mothers and fathers as they settled this land give us an excellent example of how we can do that now. They knew that they had to be unflinching in their conviction that life was centered in God. They knew equally well that they had to be completely flexible in order to meet the changed environment to which they had come. In this respect I have often said that my 95 year-old mother, who died a few years ago, made the transition from pioneer sod-house child to the 1970s "jet age" easier than I have been able to make the transition from the sixties to the seventies, because, as a pioneer, she had learned to be flexible. In the same way, it seems to me, we need to be clear that our problems rise not because the foundations of life have changed, but because the circumstances of our use of the forces of life are constantly changing. And thus, relying upon the unchangeable foundations, given to us in the witness of Scripture and the guidelines of our Confessions, we can make the decisions required of us with boldness and carry them out with courage.

We know that we will make mistakes. Thus, we must be ready to repent and not simply hold to decisions which we have made in the past, or which we even make today, as being unalterably right simply because we have made them. Determined that the resources that are our's, being God's people in this world, will not be squandered, we will constantly review what we do. We will also, by the power of the gospel, have the courage to go down untroddened paths, to do new things together. Thus, we will be open to the future, not for the sake of innovation and so-called "creativity," but because we are compelled to be where Christ will have us be in the world for others.

In our congregations, we as people and pastors will stand together, knowing we have only one ministry – the ministry of the whole gospel for the whole world. We believe that the apostolic ministry of Word and sacrament is an integral part of the way that God releases liberating love in this world. But the apostolic ministry of Word and sacrament is meaningless and ineffective unless it is attached to the universal priesthood for every Christian. Every Christian has an apostolate to carry out. And one of the exciting things for me during my years as a pastor, a chaplain, and a teacher in the seminary has been to witness the great increase there has been in the exercise of this total ministry, of all the people in all the congregations.

It is equally exciting for me to observe the steady and increasing numbers of women and men who want to prepare for the ordained ministry. And it seems to me what we need in our time is a way to put these important facts together, so that the total outreach for the gospel can be increased.

Standing at this place, I cannot help but remember, back ten years ago, when my immediate predecessor at Wartburg as president, Kent S. Knutson, concluded his statement to the Church Convention at San Antonio by saying,

> When I go to work in the morning, I see the tower of Wartburg Seminary, a tower which is a replica of the castle in Eisenach, Germany, where Luther translated the Bible. At the very top, against the sky, there silhouetted everyday for me, is a weathervane with a proud rooster. And I think of Peter, who denied his Lord to a kitchen maid. And I am reminded that love and humility go together.

To that I would add, the rooster also stands as a symbol to announce the new day. To humility, united with love, must be added hope and expectation. We come together also in repentance. And we come together likewise in joy. God calls us to this new day in the eighties.

If you should see fit to elect me to either office, relying only upon God's grace, and your total support and strength as it exists within the church, I will do what I can to be your faithful servant, to announce the new day.

Living Truth

Commencement Address
May 19, 1996

"Study to show yourself approved unto God, a worker not needing to be ashamed, rightly dividing the Word of truth." II Tim. 2:15.

This is the day you have been working for and waiting to celebrate. The last final exam has been written and passed. The last paper has been finished and approved. No more academic pressure! Tonight there is nothing more to do but walk up to this table to receive your diploma and academic hood. Afterwards you will receive the congratulations of the many loved ones and friends and faculties who have shared with you in this process of learning and growing called theological education.

Now you can settle down to a more stable and routine life. You who have come from distant lands and other cultures and churches to enrich our life together, opening our eyes to the reality of the one world we all share, can now return to your homes and family from which some of you have been separated for a long time. Now all of you can move into the so-called "real world" where study has its place but where study certainly is not the only thing.

Or is it? Whether you call it graduation or whether you designate it commencement, this event pretty much means the same thing. It marks a turning point in your vocation! Education, conceived as an expanding process of growth in knowledge and hopefully in wisdom, would indicate that you have reached a recognized level of achievement. You have made the grade from which you can commence your chosen vocation.

That chosen vocation, however, requires that you remain an inquiring student forever. In many ways one could say that actual scholarly work and serious study *begins now*!

The seasoned pastor and theologian who wrote the great motto we read at the beginning says, "The task for which you have prepared deals *with the truth!*" Though the word translated *study* in the King James version of this motto may not be totally accurate, "study" is a good word to use at the juncture of academia and vocation. The injunction to the young Timothy at the beginning of his career was: *Chart a course for your life in which the word of truth is all important.* Actualize what grace has opened up for you! I think another way of translating for you tonight is: "Become a continuing and persistent theologian *inquirer*. Living in, with, and under the word of truth, allow God who gives us the truth in Jesus Christ to guide, confirm, and approve your efforts – that is the heart of theology – the center of your vocation."

The admonition and promise given in our little text points out that dealing with the word of truth properly does not mean being clever and cute in the use of religious language and theological discourse; it means always humbly focusing attention on the One who declared: "*I am the truth.*"

In your studies through the years, I am sure that you have become increasingly aware of the fact that the quest for truth is at the heart of all serious study and inquiry. Certainly you have experienced that truth is indeed mystery. Again and again you have experienced the greatness of your created humanity in getting a glimpse of truth whenever falsehood about the universe has been unmasked through human inquiry in all the sciences. But you have also repeatedly experienced the great tragedy of this discovery. Mysteries of nature discovered through science can be turned to destruction! And so you share the longing and aspiration of a fallen humanity that waits for the truth that can save the truth that can heal!

I believe you are here tonight because you have heard the angel message that there is a place and a time in human history where the hopes and fears of all the years are met and you look forward to sharing that message for all humanity!

Through this word of truth which you share, you have come to know that in Christianity truth is also mystery, but that this mystery is an event which has taken place and takes place again and again. "It is life, personal life, revelation, and decision." In Christianity truth is new creation, realizing itself in history. Your permanent vocation is to magnify and hold up this truth.

It will be your task to proclaim the truth. And as one of my mentors, Paul Tillich, put it: the opposite of truth is not merely an opinion, a hypothesis or a conclusion as it is for scientists, philosophers, or teachers who are searching for truth in the universe. Jesus says: "I am the one who is the truth and the opposite of truth is lie." Therefore, the decision for truth or against truth is a life and death decision. Your calling will be to focus attention on the fact that the decision for truth is identical with the decision in which Christ is accepted or rejected.

The reason you are a theologian, a pastor, a teacher, a *Seelsorger*, a presider at worship is to carry out a very humble yet majestic function. Yours it is to point to the one place in human history where truth in its fullness appeared. It is your privilege to speak the truth in love, making clear that you cannot merely have an opinion about Jesus Christ after you have faced him. It is your privilege to proclaim that you can only do the truth by following Jesus Christ and that you do the lie by denying him. Above all, you will stress the fact that the heart of this truth is that it is the truth that *saves*. Consequently no statement, method, or practice is theological which does not save – and *saving truth* means *doing the truth*.

It is in this sense that you will be theological inquirers all of your life. The inquiry will take you into realms you would never have dreamed of – into the great mystery of the human spirit – into the mystery of who you are and, above all, into the expanding mystery of who your fellow human beings are – and especially into the mystery of what we all will yet become!

A lot of your inquiry will happen while you are on the run from one experience to another. You will experience the grace of truth even in your frustrations, when you are doing much that seems frivolous and pointless. The temptation will always be close at hand to think that you have only been part of the truth when it appears that you have succeeded and that you have not been doing the truth when you seemed to have failed. It is then that you will need to recall another word of truth from the great theologian, Paul, in whose spirit the words to the young theologian Timothy were framed, who said the grace of God, manifest in Jesus Christ, is perfected not in our strength but in our weaknesses.

So as we congratulate you, we wish you a joyous journey on the way to being an ongoing inquirer after the truth. Follow your mentors, Luther and Calvin. Stand forever under the Word and as John Calvin declared about this word from Timothy, you won't have to blush in shame for what you have done! And as Luther declared: *oratio, meditatio, tentatio faciunt theologum.* In English that means: the word, meditation, and testing make a theologian. That's the way you deal with the truth!

Between the Times

Sermon on Ephesians 5:15-20

It was a different day than any other day—it was the day a small anxious group of dedicated and devout Christian disciples set sail from Europe for the new world. It was on this day 6 September 1620 that our pilgrim ancestors moved from a past of difficulty in expressing and exercising their future self-understanding to a future where they hoped to be free to express their faith as they pleased. They knew there were hardships ahead but they probably were not at all prepared for the challenges and problems they would encounter. Nevertheless, they launched out and like every pilgrim found themselves between the times.

I chose the slogan — *between the times* — to focus on our time together here at Wartburg this year. In one way or another all of us are between the times – moving into a new stage in our education, or from one vocation to another, or into new challenges of life. More poignantly we are between cultural changes more a reaching than our wildest fantasy and imagination can fathom or dream up.

To be between the times is really a great time to live. Rather than something to lament, we have come here today to rejoice that we stand before the birth of a new time. It's like Ralph Waldo Emerson wrote: "If there is any period one would desire to be born in, is it not...when the old and the new stand side by side, and admit to being compared; when the energies of all men are searched by fear and by hope; when the historic glories of the old, can be compensated by the rich possibilities of the new era? This time, like all times is a very good one, if we but know what to do with it."

We are here because we are certain that by ourselves we don't know what to do with time, but nevertheless, but are both certain and doubting together that there is One who shows us the way, the truth, and the life. That's the burden of our text, the epistle for last Sunday. It only needs to be stated to make the point: "Make the most of the situation where you are— but remember you can only do it in Christ." That's why we are here. Lets' make the most of it.

Presentation, Roots and Our Life Together

Sermon on Luke 2:22

The Presentation of Jesus emphasizes that God in Christ entered the world at just the right time. Jesus was presented to the Lord in obedience to the legal prescriptions of ancient Israel. This indicates God's unrestrained compassion to enter fully into the human predicament. This lesson comes precisely at the opening eucharist of the history of our life together at Wartburg. It also comes at a time when the powerful presentation named "Roots" has appeared on television, which half of the nation watched Sunday night in the midst of the most severe winter in recorded history. What have Presentation, Roots, and life here now to do with each other? I believe much of the convergence points to the need and desire to be grafted into the tree of life where roots sink into the very heart of eternity.

What was the appeal of "Roots?" Was it just because it was well done? If so, it is just as a news viewer put it, "Roots deserved every viewer it got." Undoubtedly because as the same reviewer said, "Roots had its flaws. But at its best, it included people who are more real than those that TV usually allows us to see. It provoked emotion in the viewer, and it carried the constant possibility of surprise different from the usual stereotype. Although no American living now has ever been a slave, we all recognized why Kunta Kinte fought to be free, we all admired the resourcefulness of Chicken George, we all understood the forces that worked upon the fiddler. We did not need to have ever been whipped to understand how it hurt."

But the universal empathy "Roots" evoked is in a basic sense one everyone can identify with, a search for roots, the quest for origins that do not consist in bondage, pain, or incompleteness. Maybe "Roots" drove us to feel the oppression of spirit under which life so easily exhausts itself in endless activity when not rooted in eternity. We are all made to be free.

Another aspect of "Roots", which I could not escape thinking about, was that we, so-called white people, and citizens of the nation with this great American dream, also allowed the nightmare of slavery. Even though we know we cannot be guilty of brutality and tyranny exercised 100 or 200 years ago just by association, nevertheless we cannot evade our destiny as a nation, a people, a culture, and a history which is inexorably bound up with such abuse. We cry out for deliverance from that enslavement as we close our eyes and wonder how people could do such things, when we watch how the whip cracks and chains rattle when Kunta's foot is cut off.

In the midst of that experience comes the word about the Presentation of Jesus. And the word calls to us to hold out like Simeon in the midst of hopelessness for the day of salvation. The Presentation brings the promise that God longs for our deliverance even more than we do—so much that God comes to us under conditions of subjection to

210

prescriptions which were meant to assure remembrance of the source of life – and awaken our dedication. It appears to me that this text points us to roots that not only go back to the source of every beginning and that provide the end of every search, but thrusts us forward from the quest to *live* in dedication to our *calling*! We have a new destiny!

"Roots" and the Presentation have a connection for our beginning the Spring term of this year! All the quests that bring us together are present here with the bread and wine, so that they may be answered by the presence of the One who was presented in obedience and died in obedience, but rose from the dead and lives and reigns to all eternity!

Search to Discover God's Love

Sermon on Colossians 3:12-17

Down a million streets and paths we run, hurried, searching, looking, hoping, for inner peace, composure. We search through the past tracing back beyond all possibility of understanding – billions of years ago. Through microscopes and electronic probes, we search for the secret of inner harmony, so that finding it between ourselves and nature, perhaps we can find it with other humans too. Each in our own way is following an uncharted course, desperately looking for fulfillment and something to make life worthwhile, even if it's nothing more than watching our own television sets when we feel the need to satisfy our thirst.

The source of harmony is given through baptism in the love of God which is the cement that holds the pieces of life together. Consider the shattered pieces of broken treasure, how glue can be applied to make it whole again. This is what the author to Colossians was saying it is like to live in the world with the confidence that your life has been mended together.

In other words, in his admonitions it isn't so much following a packaged do-it-yourself program for Christian happiness by following these six guides to Christian success.

Really the admonition is to realize regularly that your life can be determined by the kind of love that is seen in the life and especially the cross, death, and resurrection of Jesus.

That's what Baptism means. Baptism is thus validated every time you listen anew to what you have in Christ and realize that your life now is determined by this love.

Remember too that this love, the source of harmony, works itself out when you realize that you are part of a total solidarity with God's entire creation.

That We May Forgive As Christ Forgives

Sermon based on Luke 7, Luke 23:24, and Ephesians 4:32

For a person or society burdened with guilt and fragmentation, who are looking for power to love, there is only one word that sums up the meaning of the gospel It seems to me, that word is forgiveness – the subject of our discussion tonight. Forgiveness describes the way God comes to our world under the condition of brokenness and meets each one of us. That's what Lent is all about! That's what the cross declares to every one of us. No wonder Alexander Pope said years ago: "To err is human, to forgive is divine!"

Forgiveness, you see, is not some kind of easy way of saying our mistakes, our failures, our wrong-doing don't make any difference! Like we might say in trying to smooth over an awkward situation that resulted from our mistake – "Oh, that's all right! It doesn't make any difference!" But we know in the agony of our guilt that it does make a difference. We can't escape the inner law of retribution which erodes away our peace of mind and says it's not all right! We feel the pain through perpetual disturbing jabs that there is too much in the life of each of us that is all wrong. It's wrong that we can't do the good we should and it's wrong we do the evil and malicious things which we wish we had not done.

This is the first thing our text on forgiveness brings to our attention on this Holy Thursday evening. Forgiveness only means something to those who have been made aware that they have lived in a way that forgiveness is needed.

Bishop Fulton J. Sheen put it aptly when he said, "The really unforgivable sin is the denial of sin because, by its nature, there is now nothing to be forgiven!" The one who feels there is nothing for which forgiveness is needed lives in self-deception and tends to look upon others as the ones who need forgiveness. It's like those who condemned Jesus. They cried, "Crucify Him, Crucify Him!" They placed him on a cross. The first words we hear from Jesus' lips as he hangs there in agony and bloody sweat are: "Father, forgive them – they don't know what they do." They have been duped and they are deceiving themselves! They would get rid of their troubles by eliminating the very one who came to give them life!

But it is not an ancient tale of misdeeds done to a tragic hero. It is the story of every one of us! In every way that we as individuals and together as people in a nation and a church attempt to push the indictment of our own estrangement onto someone or something else, avoiding our own responsibility, in our own strong drive to save and justify ourselves, we are missing the liberating power of God's Word of forgiveness from the cross. The people who placed Jesus on the cross couldn't hear the Word of forgiveness because they were totally occupied in getting rid of their problems—just as we evade the issue when we fail to acknowledge that we desperately are in need of the One who said: "I have come to seek and save the lost."

213

We recall the encounter of Jesus with Simon the Pharisee, which Luke describes in Chapter 7:36-47, about Jesus allowing the prostitute to anoint his feet and the discourse on forgiveness and love in relation to the problem this created for the righteous of that time, the Pharisees. To appreciate the full impact of what is happening in Jesus treatment of the prostitute and the Pharisee, we must remember that Jesus' conflict with the Pharisees was not a conflict over whether the Pharisees were good people or not. In the Lenten dramas we sometimes put them in a negative category. Really, they were responsible, seriously concerned, religious people. They were the guardians of the Law of God in their own time. They took their religious and moral obligations seriously.

In our time they could be compared with all of us who take active church membership and constructive citizenship seriously. The Pharisees are comparable to those of us who work hard at maintaining well-established morality and religion. Jesus calls the Pharisees of his time, and all of us like them in our time righteous and he with equally seriousness calls the sinners, sinners! There is nothing bad about being righteous. We need all the righteousness we can find. It is only out of line when we try to make our righteousness the basis for God's forgiveness of our unrighteousness. This was Simon the Pharisee's problem. Jesus word about the righteous sinner discloses the paradoxical depth of the gospel like nothing else. The disturbing, shaking, and liberating force of the good news of Jesus Christ is here disclosed in all its mystery and magnitude. The force and mystery of the gospel sounds from the word of the cross: "Forgive them for they know now what they do" – in face of the ignorant and irrational act of the leaders, the righteous who helped nail him to the cross! They too are equally the object of his healing words: "Father forgive them!" We are talking about your forgiveness and mine.

The second significant fact that impresses itself upon us as we listen to Jesus speak from the cross is that forgiveness is a word spoken by God. When Heinrich Heine, the German poet, said, "Forgiveness is God's business," he probably said more than he realized. The gospel of Jesus Christ is seeming foolishness: God was in Christ reconciling the world to Himself. The good news of the church is: God has the power to judge and condemn human rebellion and idolatry, the human abuse of freedom, the human tendency to want to live for yourself. But more importantly, God is even more the one who by nature can and does forgive! God does not desire to get rid of us by judgment! God seeks to restore us to life! God creates a new life for us and it begins with forgiveness!

The magnitude of what that implies can perhaps be illustrated by the question that the Austrian Nazi concentration camp victim, Simon Wiesenthal, poses in his book *Sunflower*. Should a Jew be asked in any way to forgive those Nazis who made them suffer so terribly?

Wiesenthal describes the predicament of a young Jew who is taken from a death camp to a German hospital. At his bedside lies a young Nazi soldier whose head is completely covered with bandages and who is dying. The dying Nazi blindly extends his hand toward the Jew and gasps out a horrible confession of how he helped to burn alive an entire village of Jews.

The young soldier, who had been raised in the Church and is terrified of dying with this burden of guilt, begs absolution from the Jew! Having listened to the young Nazi's story for hours and torn between horror and compassion for the dying man, the Jew finally walks out of the room without speaking. Do you blame him? What would you have done?

All of us could, I am sure, understand why it would be impossible for a victim of the Holocaust to forgive anyone who had anything to do with this horrendous violation of human dignity! Yet the anguish of God for rebellious humanity equals that same anguish multiplied by all the atrocities perpetrated by both the weak and the sinister throughout history. How could and how can God forgive? Only because God is God! Only because there is no conflict in God between retributive justice and reconciling love. This is God's power! This is God's highest prerogative!

The third point that the word of forgiveness from the cross brings to our attention is that forgiveness is a matter of significant change in one's relationship with other people and not just an expression of words. Forgiveness does make a difference. Without forgiveness we say "I can forgive but I cannot forget." Through God we can forgive and remember, but without lingering resentment.

To me it is quite significant that a large number of passages in the Gospels which bring us a word of Jesus about forgiveness also bring us the urging of Jesus for those who have experienced forgiveness to be forgiving to others. At times it almost seems that Jesus is imposing a condition on our forgiveness when he is pictured as saying, "So your heavenly Father will not forgive you unless you from you heart forgive your neighbor." Or, "How many times shall a person forgive? I say not seven times, but seventy times seven." Or think again of Luke 7 – the word about the penitent prostitute we have already considered.

Our text from Ephesians reminds us that we should forgive one another. To me it can be summarized by saying the church is a community of forgiven sinners—-who in turn express the meaning of their life in Christ by becoming a forgiving community.

C. S. Lewis, the great British author and Christian apologist, put it forcefully to us when he wrote: "Everyone says forgiveness is a lovely idea, until they have something to forgive." In other words, forgiveness is not pious rhetoric. Forgiveness is faith in action.

Forgiveness is an action that never comes to rest. A person who has experienced forgiveness becomes aware that this experience of God's grace moves on to the persons and groups which that very person is disinclined to like or want to forgive. For as the great preacher and theologian, Horace Bushnell, proclaimed: Forgiveness is our deepest need and also our highest possibility and achievement." It is only possible because God empowers!

You can only love, much like the woman who anointed Jesus, if you have been forgiven a lot! She was aware that she had been generously forgiven everything, so she loved much. According to Niebuhr: "Forgiving love is a possibility only for those who know they are not good, who feel themselves in need of divine mercy."

If we are to become agents of forgiveness in a society of fear, suspicion and brutality, it won't happen by the decision of any of us. It will happen by listening to the word of forgiveness and hearing that we are forgiven ourselves.

That's what the cross is all about. That's what this Lord's Supper is all about. This is the word our Lord speaks to us as we eat and drink together with him.

215

Good Bye

What does it mean to say "good bye?" The meaning of the word is "God be with you!" It is in accordance with Christ's own word, "Lo, I am always with you." (Mt 28:2). It is to acknowledge the transient character of life. Especially we the people called in love to share God's grace with each other have been led to see that we are pilgrim people and that the permanence of life is not something we are allowed to possess. Each goodbye hurts because it awakens the incompleteness and temporary character of our existence.

To say "good bye" is to acknowledge our dependence and need of each other as people and, as the people of God, especially our need of God. It is to say "thank you" for what God constantly does for us in God's word and in God's church.

To say goodbye is to experience not only the pain of separation but the courage to move into new possibilities and different opportunities. It is a time to discover anew that obedience to God in Christ is to cut incestuous ties and discover anew freedom and independence and make each goodbye a determination to see life transfigured. To say goodbye in the name of our risen Lord is to seek the presence of the living God in human relationships. Living the Good Samaritan attitude, we will discover that if Christianity in our time, which has become so self-conscious, is to recover its vigor, it must grasp this tormented, seething world in its hands and there find meaning in it because God is in it.

www.ingramcontent.com/pod-product-compliance
Lightning Source LLC
Chambersburg PA
CBHW070446100426
42812CB00004B/1221